Advanced Text Mining and Applied Principles

Advanced Text Mining and Applied Principles

Edited by **Mick Benson**

CLANRYE INTERNATIONAL

New Jersey

Published by Clanrye International,
55 Van Reypen Street,
Jersey City, NJ 07306, USA
www.clanryeinternational.com

Advanced Text Mining and Applied Principles
Edited by Mick Benson

© 2015 Clanrye International

International Standard Book Number: 978-1-63240-028-4 (Hardback)

Printed in the United States of America.

Contents

Permissions

List of Contributors

Preface

I am honored to present to you this unique book which encompasses the most up-to-date data in the field. I was extremely pleased to get this opportunity of editing the work of experts from across the globe. I have also written papers in this field and researched the various aspects revolving around the progress of the discipline. I have tried to unify my knowledge along with that of stalwarts from every corner of the world, to produce a text which not only benefits the readers but also facilitates the growth of the field.

This book discusses the topic of advanced text mining and applied principles in detail. Due to the development of computer and web technologies, we are now able to easily compile and store huge amounts of text data. It is believed that data consists of valuable knowledge. Text mining techniques have been dynamically analyzed for the extraction of knowledge from data since late 1990s. Even though many vital methods have been formulated, the text mining research field continues to expand for the needs emerging from distinct application fields. This book provides an introduction of advanced text mining techniques ranging from relation extraction to under or less resourced language. It aims at providing the readers with novel information about the field and assists them in exploring new research fields.

Finally, I would like to thank all the contributing authors for their valuable time and contributions. This book would not have been possible without their efforts. I would also like to thank my friends and family for their constant support.

Editor

Survey on Kernel-Based Relation Extraction

Hanmin Jung, Sung-Pil Choi, Seungwoo Lee and
Sa-Kwang Song

Additional information is available at the end of the chapter

1. Introduction

Relation extraction refers to the method of efficient detection and identification of prede-fined semantic relationships within a set of entities in text documents (Zelenco, Aone, & Ri-chardella, 2003; Zhang, Zhou, and Aiti, 2008). The importance of this method was recognized first at the Message Understanding Conference (MUC, 2001) that had been held from 1987 to 1997 under the supervision of DARPA[1]. After that, the Automatic Content Ex-traction (ACE, 2009) Workshop facilitated numerous researches that from 1999 to 2008 had been promoted by NIST[2] as a new project. Currently, the workshop is held every year being the greatest world forum for comparison and evaluation of new technology in the field of information extraction such as named entity recognition, relation extraction, event extrac-tion, and temporal information extraction. This workshop is conducted as a sub-field of Text Analytics Conference (TAC, 2012) which is currently under the supervision of NIST.

According to ACE, an entity in the text is a representation for naming a real object. Exempla-ry entities include the names of persons, locations, facilities and organizations. A sentence including these entities can express the semantic relationships in between them. For exam-ple, in the sentence *"President Clinton was in Washington today,"* there is the *"Located"* relation between *"Clinton"* and *"Washington"*. In the sentence *"Steve Balmer, CEO of Microsoft, said…"* the relation of *"Role (CEO, Microsoft)"* can be extracted.

Many relation extraction techniques have been developed in the framework of various tech-nological workshops mentioned above. Most relation extraction methods developed so far are based on supervised learning that requires learning collections. These methods are clas-

---

1 Defense Advanced Research Projects Agency of the U.S.

2 National Institute of Standards and Technology of the U.S.

sified into feature-based methods, semi-supervised learning methods, bootstrapping methods, and kernel-based methods (Bach & Badaskar, 2007; Choi, Jeong, Choi, and Myaeng, 2009). Feature-based methods rely on classification models for automatically specifying the category where a relevant feature vector belongs. At that, surrounding contextual features are used to identify semantic relations between the two entities in a specific sentence and represent them as a feature vector. The major drawback of the supervised learning-based methods, however, is that they require learning collections. Semi-supervised learning and bootstrapping methods, on the other hand, use a large corpora or web documents, based on reduced learning collections that are progressively expanded to overcome the above disadvantage. Kernel-based methods (Collins & Duffy, 2001), in turn, devise kernel functions that are most appropriate for relation extraction and apply them for learning in the form of a kernel set optimized for syntactic analysis and part-of-speech tagging. The kernel function itself is used for measuring the similarity between two instances, which are the main objects of machine learning. General kernel-based models will be discussed in detail in Section 3.

As one representative approach of the feature-based methods, (Kambhatla, 2004) combines various types of lexical, syntactic, and semantic features required for relation extraction by using maximum entropy model. Although it is based on the same type of composite features as that proposed by Kambhatla (2004), Zhou, Su, Zhang, and Zhang (2005) make the use of support vector machines for relation extraction that allows flexible kernel combination. Zhao and Grishman (2005) have classified all features available by that point in time in order to create individual linear kernels, and attempted relation extraction by using composite kernels made of individual linear kernels. Most feature-based methods aim at applying feature engineering algorithms for selecting optimal features for relation extraction, and application of syntactic structures was very limited.

Exemplary semi-supervised learning and bootstrapping methods are Snowball (Agichtein & Gravano, 2000) and DIPRE (Brin, 1999). They rely on a few learning collections for making the use of bootstrapping methods similar to the Yarowsky algorithm (Yarowsky, 1995) for gathering various syntactic patterns that denote relations between the two entities in a large web-based text corpus. Recent developments include KnowItAll (Etzioni, et al., 2005) and TextRunner (Yates, et al., 2007) methods for automatically collecting lexical patterns of target relations and entity pairs based on ample web resources. Although this approach does not require large learning collections, its disadvantage is that many incorrect patterns are detected through expanding pattern collections, and that only one relation can be handled at a time.

Kernel-based relation extraction methods were first attempted by Zelenco, et al. (2003). Zelenco, et al., devised contiguous subtree kernels and sparse subtree kernels for recursively measuring similarity of two parse trees in order to apply them to binary relation extraction that demonstrated relatively high performance. After that, a variety of kernel functions for relation extraction have been suggested, e.g., dependency parse trees (Culotta and Sorensen, 2004), convolution parse tree kernels (Zhang, Zhang and Su, 2006), and composite kernels (Choi et al., 2009; Zhang, Zhang, Su and Zhou, 2006), which show even better performance.

In this chapter, case analysis was carried out for kernel-based relation extraction methods, which are considered to be the most successful approach so far. Of course, some previous survey papers based on the importance and effect of the methodology have been published (Bach and Badaskar, 2007; Moncecchi, Minel and Wonsever, 2010). However, they fail to fully analyze particular functional principles or characteristics of the kernel-based relation extraction models announced so far, and just cite the contents of individual articles or describe limited analysis. Although the performance of most kernel-based relation extraction methods has been demonstrated on the basis of ACE evaluation collections, comparison and analysis of the overall performance has not been made so far.

This chapter, unlike existing case studies, makes a close analysis of operation principles and individual characteristics of five kernel-based relation extraction methods starting from Zelenco, et al. (2003) which is the source of kernel-based relation extraction studies, to the composite kernel, which is considered the most advanced kernel-based relation method (Choi, et al., 2009; Zhang, Zhang, Su, et al., 2006). The focus will be laid on the ACE collection to compare the overall performance of each method. We hope this study will contribute to further research of kernel-based relation extraction of even higher performance and to high-level general kernel studies for linguistic processing and text mining.

Section 2 outlines supervised learning-based relation extraction methods and in section 3 we discuss kernel-based machine learning. Section 4 closely analyzes five exemplary kernel-based relation extraction methods. As mentioned above, Section 5 also compares the performance of these methods to analyze advantages and disadvantages of each method. Section 6 draws a conclusion.

2. Supervised learning-based relation extraction

As discussed above, relation extraction methods are classified into three categories. The difference between feature-based and kernel-based methods is shown in the following Figure 1. With respect to machine learning procedure, these two are different from semi-supervised learning methods.

On the left of Figure 1, individual sentences that make up a learning collection have at least two entities (black square) of which the relation is manually extracted and predefined. Since most relation extraction methods studied so far work with binary relations, learning examples are modified for convenient relation extraction from the pair of entities by preprocessing the original learning collection. These modified learning examples are referred to as *relation instance*. The relation instance is defined as an element of the learning collection modified so that it can be efficiently applied to the relevant relation extraction methods on the basis of specific sentence that contains at least two entities.

The aforementioned modification is closely related to feature information used in relation extraction. Since most supervised learning-based methods use both the entity itself and the contextual information about the entity, it is important to collect contextual information efficiently for improving performance. Linguistic processing (part-of-speech tagging, base phrase recognition, syntactic analysis, etc.) for individual learning sentences in the pre-processing step contributes to making a base for effective feature selection and extraction. For example, when one sentence shown in the above Figure 1 goes through syntactic analysis, one relation instance is composed of a parse tree and the locations of entities indicated in the parse tree (Fundel, Küffner, & Zimmer, 2007; Zhang, et al., 2008; Zhou, Zhang, Ji, and Zhu, 2007). A single sentence can be represented as a feature vector or a syntactic graph (Jiang and Zhai, 2007; W. Li, Zhang, Wei, Hou, and Lu, 2008; Zhang, Zhang, and Su, 2006). The type of such relation instances depends on the relation extraction methods, and can involve various preprocessing tasks as well (D. P. T. Nguyen, Matsuo, and Ishizuka, 2007; Zhang, Zhang, and Su, 2006).

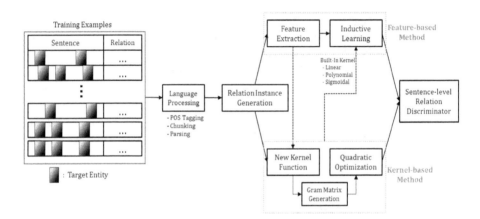

Figure 1. Learning process for supervised learning-based relation extraction.

In general, feature-based relation extraction methods follow the procedures shown in the upper part of Figure 1. That is, feature collections that *"can express individual learning examples the best"* are extracted (feature extraction.) The learning examples are feature-vectorized, and inductive learning is carried out using selected machine learning models. On the contrary, kernel-based relation extraction shown in the lower part of Figure 1 devises a kernel function that *"can calculate similarity of any two learning examples the most effectively"* to replace feature extraction process. Here, the measurement of similarity between the learning examples is not general similarity measurement in a general sense. That is, the function for enhancing similarity between the two sentences or instances that express the same relation is the most effective kernel function from the viewpoint of relation extraction. For example, two sentences *"Washington is in the U.S."* and *"Seoul is located in Korea"* use different object entities but feature the same relation (*"located."*) Therefore, an efficient kernel function would detect a high similarity between these two sentences. On the other hand, since the sentences *"Washington is the capital of the United States"* and *"Washington is located in the United States"* express the same object entities but different relations, the similarity between them should be determined as very low. As such, in kernel-based relation extraction methods, the selection and creation of kernel functions are the most fundamental part that affects the overall performance.

As shown in the Figure 1, kernel functions (linear, polynomial, and sigmoid) can be used in feature-based methods as well. They are, however, functions applied only to instances expressed with vectors. On the other hand, kernel-based methods are not limited in terms of the type of the instance, and thus can contain various kernel functions.

3. Overview of kernel-based machine learning methods

Most machine learning methods are carried out on a feature basis. That is, each instance to which an answer (label) is attached, is modified into a feature sequence or N-dimensional vector $f_1, f_2, ..., f_N$ to be used in the learning process. For example, important features for identifying the relation between two entities in a single sentence are entity type, contextual information between, before and after entities' occurrence, part-of-speech information for contextual words, and dependency relation path information for the two entities (Choi et al., 2009; Kambhatla, 2004; W. Li, Zhang, et al., 2008; Zhang, Zhang, and Su, 2006). These data are selected as a single feature, respectively, to be represented with a vector for automatic classification of the relation between the entities.

In section 2, we discussed that the essence of feature-based methods is to create a feature vector that can best express individual learning examples. However, in many cases, it is not possible to express the feature vector reasonably. For example, a feature space is required for expressing syntactic information[3] of a specific sentence as a feature vector, and it is almost impossible to express it as a feature vector in a limited space in some cases (Cristianini and Shawe-Taylor, 2000). Kernel-based methods are for learning by calculating kernel functions between two examples while keeping the original learning example without additional feature expression (Cristianini and Shawe-Taylor, 2000). The kernel function is defined as the mapping $K: X \times X \rightarrow [0, \infty)$ from the input space X to the similarity score $\phi(x) \cdot \phi(y) = \sum_i \phi_i(x)\phi_i(y)$. Here, $\phi(x)$ is the mapping function from learning examples in the input space v to the multidimensional feature space. The kernel function is symmetric, and exhibits positive semi-definite features. With the kernel function, it is not necessary to calculate all features one by one, and machine learning can thus be carried out based only on similarity between two learning examples. Exemplary models where learning is carried out on the basis of all similarity matrices between learning examples include Perceptron (Rosenblatt, 1958), Voted Perceptron (Freund and Schapire, 1999), and Support Vector Machines (Cortes and Vapnik, 1995) (Moncecchi, et al., 2010). Recently, kernel-based matching learning methods draw increasingly more attention, and are widely used for pattern recognition, data and text mining, and web mining. The per-

---

3 Dependency grammar relation, parse tree, etc. between words in a sentence.

formance of kernel methods, however, depends to a great extent on kernel function selection or configuration (J. Li, Zhang, Li, and Chen, 2008).

Kernel-based learning methods are used also for natural language processing. Linear, polynomial and Gaussian kernels are typical in simple feature vector-based machine learning. Convolutional kernel (Collins & Duffy, 2001) is used for efficient learning of structural data such as trees or graphs. The convolution kernel is a type of kernel function featuring the idea of sequence kernels (Lodhi, Saunders, Shawe-Taylor, Cristianini, & Watkins, 2002), tree kernels (Culotta & Sorensen, 2004; Reichartz, Korte, & Paass, 2009; Zelenco, et al., 2003; Zhang, Zhang, & Su, 2006; Zhang, et al., 2008), and graph kernels (Gartner, Flach, & Wrobel, 2003). The convolutional kernel can measure the overall similarity by defining "sub-kernels" for measuring similarity between the components of an individual entity and calculating similarity convolution among the components. For example, the sequence kernel divides the relevant sequence into subsequences for measuring similarity of two sequences to calculate overall similarity by means of similarity measurement between the subsequences. Likewise, the tree kernel divides a tree into its sub-trees to calculate similarity between them and then it calculates the convolution of these similarities.

As described above, another advantage of the kernel methods is that learning is possible as a single kernel function for input instance collections of different type. For example, (Choi et al., 2009; Zhang, Zhang, Su, et al., 2006) have demonstrated a composite kernel for which the convolutional parse tree kernel is combined with the entity kernel for high-performance relation extraction.

4. Kernel-based relation extraction

The most prominent characteristic of the relation extraction models derived so far is that linguistic analysis is used to carefully identify relation expressions and syntactic structures directly and indirectly expressed in specific sentences. In this section, five important research results are discussed and analyzed. Of course, there are many other important studies that have drawn much attention due to their high performance. Most of approaches, however, just modify or supplement the five basic methods discussed below. Therefore, this study can be an important reference for supplementing existing research results in the future or studying new mechanisms for relation extraction, by intuitively explaining the details of major studies. Firstly, tree kernel methods originally proposed by Zelenco, et al. (2003) are covered in detail. Then, the method proposed by Culotta & Sorensen (2004) is covered where the dependency tree kernel was used for the first time. Also, kernel-based relation extraction (Bunescu & Mooney, 2005) using dependency path between two entities in a specific sentence on the basis of similar dependency trees is discussed. Additionally, the subsequence kernel-based relation extraction method proposed by (Bunescu & Mooney (2006) is explained. Finally, the relation extraction models (Zhang, Zhang, Su, et al., 2006) based on the composite kernel for which various kernels are combined on the basis of the convolution parse tree kernel proposed by Collins & Duffy (2001) are covered in detail.

4.1. Tree kernel-based method (Zelenco, et al., 2003)

This study is known as the first application of kernel method to relation extraction. The parse trees derived from shallow parsing are used for measuring similarity between the sentences containing entities. In their study, the REES (Relation and Event Extraction System) is used to analyze part-of-speeches and types of individual words in a sentence, as well as the syntactic structure of the sentence in question. Here, the REES is a relation and event extraction system developed by Aone & Ramos-Santacruz (2000). The Figure 2 below shows example result from the REES.

"John Smith is the scientist of the Hardcom Corp."

Type	Sentence
Text	-
Head	-
Role	-

Type	Person		Type	Verb		Type	PNP
Text	John Smith		Text	-		Text	-
Head	-		Head	be		Head	scientist
Role	member		Role	-		Role	-

Type	PNP		Type	Prep		Type	Entity
Text	-		Text	of		Text	Hardcom C.
Head	scientist		Head	-		Head	-
Role	-		Role	-		Role	affiliation

Figure 2. Exemplary shallow parsing result for relation extraction.

As shown in Figure 2, when the syntactic analysis of the input sentence is completed, particular information for words of the sentence is analyzed and extracted. Four types of attribute information are attached to all words or entities other than articles and stop words. Type represents the part-of-speech or entity type of the current word. While *"John Smith"* is the *"Person"* type, *"scientist"* is specified as *"PNP"* representing a personal noun. Head represents the presence of key words of composite nouns or preposition phrases. Role represents the relation between the two entities. In Figure 2, *"John Smith"* is the *"member"* of *"Hardcom C."* In its turn, *"Hardcom C."* is an *"affiliation"* of *"John Smith"*.

As one can see, it is possible to identify and extract the relation between the two entities in a specific sentence at a given level if the REES is used. Since the system, however, was developed on the basis of rules, it has some limitations in terms of scalability and generality (Zelenco et al., 2003). Zelenco et al. (2003) have constructed tree kernels on the basis of the REES analysis result with a view of better relation extraction so as to overcome the limitations of machine learning and low performance. The kernel function defined in this study for measuring the similarity of a pair of shallow parsing trees consists of the following chain of equations. The comparison function for each individual configuration node in the trees is as follows.

$$t(P_1.p,\ P_2.p) = \begin{cases} 1, & \text{if } P_1.Type = P_2.Type \text{ and } P_1.Role = P_2.Role \\ 0, & \text{otherwise} \end{cases} \tag{1}$$

In this equation, $P_i.p$ represents a specific parent node in the parsing tree; $P_i.Type$ represents word and entity type information; and $P_i.Role$ represents relation information between the two entities. Equation 1 is called *matching function*, and is used for comparing between the part-of-speeches, entity type and relation type information for each node. If both type and role are the same as in binary comparison, 1 is returned and otherwise 0.

$$k(P_1.p,\ P_2.p) = \begin{cases} 1, & \text{if } P_1.Text = P_2.Text \\ 0, & \text{otherwise} \end{cases} \tag{2}$$

Equation 2 represents the function for deciding whether two nodes comprise the same words or entities. (Zelenco et al., 2003) named this *similarity function*. The recursive kernel function K_c for the child node of a specific parent node, is defined as follows on the basis of the two functions. Although all the functions above do not use "Head" field in each node for simplicity in (Zelenco et al., 2003), it would be valuable to use the field for better performance.

$$
\begin{aligned}
K_c(P_1.c,\ P_2.c) &= \sum_{i,j,l(i)=l(j)} SSK(P_1.c,\ P_2.c,\ i,\ j) \\
SSK(P_1.c,\ P_2.c,\ i,\ j) &= \lambda^{d(i)} \lambda^{d(i)} K(P_1[i],\ P_2[j]) \prod_{s=1,\ldots,l(i)} t(P_1[i_s],\ P_2[j_s]) \\
K(P_1[i],\ P_2[j]) &= \sum_{s=1,\ldots,l(i)} K(P_1[i_s],\ P_2[j_s]) \\
i &= \{i_1,\ i_2,\ \ldots,\ i_n \mid i_1 \leq i_2 \leq \ldots \leq i_n\} \\
d(i) &= i_n - i_1 + 1 \\
l(i) &= n
\end{aligned}
\tag{3}
$$

In Equation 3, $P_i.c$ represents the child nodes of the specific node ($P_i.p$). $SSK(P_1.c, P_2.c, i, j)$ is the function for calculating subsequence similarity between child nodes ($P_i.c$) of $P_1.p$ and $P_2.p$. Here, i is the index representing all the subsequences of the child nodes of $P_i.p$. $\lambda^{d(i)}$, $0 < \lambda < 1$ is the weight factor depending on the length of the child node subsequences. This variable determines how many subsequences of the specific child node are contained in the entire child nodes in order to lower the similarity in case of multiple matching subsequences. $d(i)$ represents the distance between the first and last nodes of the currently processing subsequence i, and $l(i)$ represents the number of the nodes of i. The kernel function between the two trees is defined as follows.

$$K(P_1,\ P_2) = \begin{cases} 0, & \text{if } t(P_1.p,\ P_2.p) = 0 \\ k(P_1.p,\ P_2.p) + K_c(P_1.c,\ P_2.c), & \text{otherwise} \end{cases} \tag{4}$$

P_i represents the tree to be compared. The similarity between the two trees is calculated by adding up the similarity function k (Equation 2) for the current node (parent node) and the similarity calculation function K_c (Equation 3) between the child nodes. The kernel calculation process for the following parse trees will be described in detail later for intuitive understanding of the kernel function.

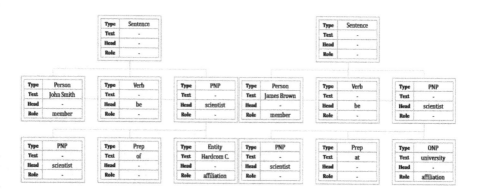

Figure 3. Two sample parse trees for illustrating kernel calculation process.

The original sentence of the parse tree on the left side is *"John Smith is a chief scientist of Hardcom C."*, and the original sentence of the tree on the right side is *"James Brown is a scientist at the University of Illinois."* For convenience, the left-side tree is referred to as P_1, and the right-side tree as P_2. For easy explanation, *"chief"* and *"University of Illinois"* are removed or abbreviated. The kernel function for the two trees is primarily expressed as in the following.

$$K(P_1, P_2) = k(P_1.Sentence.p, P_2.Sentence.p)$$
$$+ K_c([P_1.Person, P_1.Verb, P_1.PNP], [P_2.Person, P_2.Verb, P_2.PNP])$$
$$= k(P_1.Sentence.p, P_2.Sentence.p) \qquad (5)$$
$$+ \sum_{i,j,l(i)=l(j)} SSK([P_1.Person, P_1.Verb, P_1.PNP], [P_2.Person, P_2.Verb, P_2.PNP], i, j)$$

Equation 4 is used to calculate the tree kernel between the two trees P_1 and P_2. Here $P_i.Sentence.p$ represents the root node of i-th tree. Equation 3 is used to calculate K_c for each child node of the root node to expand it into the sum of the SSK function. The Figure 4 below shows the process of calculating the kernel of the SSK function.

Figure 4 shows the process of calculating the kernel function between the second-level child nodes of the two trees. Since all nodes at this level have unexpectedly the matching node type as shown in Figure 3, kernel similarity between the subsequences of each matching node as shown in the equations on the right side of Figure 3. Since matching only between subsequences of the same length is implemented as in Equation 3, non-matching subsequences are excluded from kernel calculation through conformity check among subsequences of which the length is 1, 2 and 3 respectively. The result of kernel calculation is as follows.

$$
\begin{aligned}
K(P_1, P_2) &= k(P_1.Sentence.p, P_2.Sentence.p) \\
&\quad + K_c([P_1.Person, P_1.Verb, P_1.PNP],[P_2.Person, P_2.Verb, P_2.PNP]) \\
&= \lambda^2 \{K(P_1.Person, P_2.Person) + K(P_1.Verb, P_2.Verb) + K(P_1.PNP, P_2.PNP)\} \quad \rightarrow (l(i) = 1, d(i) = 1) \\
&\quad + \lambda^4 \{K(P_1.Person, P_2.Person) + 2K(P_1.Verb, P_2.Verb) + K(P_1.PNP, P_2.PNP)\} \quad \rightarrow (l(i) = 2, d(i) = 2) \\
&\quad + \lambda^6 \{K(P_1.Person, P_2.Person) + K(P_1.PNP, P_2.PNP)\} \qquad\qquad \rightarrow (l(i) = 2, d(i) = 3) \\
&\quad + \lambda^6 \{K(P_1.Person, P_2.Person) + K(P_1.Verb, P_2.Verb) + K(P_1.PNP, P_2.PNP)\} \quad \rightarrow (l(i) = 3, d(i) = 3) \\
&= \lambda^2 \{0 + 1 + K(P_1.PNP, P_2.PNP)\} + \lambda^4 \{0 + 2 + K(P_1.PNP, P_2.PNP)\} \\
&\quad + \lambda^6 K(P_1.PNP, P_2.PNP) + \lambda^6 \{1 + K(P_1.PNP, P_2.PNP)\} \\
&= \lambda^2 + 2\lambda^4 + \lambda^6 + \{\lambda^2 + \lambda^4 + 2\lambda^6\} K(P_1.PNP, P_2.PNP)
\end{aligned}
$$

(6)

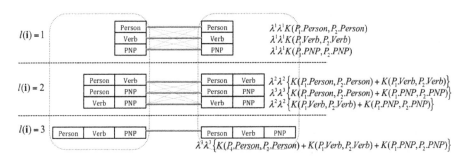

Figure 4. Executing Subsequence Similarity Kernel (SSK) function.

As Equation 6 shows, only the Equation expressed on the basis of is left, other than $K(P_1.PNP, P_2.PNP)$. The kernel function recursively compares child node subsequences at the third level to calculate resulting kernel similarity.

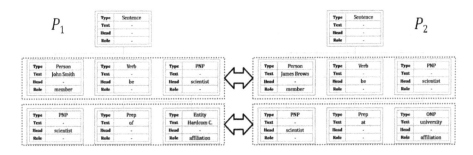

Figure 5. Process and method of calculating the tree kernel.

Figure 5 shows the process and method of calculating the kernel function. Basically, for the tree kernel, *Breadth First Search* is carried out. In calculating similarity between the two trees, trees to be compared are primarily those with the same node type and role. Since the kernel value is 0 when the text is different, nodes with the same text are substantially compared. In Figure 5, these are *"be"* and *"scientist"* nodes.

Zelenco, et al., (2003) divides tree kernel calculation into two types. One is the *sparse subtree kernel* described above, and the other one is the *continuous subtree kernel*, which is discussed below. First, the sparse subtree kernel includes two node subsequences for comparison, although two node subsequences are not continuously connected. For example, *"Person, PNP"* on the left side and *"Person, PNP"* on the right side in the middle of Figure 4 are node sequences, separated in the parse tree. The sparse subtree kernel includes such subsequences for comparison. On the contrary, the continuous subtree kernel does not approve such subsequences and excludes them from comparison. The Figure 6 below shows additional exemplary sentence for comparison and describing the effect of two tree kernels.

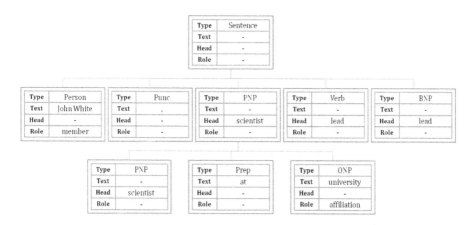

Figure 6. Additional sample sentence and parsing result.

Figure 6 shows the parsing result for *"John White, a well-known scientist at the University of Illinois, led the discussion."* Unlike the sentences discussed above, this one has an independent inserted phrase in apposition, and comprises the same contents as the second sentence of Figure 3 *"James Brown is a scientist at the University of Illinois."* If these two sentences are compared by means of the continuous subtree kernel, a very low kernel similarity will be derived because there is almost no continuous node on the parse tree although they include similar contents. The sparse subtree kernel is used overcome this deficiency. Figure 7 shows a part of the process of calculating kernel values for two sentences.

Figure 7 shows the process of calculating $K([Person, Verb, PNP], [Person, Punc, PNP, Verb, BNP])$ by means of sparse subtree kernel. When continuous subtree kernel is used, the similarity between the two sentences is very low. A better similarity value is revealed by two pairs of matching subsequences in the subsequence of which the length is 2, as shown in Figure 7.

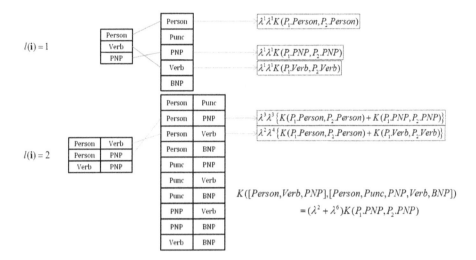

Figure 7. Process of calculating K([Person, Verb, PNP], [Person, Punc, PNP, Verb, BNP]).

For measuring the performance of the proposed two tree kernels, (Zelenco et al., 2003) used 60% of data manually constituted as a learning collection, and carried out 10-fold cross validation. Only two relations, that is, "*Person-Affiliation*" and "*Organization-Location*", were tested. The test revealed that the kernel-based method offers better performance than the feature-based method, and the continuous subtree kernel excels the sparse subtree kernel. In particular, the tree kernel proposed in their study inspired many new tree kernel researchers.

Their study is generally recognized as an important contribution for devising kernels for efficient measuring of similarity between very complex tree-type structure entities to be used later for relation extraction. Since various information other than the syntactic information is still required, the method highly depends on the performance of the REES system for creating parse trees. Because the quantity of data was not enough for the test and the binary classification test for only two types of relation was carried out, scalability or generality of the proposed kernel was not analyzed in detail.

4.2. Dependency tree kernel-based method (Culotta & Sorensen, 2004)

As the ACE collection was constituted and distributed from 2004, relation extraction has been fully studied. Culotta and Sorensen (2004) proposed a kernel-based relation extraction method, which uses the dependency parse tree structure on the basis of the tree kernel proposed by Zelenco, et al., (2003) described in section 4.1. This special parse tree, called an *Augmented Dependency Tree*, uses MXPOST (Ratnaparkhi, 1996) to carry out parsing, and then modifies some syntactic rules on the basis of the result. Exemplary rules include "*sub-*

jects are dependent on verbs", *"adjectives"* are dependent on nouns they describe, etc. In order to improve analysis result, however, this study uses even more complex node features than (Zelenco et al., 2003). The hypernym extracted from WordNet (Fellbaum, 1998) is applied to expand the matching function between nodes. The composite kernel is constructed to apply it to relation extraction for the first time.

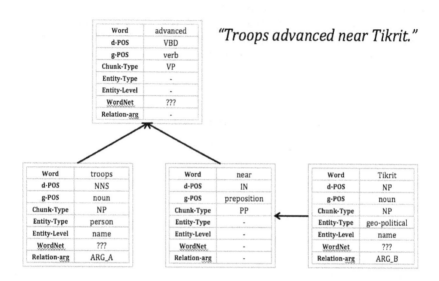

"Troops advanced near Tikrit."

Figure 8. Sample augmented dependency tree (*"Troops advanced near Tikrit"*).

Figure 8 shows a sample augmented dependency tree used in this study. The root of the tree is the verb *"advanced"*, and the resultant subject and the preposition are the child nodes of the root. The object of the preposition *"Tikrit"* is the child node of the preposition *"near"*. Each node has 8 types of node feature information. The Table below outlines each node feature.

Feature	Example
Words	troops, Tikrit
Detailed POS (24)	NN, NNP
General POS (5)	Noun, Verb, Adjective
Chunking Information	NP, VP, ADJP
Entity Type	person, geo-political-entity
Entity Level	name, nominal, pronoun
WordNet hypernyms	social group, city
Relation Argument	ARG_A, ARG_B

Table 1. Node features in the augmented dependency tree.

In Table 1, the first four features (words, part-of-speech information, and phrase information) are the information obtained from parsing, and the rest are named entity features from the ACE collection. Among them, the WordNet hypernym is the result of extracting the highest node for corresponding word from the WordNet database.

As discussed above, the tree kernel defined by (Zelenco et al., 2003) is used in this method. Since the features of each node are added, the matching function (Equaiton 1) and the similarity function (Equation 2) defined by Zelenco, et al., (2003) are accordingly modified into and applied. In detail, the features to be applied to the matching function and the features to be applied to the similarity function from among 8 features were dynamically divided to devise the following models to be applied.

t_i : feature vector representing the node i.

t_j : feature vector representing the node j.

t_i^m : subset of t_i used in matching function

t_i^s : subset of t_i used in similarity function   (7)

$$m(t_i, t_j) = \begin{cases} 1 & \text{if } t_i^m = t_j^m \\ 0 & \text{otherwise} \end{cases}$$

$$s(t_i, t_j) = \sum_{v_q \in t_i^s} \sum_{v_r \in t_j^s} C(v_q, v_r)$$

Where, m is the matching function; s is the similarity function; and t_i is a feature collection showing the node i. $C(\cdot, \cdot)$ is a function for comparing two feature values on the basis of approximate matching, not simple perfect matching. For example, recognition of "NN" and "NP" in the particular part-of-speech information of Table 1 as the same part-of-speeches is implemented by modifying the internal rule of the function. Equations 3 and 4 in section 4.1 are applied as tree kernel functions for comparing the similarity of two augmented dependency trees on the basis of two basic functions.

For the evaluation, the initial ACE collection version (2002) released in 2003 was used. This collection defines 5 entity types and 24 types of relations. Culotta & Sorensen (2004) tested relation extraction only for the higher 5 types of relation collections ("AT", "NEAR", "PART", "ROLE", "SOCIAL"). The tested kernels were the sparse subtree kernel (K_0), the continuous subtree kernel (K_1), and the bag-of-words kernel (K_2). In addition, two composite kernels for which the tree kernel was combined with the bag-of-word kernel, that is $K_3 = K_0 + K_2$, $K_4 = K_1 + K_2$ were further constituted. The test consisting of two steps of relation detection[4] and relation classification[5] revealed that all tree kernel methods, including the composite kernel, show better performance than the bag-of-words kernel. Unlike the evaluation result by (Zelenco et al., 2003), although the performance of continuous subtree kernel

---

4 Binary classification for identifying possible relation between two named entities.

5 Relation extraction for all instances with relations in the result of relation identification.

is higher, the reason for that was not clearly described, and the advantage of using the dependency tree instead of the full parse tree was not demonstrated in the experiment.

4.3. Shortest path dependency tree kernel method (Bunescu & Mooney, 2005)

In section 4.2, we have discussed relation extraction using dependency parse trees for the tree kernel proposed by Zelenco, et al., (2003). Bunescu & Mooney (2005) have studied the dependency path between the two named entities in the dependency parse tree with a view to proposing the shortest possible path dependency kernel for relation extraction. There is always a dependency path between two named entities in a sentence and Bunescu & Mooney (2005) argued that the performance of relation extraction is improved by using the syntactic paths. The Figure 9 below shows the dependency graph for a sample sentence.

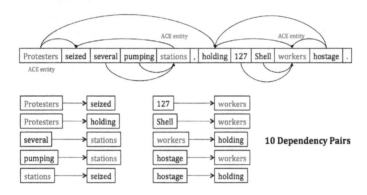

Figure 9. Dependency graph and dependency syntax pair list for the sample sentence.

The red node in Figure 9 represents the named entity specified in the ACE collection. Separation of the entire dependency graph results in 10 dependency syntax pairs. It is possible to select pairs, which include named entities in the syntax pairs to construct the dependency path as shown in Figure 10.

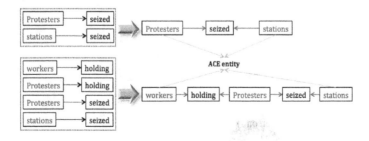

Figure 10. Extracting dependency path including named entities from dependency syntax pair collection.

As one can see from Figure 10, it is possible to construct the dependency path between the named entities, *"Protesters"* and *"stations,"* and the dependency path between *"workers"* and *"stations"*. As discussed above, the dependency path for connecting two named entities in this sentence can be extended infinitely. Bunescu & Mooney (2005) estimated that the shortest path among them contributes the most to establishing the relation between two entities. Therefore, it is possible to use kernel-based learning for estimating the relation between the two named entities connected by means of dependency path. For example, for estimating the relation for the path of *"protesters • seized • stations"*, the relation is estimated that the PERSON entity (*"protesters"*) did a specific behavior (*"seized"*) for the FACILITY entity (*"stations"*), through which PERSON (*"protesters"*) is located at FACILITY (*"stations"*) (*"LOCAT-ED_AT"*). At another complex path of *"workers • holding • protesters • seized • stations"*, it is possible to estimate the relation that PERSON (*"workers"*) is located at FACILITY (*"stations"*) (*"LOCATED_AT"*) if PERSON (*"protesters"*) did some behavior (*"holding"*) to PERSON (*"workers"*), and PERSON (*"protesters"*) did some behavior (*"seized"*) to FACILITY (*"stations"*). As such, with the dependency relation path, it is possible to identify semantic relation between two entities more intuitively.

For learning, Bunescu & Mooney (2005) have extracted the shortest dependency paths, including two entities from individual training instances as shown in the Table below.

Relations	Relation Instances
LOCATED_AT	**protesters •** seized **• stations**
LOCATED_AT	**workers •** holding **• protesters •** seized **• stations**
LOCATED_AT	**detainees •** abusing **• Jelisic •** created **• at • camp**

Table 2. Shortest path dependency tree-based sample relation extraction instance.

As shown in Table 2, each relation instance is expressed as a dependency path whose both ends are named entities. In terms of learning, however, it is not easy to extract sufficient features from such instances. Therefore, as discussed in section 4.2, various supplementary information is created, such as part-of-speech, entity type and WordNet synset. As a result, individual nodes which make up the dependency path comprise a plurality of information elements, and a variety of new paths are finally created as shown in Figure 11.

$$\begin{bmatrix} protesters \\ NNS \\ Noun \\ Person \end{bmatrix} \times [\rightarrow] \times \begin{bmatrix} seized \\ VBD \\ Verb \end{bmatrix} \times [\leftarrow] \times \begin{bmatrix} stations \\ NNS \\ Noun \\ Facility \end{bmatrix}$$

Figure 11. New dependency path information created in a single instance.

As shown in Figure 11, with more information available for individual nodes, new 48 dependency paths can be created through Cartesian product of the node values. Here, relation extraction is carried out by applying the dependency path kernel for calculating redundancy of the information included in each node rather than comparing all newly created paths, as shown below.

$$x = x_1 x_2 \cdots x_m, \quad y = y_1 y_2 \cdots y_n$$

$$K(x, y) = \begin{cases} 0, & m \neq n \\ \prod_{i=1}^{n} c(x_i, y_i) & m = n \end{cases} \tag{8}$$

$$c(x_i, y_i) = |\, x_i \cap y_i \,|$$

In the above Equation 8, x and y represent extended individual instances; m and n denote the lengths of the dependency path; $K(\,\bullet\,,\,\bullet\,)$ presents the dependency path kernel; and $c(\,\bullet\,,\,\bullet\,)$ is a function for calculating the level of information element redundancy between the two nodes. The Figure below shows the process of calculating the kernel value on the basis of Equation 8.

- *'his actions in Brcko'* ➔ his ➔ actions ← in ← **Brcko**
- *'his arrival in Beijing'* ➔ his ➔ arrival ← in ← **Beijing**

his PRP Person	→	actions NNS Noun	←	in IN	←	Brcko NNP Noun Location	
his PRP Person	→	arrival NN Noun	←	in IN	←	Beijing NNP Noun Location	
3	1	1	1	2	1	3	18

Figure 12. Calculating dependency path kernel.

As shown in Figure 12, the process of comparing two dependency paths is very simple. If the length of two paths is different, the kernel function simply returns zero (0). Otherwise, the level of information redundancy is then calculated for each node with respect to two paths. Since all the corresponding values are identical in the first node ("his", "PRP" and "Person"), the output is set to 3. As one matches in the second node, 1 is returned. By exponentiating all the calculated values, the kernel value is found to be 18.

On the basis of the same test environment as the collection used by Culotta & Sorensen (2004), two parsing systems, the CCG parser (Hockenmaier & Steedman, 2002) and the CFG parser (Collins, 1997) have been used to construct the shortest dependency path. The test included K_4 (bag-of-words kernel + continuous subtree kernel) that demonstrated the best performance by Culotta & Sorensen (2004) for comparing performance. The test revealed that the CFG-based shortest dependency path kernel offers better performance by using the CFG parser than the CCG parser for the same kernel.

With regard to relation extraction, the shortest dependency path information is considered to be very useful, and is highly likely to be used in various fields. However, the kernel structure is too simple. Yet another limitation is that only the paths of the same length are included in calculating similarity of two dependency paths.

4.4. Subsequence kernel-based method (Bunescu & Mooney, 2006)

The tree kernel presented by Zelenco, et al., (2003) is to compare two sibling nodes basically at the same level and uses the subsequence kernel. Bunescu & Mooney (2006) introduced the subsequence kernel and attempted relation extraction only with the base phrase analysis (chunking), without applying the syntactic structure. Since kernel input is not of a complex syntactic structure, but base phrase sequences, the assumption was that the feature space can be divided into 3 types to comprise maximum 4 words for each type of features as follows, by using the advantage of easy selection of contextual information essential for relation extraction.

- [FB] Fore-Between
  - 'interaction of [P1] with [P2]'
  - 'activation of [P1] by [P2]'
- [B] Between
  - '[P1] interacts with [P2]'
  - '[P1] is activated by [P2]'
- [BA] Between-After
  - '[P1] – [P2] complex'
  - '[P1] and [P2] interact'

Figure 13. Contextual location information for feature extraction.

In Figure 13, [FB] represents the words positioned before and between the two entities; [B] means only the word between them; and [BA], accordingly, means word collections between and after. The 3 types of feature collections can accept individual relation expressions, respectively. Furthermore, various types of supplementary word information (part-of-speech, entity type, WordNet synset, etc.) are used to expand them as in the methods described above.

Zelenco et al., (2003) described how to calculate the subsequence kernel, which will be described in detail again later. The kernel calculation function $K_n(s, t)$ is defined as shown below based on all n-length subsequences included in two sequences s, t.

$$K_n(s, t, \lambda) = \sum_{i:|i|=n} \sum_{j:|j|=n} \lambda^{l(i)+l(j)} \prod_{k=1}^{n} c(s_{i_k}, t_{j_k}) \qquad (9)$$

Where, i and j represent subsequences contained in s, t respectively; $c(\,\bullet\,,\,\bullet\,)$ is a function for deciding the homogeneity of the two inputs; and λ is a weight given to matching subsequences. $l(i)$ and $l(j)$ are the values indicating how far each relevant subsequence is positioned from the entire sequences. In order to calculate the weighted length, equation 9 selects among s and t only n-length subsequences, which exist in both sequences. For easy description, the following two sentences and base phrase analysis result will be used to explain the process of calculating the kernel value.

s = "Troops advanced near Tikrit."

Word	troops
d-POS	NNS
g-POS	noun
Chunk-Type	NP
Entity-Type	person
Entity-Level	name
WordNet	???
Relation-arg	ARG_A

Word	advanced
d-POS	VBD
g-POS	verb
Chunk-Type	VP
Entity-Type	-
Entity-Level	-
WordNet	???
Relation-arg	-

Word	near
d-POS	IN
g-POS	preposition
Chunk-Type	PP
Entity-Type	-
Entity-Level	-
WordNet	???
Relation-arg	-

Word	Tikrit
d-POS	NP
g-POS	noun
Chunk-Type	NP
Entity-Type	geo-political
Entity-Level	name
WordNet	???
Relation-arg	ARG_B

Word	forces
d-POS	NNS
g-POS	noun
Chunk-Type	NP
Entity-Type	person
Entity-Level	name
WordNet	???
Relation-arg	ARG_A

Word	moved
d-POS	VBD
g-POS	verb
Chunk-Type	VP
Entity-Type	-
Entity-Level	-
WordNet	???
Relation-arg	-

Word	quickly
d-POS	RB
g-POS	adverb
Chunk-Type	ADVP
Entity-Type	-
Entity-Level	-
WordNet	???
Relation-arg	-

Word	toward
d-POS	IN
g-POS	preposition
Chunk-Type	PP
Entity-Type	-
Entity-Level	-
WordNet	???
Relation-arg	-

t = "Forces moved quickly toward Baghdad."

$$[K_3(s, t, 0.5)]?$$

Word	Baghdad
d-POS	NP
g-POS	noun
Chunk-Type	NP
Entity-Type	geo-political
Entity-Level	name
WordNet	???
Relation-arg	ARG_B

Figure 14. Two sentences and base phrase analysis result to illustrate the process of calculating subsequence kernel.

As shown in Figure 14, each of the nodes that consist of analysis result has 8 types of lexical information (word, part-of-speech, base phrase type, entity type, etc.) The kernel value, $K_3(s, t, 0.5)$, of two analysis sequences is calculated according to the process shown in Figure 15, with features of the subsequence of which the length is 3.

There are three subsequence pairs which are decided that the node of all subsequence is at least 0 by means of the homogeneity decision function $c(\,\cdot\,,\,\cdot\,)$, among the subsequences in s and t. Scores for each of matching subsequences are derived by calculating the cumulative factorial of $c(\,\cdot\,,\,\cdot\,)$ for each of them and then multiplying it by the weight. For example, the similarity of 0.84375 is obtained for *"troops advanced near"* and *"forces moved toward"*. On the contrary, the similarity of *"troops advanced ...Tikrit"* and *"forces moved ...Bagdhad"* is 0.21093. This results from the lowered weight because the two subsequences are positioned apart. At last, the similarities of the subsequences are introduced to Equation 8 that gives 1.477.

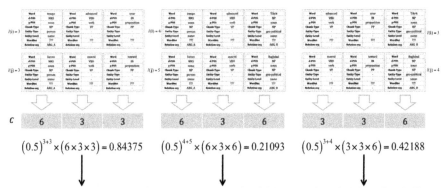

$$\left(0.5\right)^{3+3} \times \left(6 \times 3 \times 3\right) = 0.84375 \qquad \left(0.5\right)^{4+5} \times \left(6 \times 3 \times 6\right) = 0.21093 \qquad \left(0.5\right)^{3+4} \times \left(3 \times 3 \times 6\right) = 0.42188$$

$$K_3(\text{"Troops advanced near Tikrit"},\text{"Forces moved quickly toward Baghdad"},0.5) = 1.47656$$

Figure 15. Process of calculating K_3(s, t, 0.5).

As described above, it is possible to construct the subsequence kernel function based on the subsequences of all lengths by using contextual location information and Equation 8 as described above. Figure 16 shows surrounding contextual location where named entities occur in the sentence.

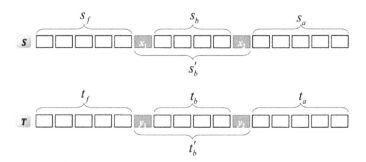

Figure 16. Specifying contextual information depending on named entity location and defining variables.

$$K(s, t) = K_{fb}(s, t) + K_b(s, t) + K_{ba}(s, t)$$

$$K_{b,i}(s, t) = K_i(s_b, t_b, 1) \cdot c(x_1, y_1) \cdot c(x_2, y_2) \cdot \lambda^{l(s'_b) + l(t'_b)}$$

$$K_{fb}(s, t) = \sum_{i \geq 1, j \geq 1, i+j f b_{\max}} K_{b,i}(s, t) \cdot K'_j(s_f, t_f)$$

$$K_b(s, t) = \sum_{1 \leq i \leq b_{\max}} K_{b,i}(s, t)$$

$$K_{ba}(s, t) = \sum_{i \geq 1, j \geq 1, i+j ba_{\max}} K_{b,i}(s, t) \cdot K'_j(\tilde{s}_f, \tilde{t}_f)$$

(10)

In Figure 16, x_i and y_i represent named entities; s_f and t_f denote the word lists before named entities; and s_a and t_a presents contextual word collections after two entities. s_b' and t_b' represent contextual information including two entities. Thus, the subsequence kernel for two sequences s and t is defined with the following Equation 10.

The subsequence kernel $K(s, t)$ consists of the sum of the contextual kernel before and between entity pairs, K_{fb}, the intermediate contextual kernel K_b of the entities, and the contextual kernel between and after entity pairs K_{ba}. fb_{max} is the length of the target context "Fore-Between" and b_{max} is the length of "Between" context. Also, ba_{max} is the target length of the context "Between-After" as seen in the figure 13. $\tilde{s}$ and $\tilde{t}$ are the reverse versions of strings of s and t respectively. The definition of the individual contextual kernel is described from the third to the fifth line of Equation 10. Here, K'_n is the same as K_n, with the exception that it specifies the length of the relevant subsequence from the location where the subsequence starts to the end of the entire sequence, and is defined as follows.

$$K_n'(s, t, \lambda) = \sum_{i:|i|=n} \sum_{j:|j|=n} \lambda^{|s|+|t|-i_1-j_1+2} \prod_{k=1}^{n} c(s_{i_k}, t_{j_k}) \tag{11}$$

In Equation 11, i_1 and j_1 represent the starting positions of subsequences i and j respectively. The individual contextual kernel calculates the similarity between the two sequences for the subsequences in the location divided on the basis of the locations specified in Figure 16, with Equation 10, and totalizes the kernel values to calculate resulting kernel values.

The performance evaluation in the same test environment as used in Sections 4.2 and 4.3 shows increased performance, even without complicated pre-processing, such as parsing, and without any syntactic information. In conclusion, the evaluation shows that this method is very fast in terms of learning speed and is an approach with a variety of potentials for improving performance.

4.5. Composite kernel-based method (Zhang, Zhang, Su, et al., 2006)

The release of ACE 2003 and 2004 versions contributed to full-scale study on relation extraction. In particular, the collection is characterized by even richer information for tagged entities. For example, ACE 2003 provides various entity features, e.g., entity headwords, entity type, and entity subtype for a specific named entity, and the features have been used as an important clue for determining the relation between two entities in a specific sentence. In this context, Zhang, Zhang, Su, et al., (2006) have built a composite kernel for which the convolution parse tree kernel proposed by Collins & Duffy, (2001) is combined with the entity feature kernel. Equation 11 gives the entity kernel definition.

$$K_L(R_1, R_2) = \sum_{i=1,2} K_E(R_1.E_i, R_2.E_i)$$

$$K_E(E_1, E_2) = \sum_i C(E_1.f_i, E_2.f_i)$$

$$C(f_1, f_2) = \begin{cases} 1, & \text{if } f_1 = f_2 \\ 0, & \text{otherwise} \end{cases} \tag{12}$$

In Equation 12, R_i represents the relation instance; and $R_i.E_j$ are the j-th entity of R_i. $E_i.f_j$ represents the j-th entity feature of entity E_i; and $C(\cdot , \cdot)$ is a homogeneity function for the two entities. It is possible to calculate the entity kernel K_L by summation on the basis of feature redundancy decision kernel K_E for a pair of entities.

Second, the convolution parse tree kernel expresses one parse tree as an occurrence frequency vector of a subtree as follows so as to measure the similarity between the two parse trees.

$$\phi(T)=\left(\# subtree_1(T),\ ...,\ \# subtree_i(T),\ ...,\ \# subtree_n(T)\right) \qquad (13)$$

In Equation 13, #subtree$_i$(T) represents the occurrence frequency of the i-th subtree. All parse trees are expressed with the vector as described above, and the kernel function is calculated as the inner product of two vectors as follows.

$$K(T_1,\ T_2)=\langle\phi(T_1),\ \phi(T_2)\rangle \qquad (14)$$

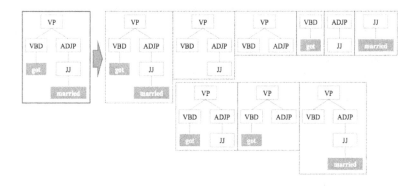

Figure 17. Parsing tree and its subtree collection.

Figure 17 shows all subtrees of a specific parse tree. There are nine subtrees in the figure altogether, and each subtree is an axis of the vector, which expresses the left side parse tree. If the number of all unified parse trees that can be extracted for N parse trees is M, each of extracted subtrees can be expressed as an M-dimension vector.

As shown in Figure 17, there are two constraints for a subtree of a specific parse tree. First, the number of nodes of the subtree must be at least 2, and the subtree should comply with production rules used by syntactic parser to generate parse trees of sentences (Collins & Duffy, 2001). For example, [VP $\cdot$ VBD $\cdot$ "got"] cannot become a subtree.

It is necessary to investigate all subtrees in the tree T, and calculate their frequency so as to build the vector for each of parse trees. This process is quite inefficient, however. Since we need only to compute the similarity of two parse trees in the kernel-based method, we can come up with indirect kernel functions without building the subtree vector for each parse tree as with Equation 13. The following Equation 15, proposed by Collins & Duffy (2001), is used to calculate efficiently the similarity of two parse trees

$$K(T_1, T_2) = \langle \phi(T_1), \phi(T_2) \rangle$$

$$= \sum_i \# subtree_i(T_1) \cdot \# subtree_i(T_2)$$

$$= \sum_i \left(\sum_{n_1 \in N_1} I_{subtree_i}(n_1) \right) \cdot \left(\sum_{n_2 \in N_2} I_{subtree_i}(n_2) \right)$$

$$= \sum_{n_1 \in N_1} \sum_{n_2 \in N_2} \Delta(n_1, n_2)$$

$$N_1, N_2 \rightarrow \text{the set of nodes in trees } T_1 \text{ and } T_2.$$

$$(15)$$

$$I_{subtree_i}(n) = \begin{cases} 1 & \text{if } ROOT(subtree_i) = n \\ 0 & \text{otherwise} \end{cases}$$

$$\Delta(n_1, n_2) = \sum_i I_{subtree_i}(n_1) \cdot I_{subtree_i}(n_2)$$

In Equation 15, T_i represents a specific parse tree, and N_i represents all node collections of the parse tree. $I_{st}(n)$ is the function for checking whether the node n is the root node of the specific subtree st. The most time-consuming calculation in Equation 15 falls on calculating $\varnothing(n_1, n_2)$. To enhance this, Collins & Duffy (2001) came up with the following algorithm.

1. If CFP Production rules of n_1 and n_2 are different each other,

$$\Delta(n_1, n_2) = 0$$

2. If both n_1 and n_2 are pre-terminals (POS-tag),

$$\Delta(n_1, n_2) = 1 \times \lambda$$

3. Otherwise,

$$\Delta(n_1, n_2) = \lambda \prod_{j=1}^{nc(n_1)} \left(1 + \Delta\left(ch(n_1, j), ch(n_2, j) \right) \right)$$

$$nc(n_1) \rightarrow \text{the child number of } n_1,$$

$$ch(n, j) \rightarrow j^{th} \text{ child of node } n$$

$$\lambda \rightarrow \text{decay factor}$$

Figure 18. Algorithm for calculating $\varnothing(n_1, n_2)$

The function $\varnothing(n_1, n_2)$ defined in (3) of Figure 18 compares the child nodes of the input node to calculate the frequency of subtrees contained in both parse trees and the product thereof, until the end conditions defined in (1) and (2) are satisfied. In this case, the decay factor , which is a variable for limiting large subtrees so as to address the issue that larger subtrees among the subtrees of the parse tree comprise another subtrees therein, can be applied repeatedly for calculating the inner product of the subtree vector.

Two kernels built as described above, that is, the entity kernel and the convolution parse tree kernel, are combined in the following two manners.

$$K_1(R_1, R_2) = \alpha \cdot \frac{K_L(R_1, R_2)}{\sqrt{K_L(R_1, R_1) \cdot K_L(R_2, R_2)}} + (1-\alpha)\frac{K(T_1, T_2)}{\sqrt{K(T_1, T_1) \cdot K(T_2, T_2)}} \qquad (16\text{-}1)$$

$$K_2(R_1, R_2) = \alpha \cdot \left(\frac{K_L(R_1, R_2)}{\sqrt{K_L(R_1, R_1) \cdot K_L(R_2, R_2)}} + 1\right)^2 + (1-\alpha)\frac{K(T_1, T_2)}{\sqrt{K(T_1, T_1) \cdot K(T_2, T_2)}} \qquad (16\text{-}2)$$

In the above equations 16-1 and 16-2, K_L represents the entity kernel and K stands for the convolution parse tree kernel. Equation 16-1 shows the composite kernel being a linear combination of the two kernels, and Equation 16-2 defines the composite kernel constructed using quadratic polynomial combination.

Furthermore, Zhang, Zhang, Su, et al., (2006) proposed the method for pruning relation instance by leaving a part of the parse tree and removing the rest, so as to improve similarity measurement performance of the kernel function, and to exclude unnecessary contextual information in learning.

Tree Pruning Methods	Details
Minimum Complete Tree (MCT)	Minimum complete sub-tree encompassing two entities
Path-enclosed Tree (PT)	Sub-tree belong to the shortest path in between two entities
Chunking Tree(CT)	Sub-tree generated by discarding all the internal nodes excpet nodes for base phrases and POS from PT
Context-sensitive PT(CPT)	Sub-tree generated by adding two additional terminal nodes outside PT
Context-sensitive CT(CCT)	Sub-tree generated by adding two additional terminal nodes outside CT
Flattened PT(FPT)	Sub-tree generated by discarding all the nodes having only one paraent and child node from PT
Flattened CPT(FCPT)	Sub-tree generated by discarding all the nodes having only one paraent and child node from CT

Table 3. Relation instance pruning (Zhang, Zhang, Su, et al., 2006; Zhang et al., 2008).

For the evaluation, Zhang, Zhang, Su, et al., (2006) used both ACE 2003 and ACE 2004. They parsed all available relation instances with Charniak's Parser (Charniak, 2001), and on the basis of the parsing result carried out instance conversion using the method described in Table 3. To this end, Moschitti (2004) has developed a kernel tool, while SVMLight (Joachims, 1998) was used for learning and classification.

The test shows that the composite kernel features better performance than a single syntactic kernel. The combination of quadratic polynomial type shows performance between the two kernels. This means that flat feature (entity type feature) and structural feature (syntactic feature) can be organically combined as a single kernel function. In consideration that the Path-enclosed Tree method shows the best performance among all relation instance pruning methods, it is possible to achieve the effect only with core related syntactic information, so as to estimate the relation of two entities in a specific sentence.

4.6. Other recent studies

Choi, et al., (2009) have constructed and tested a composite kernel where various lexical and contextual features are added by expanding the existing composite kernel. In addition to the syntactic feature, called flat feature, they extended the combination range of lexical feature from the entity feature to the contextual feature in order to achieve high performance. Mintz, Bills, Snow, and Jurafsky (2009) proposed a new method of using Freebase, which is a semantic database for thousands relation collections, to gather exemplary sentences for a specific relation and making relation extraction on the basis of the obtained exemplary sentences. In the test, the collection of 10,000 instances corresponding to 102 types of relations has shown the accuracy of 67.6%. In addition, T.-V. T. Nguyen, Moschitti, and Riccardi (2009) have designed a new kernel, which extends the existing convolution parse tree kernel, and Reichartz, et al., (2009) proposed a method, which extends the dependency tree kernel. As described above, most studies published so far are based on the kernels described in Sections 4.1 to 4.5.

5. Comparison and analysis

In the previous section, five types of kernel-based relation extraction have been analyzed in detail. Here, we discuss the results of comparison and analysis of these methods. Section 5.1 will briefly describe the criteria for comparison and analysis of the methods. Section 5.2 compares characteristics of the methods. Section 5.3 covers performance results in detail. Section 5.4 sums up the advantages and disadvantages of each of the method.

5.1. Criteria for comparison and analysis

Generally, a large variety of criteria can be used for comparing kernel-based relation extraction methods. The following 6 criteria, however, have been selected and used in this study. First, (1) linguistic analysis and pre-processing method means the pre-processing analysis methods and types for individual instances which are composed of learning collections and evaluation collections, e.g., the type of parsing method or the parsing system used. (2) The level of linguistic analysis, which is the criterion related to the method (1), is a reference to what level the linguistic analysis will be carried out in pre-processing and analyzing instances. Exemplary levels include part-of-speech tagging, base phrase analysis, dependency parsing or full parsing. In addition, (3) the method of selecting a feature space is a reference for deciding if the substantial input of the kernel function is an entire sentence or a part thereof. Also, (4) the applied lexical and supplementary feature information means various supplementary feature information used for addressing the issue of sparse data. (5) The relation extraction method is a practical relation extraction method based on learning models already constituted. Exemplary relation extraction methods include multi-class classification at a time and a single mode method of separating instances with relations from those without relations by means of processing multiple classifications at a time or binary classification, then to carry out relation classification only for the instances with relations. (6) The manual work requirement is a reference to decide if the entire process is fully automatically carried out or manual work is required only at some step. The aforementioned 6 criteria were used to analyze the kernel-based relation extraction methods and the result of the analysis is shown in the following Table 6.

In addition, for the purpose of describing the characteristics of the kernel function, the description in section 4 will be summarized, and each structure of factors to be input of the kernel function will be described. Modification of the kernel function for optimized speed will be included in the analysis criteria and described. For performance comparison of the individual methods, types and scale of the tested collections and tested relations will be analyzed and described in detail. The following Table 4 describes the ACE collection generally used among the tested collections for relation extraction developed so far.

Items	ACE-2002	ACE-2003	ACE-2004
# training documents	422	674	451
# training relation instances	6,156	9,683	5,702
# test documents	97	97	N/A
# test relation instances	1,490	1,386	N/A
# entity types	5	5	7
# major relation types	5	5	7
# relation sub-types	24	24	23

Table 4. Description of ACE Collection.

As shown in Table 4, the ACE collection is generally used and can be divided into 3 types. ACE-2002, however, is not widely used because of consistency and quality problems. There are 5 to 7 types of entities, e.g., Person, Organization, Facility, Location, Geo-Political Entity, etc. For relations, all collections are structured to be at two levels, consisting of 23 to 24 types of particular relations corresponding to 5 types of Role, Part, Located, Near, and Social. As the method of constructing those collections is advanced and the quality thereof is improved, the tendency is that the scale of training instances is reduced. Although subsequent collections have already been constituted, they are not publicized according to the principle of non-disclosure, which is the policy of ACE Workshop. This should be improved for active studies.

5.2. Comparison of characteristics

Table 5 summarizes each of kernel functions with respect to the concept, before analyzing the kernel-based relation extraction method, in conformity to 6 types of comparison and analysis criteria described in 5.1.

Kernel types	Description of concept
Tree Kernel (TK)	Compares each node which consists of two trees to be compared.
Dependency Tree Kernel (DTK)	Based on BFS, applies subsequence kernel to the child nodes located at the same level. The decay factor is adjusted and applied to the similarity depending on the length of subsequences at the same level or on the level itself.
Shortest Path Dependency Kernel (SPDK)	Compares each element of the two paths to cumulatively calculate the common values for the elements in order to compute the similarity by multiplying all values. Similarity is 0 if the length of two paths is different.
Subsequence Kernel (SK)	For the example of measuring similarity of two words, extracts only the subsequences which exist in both words, and expresses the two words with a vector ($\Phi(x)$) by using the subsequences, among all of the subsequences which belong to two words and of which the length is n. Afterwards, obtains the inner product of the two vectors to calculate the similarity. Generalizes and uses SSK to compare planar information of the tree kernel (sibling node).
Composite Kernel (CK)	Finds all subtrees in the typical CFG-type syntactic tree, and establishes them as a coordinate axis to represent the parse tree as a vector ($\Phi(x)$). In this case, the following constraints hold true: (1) the number of nodes must be at least 2, and (2) the subtree should comply with the CFG creation rule. Since there can be multiple subtrees, each coordinate value can be at least 1, and similarity is calculated by obtaining the inner product of the two vectors created as such.

Table 5. Summary of kernel-based relation extraction methods.

Table 6 shows comparison and analysis of the kernel-based relation extraction methods. As it is closer to the right side, the method is more recent one. The characteristic found in all of the above methods is that various feature information in addition to the syntactic information is used as well. Such heterogeneous information was first combined and used in a single kernel function, but is separated from the composite kernel and applied.

With respect to selecting the feature space, most of sentences or a part of the parse tree are applied other than the tree kernel. Manual work was initially required for extracting relation instances and building the parse tree. The recently developed methods, however, offer full automation. In the relation extraction methods, multi-class classification is used, in which the case with no relation is included as one relation.

	TK	DTK	SPDK	SK	CK
Language Processor	Shallow Parserx (REES)	Statistical Parserx (MXPOST)	Statistical Parser (Collins' Parser)	Chunker (OpenNLP)	Statistical Parser (Charniak's Parser)
Level of Language Processing	PLO Tagging Parsing	Parsing	Parsing	Chunking	Parsing
Feature Selection Methods	Extracts features from parse trees manually	Selects small sub-tree including two entities from the entire dependency tree	Selects the shortest dependency path which starts with one entity and ends with the other one	Before Entities After Entities Between Entities	MCT PT CPT FPT FCPT
Features used in Kernel Computation	Entity Headword Entity Role Entity Text	Word POS Chunking Info. Entity Type Entity Level WordNet Hypernym Relation Parameter	Word POS Chunking Info. Entity Type	Word POS Chunking Info. Entity Type Chunk Headword	Entity Headword Entity Type Mention Type LDC mention Type Chunking Info.
Relation Extraction Methods	Single Phase (Multiclass SVM)	Cascade Phase (Relation Detection and Classification)	Single Phase Cascade Phase	Single Phase (Multiclass SVM)	Single Phase (Multiclass SVM)
Manual Process	Necessary (Instance Extraction)	Necessary (Dependency Tree)	Necessary (Dependency Path)	N/A	N/A

Table 6. Comparison of characteristics of kernel-based relation extraction.

5.3. Comparison of performance

Table 7 shows the parameter type of each kernel function and computation complexity in calculating the similarity of two inputs. Most of them show complexity of $O(N^2)$, but SPDK exceptionally demonstrates the complexity of the order of $O(N)$ and can be considered as the most efficient kernel.

Kernels	Parameter Structure	Time Complexity
TK	Shallow parse trees	CSTK : $O(|N_{i,1}|*|N_{i,2}|)$
DTK	Dependency trees	SSTK : $O(|N_{i,1}|*|N_{i,2}|^3)$
		$|N_1|$: #(1st input's nodes in level i)
		$|N_2|$: #(2nd input's nodes in level i)
SPDK	Dependency paths	$O(|N_1|)$
		$|N_1|$: #(1st input's nodes)
SK	Chunking results	$O(n*|N_1|*|N_2|)$
		n : subsequence length
		$|N_1|$: #(1st input's nodes)
		$|N_2|$: #(2nd input's nodes)
CK	Full parse trees	$O(|N_1| *|N_2|)$
		$|N_1|$: #(1st input's nodes)
		$|N_2|$: #(2nd input's nodes)

Table 7. Parameter structure and calculation complexity of each kernel.

It should be noted that the complexity shown in Table 7 is just kernel calculation complexity. The overall complexity of relation extraction can be much higher when processing time for parsing and learning is also considered.

Articles	Year	Methods	Test Collection	F1
(Zelenco et al., 2003)	2003	TK	200 News Articles (2-relations)	**85.0**
(Culotta & Sorensen, 2004)	2004	DTK	ACE-2002 (5-major relations)	**45.8**
(Kambhatla, 2004)	2004	ME	ACE-2003 (24-relation sub-types)	**52.8**
(Bunescu & Mooney, 2005)	2005	SPDK	ACE-2002 (5-major relations)	**52.5**
(Zhou et al., 2005)	2005	SVM	ACE-2003 (5-major relations)	**68.0**
			ACE-2003 (24-relation sub-types)	**55.5**
(Zhao & Grishman, 2005)	2005	CK	ACE-2004 (7-major relations)	**70.4**
(Bunescu & Mooney, 2006)	2006	SK	ACE-2002 (5-major relations)	**47.7**
(Zhang, Zhang, Su, et al., 2006)	2006	CK	ACE-2003 (5-major relations)	**70.9**
			ACE-2003 (24-relation sub-types)	**57.2**
			ACE-2004 (7-major relations)	**72.1**
			ACE-2004 (23-relation sub-types)	**63.6**
(Zhou et al., 2007)	2007	CK	ACE-2003 (5-major relations)	**74.1**
			ACE-2003 (24-relation sub-types)	**59.6**
			ACE-2004 (7-major relations)	**75.8**
			ACE-2004 (23-relation sub-types)	**66.0**
(Jiang & Zhai, 2007)	2007	ME/SVM	ACE-2004 (7-major relations)	**72.9**

Table 8. Comparison of performance of each model of kernel-based relation extraction.

Articles and Approaches	Relation Sets	Test Collection																						
		200 News			ACE-2002						ACE-2003						ACE-2004					
		PLO-2			Main-5			Sub-24			Main-5			Sub-24			Main-7			Sub-23		
Precision/Recall/F-measure		P	R	F	P	R	F	P	R	F	P	R	F	P	R	F	P	R	F	P	R	F
(Zelenco et al., 2003)	TK	91.6	79.5	85.0																		
(Culotta & Sorensen, 2004)	DTK				67.1	35.0	45.8															
(Kambhatla, 2004)	ME													63.5	45.2	52.8						
(Bunescu & Mooney, 2005)	SPDK				65.5	43.8	52.5															
(Zhou et al., 2005)	SVM										77.2	60.7	68.0	63.1	49.5	55.5						
(Zhao & Grishman, 2005)	CK																69.2	70.5	70.4			
(Bunescu & Mooney, 2006)	SK							73.9	35.2	47.7												
(Zhang, Zhang, Su, et al., 2006)	CK										77.3	65.6	70.9	64.9	51.2	57.2	76.1	68.4	72.1	68.6	59.3	63.6
(Zhou et al., 2007)	CK										80.8	68.4	74.1	65.2	54.9	59.6	82.2	70.2	75.8	70.3	62.2	66.0
(Jiang & Zhai, 2007)	ME/ SVM																74.6	71.3	72.9			

Table 9. Comparison of performance of each kernel-based relation extraction method.

ACE-2002, which is the first version of ACE collection, had the issue with data consistency. In the subsequent versions this problem has been continuously addressed, and finally resolved in version ACE-2003. Starting from 52.8% achieved by Kambhatla (2004) on the basis of the performance of ACE-2003 with respect to 24 relation collections, the performance was improved up to 59.6% recently announced by Zhou, et al., (2007). Similarly, the maximum relation extraction performance for 23 particular relations on the ACE-2004 collection is currently 66%.

Although each model has different performance in differently sized relation collections, the composite kernel generally shows better results. In particular, Zhou, et al., (2007) have demonstrated high performance for all collections or relation collections based on extended models initially proposed by Zhang, Zhang, Su, et al., (2006). As described above, it is considered that various features for relation extraction, that is, the syntactic structure and the vocabulary, can be efficiently combined in a composite kernel for better performance.

Although the described research results do not represent all studies on relation extraction, there are many parts not evaluated yet although a lot of study results have been derived so far as seen in Table 9. It is necessary to carry out evaluation on the basis of various collections for comprehensive performance evaluation of a specific relation extraction model, but this is a challenge that more studies should be done. In particular, the key issue is to check whether the performance of relation extraction is achieved as high as described in the above without the characteristics of ACE collections, in that they provide supplementary information (entity type information) of a considerable scale for relation extraction.

5.4. Comparison and analysis of advantages and disadvantages of each method

In Section 5.4, advantages and disadvantages of five kernel-based relation extraction methods are discussed and outlined in Table 10.

Method	Advantage	Disadvantage
Feature-based SVM/ME	Applies the typical automatic sentence classification without modification. Performance can be further improved by applying various feature information. Relatively high speed	A lot of effort is required for feature extraction and selection. Performance can be improved only through feature combination.
Tree Kernel (TK)	Calculates particular similarity between shallow parse trees. Uses both structural (parenthood) and planar information (brotherhood). Optimization for speed improvement.	Very limited use of structural information (syntactic relations) Slow similarity calculation speed in spite of optimized speed
Dependency TK (DK)	Addressed the issue of insufficient use of structural information, which is a disadvantage of TK.	Predicates and key words in a dependency tree are emphasized only by means of decay factors (low emphasis capability)

Method	Advantage	Disadvantage
	Uses key words which are the core of relation expression in the sentence, as feature information, on the basis of the structure that the predicate node is raised to a higher status, which is a structural characteristic of a dependency tree.	Slow similarity calculation speed
Shortest Path DTK (SPTK)	Creates a path between two named entities by means of dependency relation to reduce noise not related to relation expression. Shows very fast computation speed because the kernel input is not trees, but paths, different from previous inputs. Adds various types of supplementary feature information to improve the performance of similarity measurement, thanks to the simple structure of paths.	Too simple structure of the kernel function Too strong constraints because the similarity is 0 if the length of two input paths is different.
Subsequence Kernel (SK)	Very efficient because syntactic analysis information is not used. Adds various supplementary feature information to improve the performance.	Can include many unnecessary features
Composite Kernel (CK)	Makes all of constituent subtrees of a parse tree have a feature, to perfectly use structure information in calculating similarity. Optimized for improved speed	Comparison is carried out only on the basis of sentence component information of each node (phrase info.) (kernel calculation is required on the basis of composite feature information with reference to word class, semantic info, etc.)

Table 10. Analysis of advantages and disadvantages of kernel-based relation extraction.

As one can see in Table 10, each method has some advantages and disadvantages. A lot of efforts are required for the process of feature selection in general feature-based relation extraction. The kernel-based method does not have this disadvantage, but has various limitations instead. For example, although the shortest dependency path kernel includes a variety of potentials, it showed low performance due to the overly simple structure of the kernel function. Since the composite kernel constitutes and compares subtree features only on the basis of part-of-speech information and vocabulary information of each node, generality of similarity measurement is not high. A scheme to get over this is to use word classes or semantic information.

A scheme can be suggested for designing a new kernel in order to overcome the above shortcomings. For example, a scheme may be used for interworking various supplementary feature information (WordNet Synset, thesaurus, ontology, part-of-speech tag, thematic role information, etc.), so as to ensure general comparison between subtrees in the composite kernel. The performance can be improved by replacing the current simple linear kernel with the subsequence or another composite kernel and applying all sorts of supplementary feature information in order to address the shortcomings of the shortest path dependency kernel.

6. Conclusion

In this chapter, we analyzed kernel-based relation extraction method, which is considered the most efficient approach so far. Previous case studies did not fully covered specific operation principles of the kernel-based relation extraction models, just cited contents of individual studies or made an analysis in a limited range. This chapter, however, closely examines operation principles and individual characteristics of five kernel-based relation extraction methods, starting from the original kernel-based relation extraction studies (Zelenco et al., 2003), to composite kernel (Choi et al., 2009; Zhang, Zhang, Su, et al., 2006), which is considered the most advanced kernel-based method. The overall performance of each method was compared using ACE collections, and particular advantages and disadvantages of each method were summarized. This study will contribute to researchers' kernel study for relation extraction of higher performance and to general kernel studies of high level for linguistic processing and text mining.

Author details

Hanmin Jung*, Sung-Pil Choi, Seungwoo Lee and Sa-Kwang Song

*Address all correspondence to: jhm@kisti.re.kr

Korea Institute of Science and Technology Information, Korea

References

[1] ACE. (2009). *Automatic Content Extraction*, Retrieved from, http://www.itl.nist.gov/iad/mig//tests/ace/.

[2] Agichtein, E., & Gravano, L. (2000). Snowball: extracting relations from large plaintext collections. *Proceedings of the fifth ACM conference on Digital libraries*, 85-94, New York, NY, USA, ACM, doi:10.1145/336597.336644.

[3] Bach, N., & Badaskar, S. (2007). A Survey on Relation Extraction. *Literature review for Language and Statistics II*.

[4] Brin, S. (1999). Extracting Patterns and Relations from the World Wide Web. Lecture Notes in Computer Science, , 1590, 172-183.

[5] Bunescu, R., & Mooney, R. J. (2005). A Shortest Path Dependency Kernel for Relation Extraction. *Proceedings of the Human Language Technology Conference and Conference on Empirical Methods in Natural Language Processing*, 724-731.

[6] Bunescu, R., & Mooney, R. J. (2006). Subsequence Kernels for Relation Extraction. *Proceeding of the Ninth Conference on Natural Language Learning (CoNLL-2005)*, Ann Arbor, MI, Retrieved from, http://www.cs.utexas.edu/users/ai-lab/pub-view.php?PubID=51413.

[7] Charniak, E. (2001). Immediate-head Parsing for Language Models. *Proceedings of the 39th Annual Meeting of the Association for Computational Linguistics.*

[8] Choi, S.-P., Jeong, C.-H., Choi, Y.-S., & Myaeng, S.-H. (2009). Relation Extraction based on Extended Composite Kernel using Flat Lexical Features. *Journal of KIISE⟲: Software and Applications*, 36(8).

[9] Collins, M. (1997). Three Generative, Lexicalised Models for Statistical Parsing. Madrid. *Proceedings of the 35th Annual Meeting of the ACL (jointly with the 8th Conference of the EACL).*

[10] Collins, M., & Duffy, N. (2001). Convolution Kernels for Natural Language. *NIPS-2001.*

[11] Cortes, C., & Vapnik, V. (1995). Support-Vector Networks. *Machine Learning*, 20(3), 273-297, Hingham, MA, USA, Kluwer Academic Publishers, doi:10.1023/A: 1022627411411.

[12] Cristianini, N., & Shawe-Taylor, J. (2000). *An Introduction to Support Vector Machines and Other Kernel-based Learning Methods*, Cambridge University Press.

[13] Culotta, A., & Sorensen, J. (2004). Dependency Tree Kernels for Relation Extraction. *Proceedings of the 42nd Annual Meeting on Association for Computational Linguistics.*

[14] Etzioni, O., Cafarella, M., Downey, D., Popescu, A., , M., Shaked, T., Soderland, S., Weld, D. S., et al. (2005). Unsupervised named-entity extraction from the Web: An experimental study. *Artificial Intelligence*, 165(1), 91-134, Retrieved from, http://www.sciencedirect.com/science/article/pii/S0004370205000366.

[15] Fellbaum, C. (1998). WordNet: An Electronic Lexical Database. MIT Press Cambridge, MA

[16] Freund, Y., & Schapire, R. E. (1999). Large margin classification using the perceptron algorithm. *Machine learning*, 37(3), 277, 296, Retrieved from, http://www.springerlink.com/index/q3003163876k7h81.pdf.

[17] Fundel, K., Küffner, R., & Zimmer, R. (2007). RelEx-Relation extraction using dependency parse trees. *Bioinformatics*, 23(3), 365-371.

[18] Gartner, T., Flach, P., & Wrobel, S. (2003). On graph kernels: Hardness results and efficient alternatives. *Learning Theory and Kernel Machines*, 129-143.

[19] Hockenmaier, J., & Steedman, M. (2002). Generative Models for Statistical Parsing with Combinatory Categorial Grammar. Philadelphia, PA. *Proceedings of 40th Annual Meeting of the Association for Computational Linguistics.*

[20] Jiang, J., & Zhai, C. (2007). A Systematic Exploration of the Feature Space for Relation Extraction. *NAACL HLT.*

[21] Joachims, T. (1998). Text Categorization with Support Vecor Machine: learning with many relevant features. *ECML-1998.*

[22] Kambhatla, N. (2004). Combining lexical, syntactic and semantic features with Maximum Entropy models for extracting relations. *ACL-2004.*

[23] Li, J., Zhang, Z., Li, X., & Chen, H. (2008). Kernel-based learning for biomedical relation extraction. *Journal of the American Society for Information Science and Technology,* 59(5), 756-769, Wiley Online Library.

[24] Li, W., Zhang, P., Wei, F., Hou, Y., & Lu, Q. (2008). A novel feature-based approach to Chinese entity relation extraction. *Proceedings of the 46th Annual Meeting of the Association for Computational Linguistics on Human Language Technologies: Short Papers,* 89-92.

[25] Lodhi, H., Saunders, C., Shawe-Taylor, J., Cristianini, N., & Watkins, C. (2002). Text classification using string kernels. *Journal of Machine Learning Research,* 2, 419-444.

[26] MUC. (2001). *The NIST MUC Website,* Retrieved from, http://www.itl.nist.gov/iaui/894.02/related_projects/muc/.

[27] Mintz, M., Bills, S., Snow, R., & Jurafsky, D. (2009). Distant supervision for relation extraction without labeled data. *Proceedings of the Joint Conference of the 47th Annual Meeting of the ACL and the 4th International Joint Conference on Natural Language Processing of the AFNLP,* 2, 1003-1011, Stroudsburg, PA, USA, Association for Computational Linguistics, Retrieved from, http://dl.acm.org/citation.cfm?id=1690219.1690287.

[28] Moncecchi, G., Minel, J. L., & Wonsever, D. (2010). A survey of kernel methods for relation extraction. *Workshop on NLP and Web-based technologies (IBERAMIA 2010).*

[29] Moschitti, A. (2004). A Study on Convolution Kernels for Shallow Semantic Parsing. *ACL-2004.*

[30] Nguyen, D. P. T., Matsuo, Y., & Ishizuka, M. (2007). Exploiting syntactic and semantic information for relation extraction from wikipedia. *IJCAI Workshop on Text-Mining & Link-Analysis (TextLink 2007).*

[31] Nguyen, T.-V. T., Moschitti, A., & Riccardi, G. (2009). Convolution kernels on constituent, dependency and sequential structures for relation extraction. *Proceedings of the 2009 Conference on Empirical Methods in Natural Language Processing,* 3, 1378-1387.

[32] Ratnaparkhi, A. (1996). A Maximum Entropy Part-Of-Speech Tagger. *Proceedings of the Empirical Methods in Natural Language Processing Conference,* Retrieved from, http://onlinelibrary.wiley.com/doi/10.1002/cbdv.200490137/abstract.

[33] Reichartz, F., Korte, H., & Paass, G. (2009). Dependency tree kernels for relation extraction from natural language text. *Machine Learning and Knowledge Discovery in Databases*, 270-285, Springer.

[34] Rosenblatt, F. (1958). The Perceptron: A Probabilistic Model for Information Storage and Organization in the Brain. *Psychological Review*, 65(6), 386-408.

[35] TAC. (2012). *Text Analysis Conference*, Retrieved from, http://www.nist.gov/tac/.

[36] Yarowsky, D. (1995). Unsupervised word sense disambiguation rivaling supervised methods. *Proceedings of the 33rd annual meeting on Association for Computational Linguistics*, 189-196, Morristown, NJ, USA, Association for Computational Linguistics, doi:10.3115/981658.981684.

[37] Yates, A., Cafarella, M., Banko, M., Etzioni, O., Broadhead, M., & Soderland, S. (2007). TextRunner: open information extraction on the web. Proceedings of Human Language Technologies: The Annual Conference of the North American Chapter of the Association for Computational Linguistics: Demonstrations Stroudsburg, PA, USA: Association for Computational Linguistics Retrieved from http://dl.acm.org/citation.cfm?id=1614164.1614177 , 25-26.

[38] Zelenco, D., Aone, C., & Richardella, A. (2003). Kernel Methods for Relation Extraction. *Journal of Machine Leanring Research*, 3, 1083-1106.

[39] Zhang, M., Zhang, J., & Su, J. (2006). Exploring syntactic features for relation extraction using a convolution tree kernel. *Proceedings of the main conference on Human Language Technology Conference of the North American Chapter of the Association of Computational Linguistics*, 288-295, Stroudsburg, PA, USA, Association for Computational Linguistics, doi:10.3115/1220835.1220872.

[40] Zhang, M., Zhang, J., Su, J., & Zhou, G. (2006). A Composite Kernel to Extract Relations between Entities with both Flat and Structured Features. *21st International Conference on Computational Linguistics and 44th Annual Meeting of the ACL*, 825-832.

[41] Zhang, M., Zhou, G., & Aiti, A. (2008). Exploring syntactic structured features over parse trees for relation extraction using kernel methods. *Information processing & management*, 44(2), 687-701, Elsevier.

[42] Zhao, S., & Grishman, R. (2005). Extracting Relations with Integrated Information Using Kernel Methods. *ACL-2005*.

[43] Zhou, G., Su, J., Zhang, J., & Zhang, M. (2005). Exploring Various Knowledge in Relation Extraction. *ACL-2005*.

[44] Zhou, G., Zhang, M., Ji, D., & Zhu, Q. (2007). Tree Kernel-based Relation Extraction with Context-Sensitive Structured Parse Tree Information. *The 2007 Joint Conference on Empirical Methods in Natural Language Processing and Computational Natural Language Learning*, 728-736.

## Chapter 2

Text Clumping for Technical Intelligence

Alan L. Porter and Yi Zhang

Additional information is available at the end of the chapter

1. Introduction: Concepts, Purposes, and Approaches

This development responds to a challenge. Text mining software can conveniently generate very large sets of terms or phrases. Our examples draw from use of VantagePoint (or equivalently, Thomson Data Analyzer – TDA) software [1] to analyze abstract record sets. A typical search on an ST&I topic of interest might yield, say, 5,000 records. One approach is to apply VantagePoint's Natural Language Processing (NLP) to the titles, and also to the abstracts and/or claims. We also take advantage of available topic-rich fields such as keywords and index terms. Merging these fields could well offer on the order of 100,000 terms and phrases in one field (list). That list, unfortunately, will surely contain much noise and redundancy. The text clumping aim is to clean and consolidate such a list to provide rich, usable content information.

As described, the text field of interest can contain terms (i.e., single words or unigrams) and/or phrases (i.e., multi-word noun + modifiers term sets). Herein, we focus on such NLP phrases, typically including many single words also. Some of the algorithms pertain especially to multi-word phrases, but, in general, many steps can usefully be applied to single-word term sets. Here we focus on analyzing NLP English noun-phrases – to be called simply „phrases."

Our larger mission is to generate effective Competitive Technical Intelligence (CTI). We want to answer basic questions of „Who is doing What, Where and When?" In turn, that information can be used to build „innovation indicators" that address users' CTI needs [2]. Typically, those users might be:

• Information professionals (compiling most relevant information resources)

• Researchers (seeking to learn about the nearby „research landscape")

• R&D managers (wanting to invest in the most promising opportunities)

- Science, Technology and Innovation (ST&I) policy-makers (striving to advance their country's competitiveness)

We focus on ST&I information sets, typically in the form of field-structured abstract records retrieved from topical database searches [e.g., Web of Science (WoS), Derwent World Patent Index, Factiva]. These records usually contain a mix of free text portions (e.g., abstracts) and structured text fields (e.g., keywords, publication years). The software uses an import filter to recognize fields (i.e., to know where and how to find the authors and parse their names properly) for particular source sets, such as WoS. VantagePoint can merge multiple datasets from a given source database or from different sources (with guidance on field matching and care in interpreting).

Figure 1 presents our framework for „term clumping." We combine established and relatively novel bibliometric and text mining techniqueswithin this framework. Itincludesa number of steps to process alarge phrase list. The top portion of the figure indicates choices to be made concerning which data resources to mine and selection criteria for the records to be analyzed. The next tier notes additional choices regarding which content-laden fields to process. The following two blocks contain the major foci of this chapter. "Text Cleanup" includes stopword and common term handling, through several steps to consolidate related terms. "Consolidateion of terms into informative topical factors" follows. Here we treat basic "inductive methods." The elements of the Figure flagged with an asterisk (*) are addressed in depth herein.

Figure 1 also points toward interests for future work. These include"purposive methods," wherein our attention focuses on particular terms based on external criteria – e.g., semantic TRIZ (Theory of Inventive Problem Solving) suggests vital functions and actions indicative of technological innovative potential [3, 4]. The idea is to search the target text fields for occurrences of theory-guided terms and adjacent content.

We are also keenly interested in pursuing single word analyses via Topic Modeling (TM) methods to get at themes of the record set under study. These hold appeal in providing tools that will work well in multiple languages and character sets (e.g., Chinese). The main language dependency that we confront is the use of NLP to extract noun phrases (e.g., VantagePoint's NLP is developed for English text).

The bottom portion of Figure 1 indicates interest in how best to engage experts in such topic identification processes. We distinguish three roles:

- Analyst: Professionals in data retrieval and analysis, who have analytical skills in handling text, but usually don't have domain knowledge

- Expert: Professional researchers in the specific domain, knowledgeable over the domain, and able to describe the current status of the domain at both macro and micro levels;

- Information & Computer Scientist: Covering a range of skills from in-depth programming, through preparation of macros, to operating software to accomplish particular text manipulations.

So defined, engagement of experts presents challenges in terms of motivation, time required, and communication of issues so that the domain experts can readily understand and respond to the analyst's needs. Simple, intermediate stage outputs could have value in this regard.

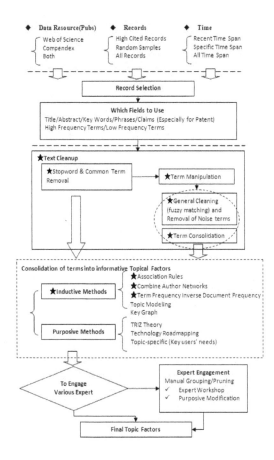

Figure 1. Term Clumping for Technical Intelligence

In summary, this chapter addresses how best to clean and consolidate ST&I phrase lists from abstract record sets. The target is to semi-automate this „inductive" process (i.e., letting the data speak without predetermined identification of target terms). We aim toward semi-automation because the process should be tailorable to study needs. We are exploring a series of text manipulations to consolidate phrase lists. We are undertaking a series of experiments that vary how technical the content is, which steps are performed, in what sequence, and what statistical approaches are then used to further cluster the phrases or terms. In particular, we also vary and assess the degree of human intervention in the term clumping. That ranges from almost none, to analyst tuning, to active domain expert participation [5-7].

2. Review of Related Literatures

Given the scope of Figure 1, several research areas contribute. This chapter does not address the purposive analyses, so we won't treat literatures on importing index terms, or on TRIZ and Technology RoadMapping (TRM) -- of great interest in suggesting high value terms for CTI analyses.

Several of the steps to be elaborated are basic. Removal of „stopwords" needs little theoretical framing. It does pose some interesting analytical possibilities, however. For instance, Cunningham found that the most common modifiers provided analytical value in classifying British science [8]. He conceives of an inverted U shape that emphasizes analyzing moderately high frequency terms -- excluding both the very high frequency (stopwords and commonly used scientific words, that provide high recall of records, but low precision) and low frequency words (suffering from low recall due to weak coverage, but high precision). Pursuing this notion of culling common scientific words, we remove „common words." In our analyses we apply several stopword lists of several hundred terms (including some stemming), and a common words in academic/scientific writing thesaurus of some 48,000 terms [9]. We are interested in whether removal of these enhances or, possibly, degrades further analytical steps' performance (e.g., Topic Modeling).

To state the obvious -- not all texts behave the same. Language and the venue for the discourse, with its norms, affect usage and text mining. In particular, we focus on ST&I literature and patent abstracts, with outreach to business and attendant popular press coverage of topics (e.g., the Factiva database). English ST&I writing differs somewhat from „normal" English in structure and content. For instance, scientific discourse tends to include many technical phrases that should be retained, not parsed into separate terms or part-phrases by NLP. VantagePoint's NLP routine [1] strives to do that. It also seeks to retain chemical formulas.

A research community has built around bibliometric analyses of ST&I records over the past 60 or so years, see for instance [10-12]. DeBellis nicely summarizes many facets of the data and their analyses [13]. Our group at Georgia Tech has pursued ST&I analyses aimed especially at generating Competitive Technical Intelligence (CTI) since the 1970's, with software development to facilitate mining of abstract records since 1993 [1, 2, 14]. We have explored ways to expedite such text analyses, c.f. [15, 16], as have others [17]. We increasingly turn toward extending such „research profiling" to aid in Forecasting Innovation Pathways (FIP), see for example [18].

Over the years many techniques have been used to model content retrieved from ST&I text databases. Latent Semantic Indexing (LSI) [19], Principal Components Analysis (PCA), Support Vector Machines (SVM), and Topic Modeling (TM) are among the key methods that have come forth [20].

PCA is closely related to LSI. Both use Singular Value Decomposition (SVD) to transform the basic terms by documents matrix to reduce ranks (i.e., to replace a large number of terms by a relatively small number of factors, capturing as much of the information value as possible). PCA eigen-decomposes a covariance matrix, whereas LSI does so on the term-document matrix. [See wikipedia for basic statistical manipulations.]

VantagePoint uses a special variant of PCA developed to facilitate ST&I text analyses (used in the analyses reported here). This PCA routine generates a more balanced factor set than LSI (which extracts a largest variance explaining factor first; then a second that best explains remaining variance, etc.). The VantagePoint factor map routine applies a small-increment Kaiser Varimax Rotation (yielding more attractive results, but running slower, than SPSS PCA in developmental tests). Our colleague, Bob Watts of the U.S. Army, has led development of a more automated version of PCA, with an optimization routine to determine a best solution (maximizing inclusion of records with fewest factors) based on selected parameter settings -- (Principal Components Decomposition – PCD)[21] He has also empirically compared PCD (inductive) results with a deductive approach based on use of class codes [22].

We apply PCA to term sets to generate co-occurrence based principal components. Because of the familiar use of "clusters," we also use that terminology, although other clustering approaches can yield different forms (e.g., K-means, hierarchical clustering). This PCA approach allows terms to appear in multiple factors

We use the concept, „term clumping," as quite general – entailing various means of text consolidation (e.g., application of thesauri, fuzzy matching, stemming) with noise removal. Bookstein, Raita, and collegues offer a somewhat more specialized, but related, interpretation pointing toward the aim of condensing terminology to better identify content-bearing words [23-25]. Term clumping addresses text (not document) „clustering." Any type of text clustering is based on co-occurrence of words in records (documents). Clustering, in turn, includes many variations plus additional statistical analyses with considerable commonality -- in particular, factor analysis. PCA can be considered as a basic factoring approach; indeed, we call its output principal components „factors. "Similarity among these term grouping approaches arises in that they generally aim to maximize association within clusters and minimize association among clusters. Features to keep in mind include whether terms or phrases being clustered are allowed to be included in multiple clusters or not; whether algorithms yield the same results on rerun or may change (probabilistic methods); and whether useful visualization are generated. Many further variations are available – e.g., hierarchical or non-hierarchical; building up or partitioning down; neural network based approaches (e.g., Kohonen Self-Organizing Maps), and so forth [26]. Research is actively pursuing many refinements, for many objectives, for instance [27]. Our focus is on grouping terms, but we note much complementary activity on grouping documents (based on co-occurrence with particular terms) [26], with special interest in grouping web sites, for instance [28].

Latent Semantic Indexing (LSI) or Latent Semantic Analysis, is a classical indexing method based on a Vector Space Model that introduces Singular-Value Decomposition (SVD) to uncover the underlying semantic structure in the text set. The key feature of LSI is to map those terms that occur in similar contexts into a smaller "semantic space" and to help determine the relationships among terms (synonymy and polysemy) [17, 29, 30]. When applied on co-occurrence information for large text sources, there is no need for LSI to import domain literatures or thesauri (what we call „purposive" or aided text clumping). There are also various extended LSI methods [31]. Researchers are combining LSI with term clumping variations in order to relate synonymous terms from massive content.For example, Maletic and Marcus combine semantic and structural information [32] and Xu et al. seek to associate genes based on text mining of abstracts [30].

Topic modeling is a suite of algorithms that automatically conforms topical themes from a collection of documents [33, 34]. This stream of research begins with Latent Dirichlet Allocation (LDA), which remains the basic algorithm. Topic modelling is an extended LSI method, that treats association probabilistically. Various topic modeling algorithms extend the basic approach, for example [35-44]. Topic modeling is being applied in many contexts – e.g., NLP extension, sentiment analysis, and topic detection.

We are pursuing topic modeling in conjunction with our text clumping development in several ways. We are experimenting to assess whether and which term clumping steps can refine term or phrase sets as input into topic modeling to enhance generation of meaningful topics. We also compare topic modeling outputs to alternative processes, especially PCA performed on clumped phrases. We additionally want to assess whether some form of text clumping can be applied after topic modeling to enhance topic interpretability.

We have also tried, but are not actively pursuing, Key Graph, a kind of visualization technique that treats the documents as a building constructed by a series of ideas and then retrieves these ideas and posts as a summary of original points on the segmentation of a graph [45-47]. Usually, Key Graph has 3 major components: (1) Foundations, which are the subgraphs of highly associated and frequent terms; (2) Roofs, which are terms highly related to the foundations; and (3) Columns, which are keywords representing the relationships between foundations and roofs.

We are especially interested in term grouping algorithms to refine large phrase sets through a sequence of steps. These typically begin with noise removal and basic cleaning, and end with some form of clustering of the resulting phrases (e.g., PCA). „In-between" we are applying several intermediate stage term consolidation tools. Kongthon has pursued an object oriented association rule mining approach [48], with a „concept grouping" routine [49] and a tree-structured network algorithm that associates text parent-child and sibling relationships [50].

Courseault-Trumbach devised a routine to consolidate related phrases, particularly of different term lengths based on term commonality [51]. Webb Myers developed another routine to combine authors. The notion was that, say, we have three papers authored by X. Perhaps two of those are co-authored with Y, and one with Z; and Y and Z never appear as authors on another paper without X. In that case, the operation surmises that Y and Z are likely junior authors, and eliminates them so that further author analyses can focus on the senior authors or author team. The macro [available at www.theVantagePoint.com] adds major co-authors into the term name. We incorporate these two routines in the present exercises.

Lastly, we consider various quality assessment approaches. Given that one generates clustered text in various forms, which are best? We look toward three approaches. First, we want to ask the target users. While appealing, this also confronts issues – e.g., our PCA output „names" the resulting factors, whereas topic modeling does not. How can we compare these even-handedly? Second are statistical approaches that measure some form of the degree of coherence within clusters vs. among clusters [52]. Third are record assignment tests – to what extent do alternative text clumping and clustering sequences correctly distinguish mixed dataset components? Here we seek both high recall and precision.

3. Empirical Investigation:Two Case Analyses

Figure 1 arrays a wide range of possible term clumping actions. As introduced in the previous sections, we are interested in many of those, but within the scope of this chapter we focus on many of the following steps and comparisons:

Term Clumping STEPS:

a. Fuzzy matching routines

b. Thesauri to reduce common terms

c. Human-aided and topic tailored cleaning

d. Phrase consolidation macro (different lengths)

e. Pruning of extremely high and low frequency terms

f. Combine term networks (parent-child) macro

g. g.TFIDF (Term Frequency Inverse Document Frequency)

h. Term normalization vs. parent database samples

i. PCA variations to generate high, medium, and low frequency factors

j. Topic Modeling

k. Quality assessment of the resulting factors – comparing expert and statistical means

We are running multiple empirical comparisons. Here we compare results on two topical datasets:

"MOT" (for Management of Technology) – 5169 records covering abstract records of the PICMET (Portland International Conference on Management of Engineering and Technology) from 1997 through 2012.

"DSSCs" (for Dye-Sensitized Solar Cells) – 5784 abstract records compiled from searches for 2001-2010 in WoS and in EI Compendex, merged in VantagePoint

Elsewhere, we elaborate on these analyses in various ways. Substantive interpretations of the topical MOT thrusts based on the human-selected MOT terms are examined over time and regions [55]. Comparisons of three MOT analyses -- 1) 3-tier, semi-automatic PCA extraction, 2) PCA based on human-selected MOT terms, and 3) Topic Modeling of unigrams – found notably different factors extracted. Human quality assessment did not yield a clear favorite, but the Topic Modeling results edged ahead of the different PCA's [7]. Additional explorations of the WoS DSSC data appear in [6], comparing Topic Modeling and term clumping-to-PCA – finding quite different emphases in the extracted factors. Zhang et al. [54] track through a similar sequence of term clumping steps on the combined WoS-Compendex DSSC dataset.

Here, we focus on stepping through most of the term clumping operations for these two cases. To avoid undue complexity, we set aside data variations (e.g., stepping through for the WoS DSSC set alone), Topic Modeling comparisons, and quality assessment. As noted, we have done one version of human assessment for the MOT data [7]. We are pursuing additional quality assessments via statistical measures [52] and by comparing how well the alternative analytics are able to separate out record sets from a combination of 7 searches. We also intend to pursue Step h – term normalization based on external (e.g., entire database) frequencies. So, here we treat Steps a-g and i, not Steps h, j, or k.

Table 1 provides the stepwise tally of phrases in the merged topical fields undergoing term clumping. It is difficult to balance precision with clarity, so we hope this succeeds. The first column indicates which text analysis action was taken, coresponding to the list of steps just above.The second column shows the results of those actions applied in sequence on the MOT data. Blank cells indicate that particular action was not performed on the MOT (or DSSC) dataset. The last row notes additional human-informed analyses done on the MOT data, but not treated here (to recognize that this is a selective presentation). The third column relates the results of application of the steps to the DSSC data, but here we indicate sequence within the column, also showing the resulting term reduction. [So, the Table shows the Term Clumping Steps in the order performed on MOT; this was arbitrary. It could as well have been ordered by the list (above) or in the order done for DSSC data.]

Term Clumping Steps	MOT	DSSCs
	5169 PICMET records	5784 records (WoS+Compendex), 2001-2010
Field selection	Title&Abstract NLP phrases	Title&Abstract NLP phrases + keywords
Phrases with which we begin	86014	90980
a-1) Apply general.fuz routine	76398	Applied 10th, reducing 82701 to 74263
b-1) Apply stopwords thesaurus	76105	Applied 1st, reducing 90980 to 89576) and applied 7th, reducing 85960 to 84511

Term Clumping Steps	MOT 5169 PICMET records	DSSCs 5784 records (WoS+Compendex), 2001-2010
b-2) Apply common academic/scientific terms thesaurus	73232	Applied 2d, reducing 89576 to 89403; and applied8th, reducing 84511 to 82739
b-3) multiple tailored cleaning routines -- trash term remover.the; topic variations consolidator.the; DSSC data fuzzy matcher results.the*		Applied such actions as 3d-6th steps, reducing 89403 to 85960; applied 9th, reducing 82739 to 82701;
a-2) Apply general-85cutoff-95fuzzywordmatch-1exact.fuz	69677	Applied 11th, reducing 74263 to 65379
d) Apply phrase consolidation macro (different lengths)	68062	Applied 4th, reducing 89355 to 86410
e) Prune (remove phrases appearing in only 1 record)	13089	Applied 12th, reducing 65379 to 23311
c-1) Apply human-aided and general.fuz routine		Applied 13th, reducing 23311 to 21645
c-2) Manual noise screens (e.g., copyrights, stand-alone numbers)		Applied 14th, reducing 21645 to 20172
f) Apply combine term networks (parent-child) macro	10513	Applied 15th, reducing 20172 to 8181
g) Apply TFIDF	1999	Applied 16th, reducing 8181 to 2008
i) Auto-PCA: highest frequency; 2d highest; 3d highest	201, 256, 299	203;214;230
PCA factors	9 factors (only top tier)	12 (only top tier)
c-3) Tuned phrases to 7164; reviewed 15 factors from 204 top phrases; reran to get final PCA		

Table 1. Term Clumping Stepwise Results

*a compilation of phrase variations that VantagePoint's "List Cleanup" routine suggested combining [e.g. – various singular and plural variations; hyphenation variations; and similar phrases such as "nanostructured TiO2 films" with "nanostructured TiO2 thin films"]

Some steps are broken out in more detail – e.g., Step a -- Fuzzy matching routines – is split into use of VantagePoint's general matching routine (a-1) and application of a variant tuned-for this term clumping (a-2). Note also that some steps appear more than once, especially for the DSSC clumping.

For Step b – application of thesauri to remove common terms – we distinguish the use of a modest size stopwords thesaurus (fewer than 300 words) as Step b-1 and the application of the 48,000 term thesaurus of common academic/scientific terms as Step b-2.

Step c -- Human-aided and topic tailored cleaning (Steps c-1, c-2 & c-3) groups a variety of „obvious" cleaning routines. Our dilemma is whether to eliminate these, to facilitate development of semi-automated routines, or to include them, for easy improvement of the term consolidation? In the MOT term clumping reported in Table 1, we essentially avoid such cleaning. In the DSSC step-through, we include limited iterations of human-aided cleaning to see whether this makes a qualitative difference by the time the progression of steps is completed. [It does not seem to do so.]

Step d -- Phrase consolidation macro – consolidates only a modest percentage of the phrases (as applied here, reducing the phrase count by 2.3% for MOT and by 3.3% for DSSCs), but the improvements appear worthwhile. For instance, combining "Dye-Sensitized Solar Cells" with "Sensitized Solar Cells" can provide important conceptual concentration.

Step e – Pruning – is simply discarding the phrases that appear in only one record. Those would not add to co-occurrence based analyses. The challenge is to sequence pruning after consolidation so that potentially useful topical information is not discarded. Pruning is the overwhelmingly potent step in reducing the term or phrase counts. For MOT, it effects a reduction of 81%; for DSSCs, 64%.

Step f -- Combine term networks (parent-child) – appears a powerful reducer. As discussed, Webb Myers devised this macro to consolidate author sets.We apply the macro to the phrases field, showing sizable reductions for MOT (19.7%) and DSSCs (59.4%). The macro will combine major co-occurring terms in the new phrase name with a "&" between them. It also results in terms that appear in a single record being combined into a single phrase [hence, we perform the Pruning step prior to applying this macro].

Step g – TFIDF – strives to distinguish terms that provide specificity within the sample set.For example, if some form of „DSSC" appears in nearly every DSSC record, this would not be a high-value term in distinguishing patterns within the dataset. VantagePoint offers three TFIDF routines – A) un-normalized, B) log, and C) square root. We compared these and proceed with the square root term set for DSSCs, whose 2008 terms are all included in sets A or B. Of the 2008 phrases, 1915 are in both A and B (so differences in this regard are small), with 42 in set A and 51 in set B. For the MOT data, B and C yield the same 1999 terms, whereas A yields 2052. Inspection of the distinct terms find the 78 only in sets B & C to appear more substantive than the 131 terms only in set A, so we opt for the 1999 term result.

Step h is included as a place-holder.On the one hand, Step b aims to remove generally common terms.On another, Step g favors more specific terms within the document set being analyzed. With access to full databases or general samples from sources such as WoS, one could sort toward terms or phrases that are relatively unique to the search set.We have not done that here.

At this stage, we have very large, but clumped, phrase sets. In our two cases, these consist of about 2000 phrases. Consider the illustrative „post-TFIDF" tabulations in Table 2. We believe these offer rich analytical possibilities. For instance, we could scan their introduction and frequency over time to identify „hot" topics in the field. Or, we could compare organizational emphases across these phrases to advance CTI interests. We might ask technical and/or business experts in the field to scan those 2000 phrases to identify particularly important or novel ones for in-depth analyses.

Steps i and j represent a major „last step" for these sorts of term analyses. Here we explore select PCA steps; elsewhere, as noted, we pursue Topic Modeling [6, 7]. This factoring (~clustering) step reduces thousands of phrases to tens of phrases. If done accurately, this can be game-changing in terms of opening conceptual insights into topical emphases in the field under study.

VantagePoint's PCA routine is now applied as Step i. In these cases we have tried to minimize human-aiding, but we explore that elsewhere [6, 7]. We select three top tiers of terms to be subjected to separate Principal Components Analysis. Such selection can be handled by various coverage rules – e.g., terms appearing in at least 1% of the records. In the present exercises, we set thresholds to provide approximately 200 phrases as input to each of three PCA analyses. We run the default requested number of factors to extract – this is the square root of the number of terms submitted. We review the resulting three sets of factors in terms of recall (record coverage) and determine to focus on just the top tier PCA results here. For DSSCs, the top-tier PCA yields 12 factors that cover 98% of the records, whereas the 2d tier factors cover 47% and the 3d tier only 18%.For the MOT analyses, results are comparable – the 9 top-tier factors cover 90% of the records; 2d tier, 36%; 3d tier, 17%. [We have performed additional analyses of these data, exploring various PCA factor sets, including ones in which we perform post-PCA term cleaning based on inspection of initial results., then re-run PCAFor instance, a very high frequency term might be removed, or simple relations handled by refining a thesaurus (e.g., in one result „Data Envelopment Analysis" and its acronym, DEA, constituted a factor).

Step j is of high interest, and we are exploring several alternative approaches, as mentioned. Here, we just present the high tier set of PCA factors for face validity checks.

4. Term Clumping Case Results

Having stepped through multiple term clumping steps, what do we get? One has many reasonable choices as to which term clumping steps to apply, in what sequence. To get a feel for the gains, let's compare sample results at four Stages:

1. Initial phrase set

2. After the term clumping steps up to TFIDF

3. After TFIDF

4. After PCA

Referring to Figure 1, the Text Cleaning stage, in general, would be carried out in preparation for nearly all further analyses. We would not anticipate aborting that processing partway, except in special cases (e.g., as mentioned in Cunningham's analysis of British science titles). The next stage of consolidating the cleaned and, therefore, partly consolidated phrases, is where interesting choices arrive. Based on the analyses of the MOT and DSSC data, we note the significant effect of selecting the high TFIDF terms. We thus compare the phrase sets at Stage 1 (before cleaning and clumping), Stage 2 (before filtering to the top TFIDF terms), Stage 3 (after TFIDF), and Stage 4 (after applying one of the clustering family of techniques – PCA).

Stage 1 - Initial			Stage 2 - Clumped		
Top 10	# Records	# Instances	Top 10	# Records	#Instances
study	1177	1874	technology	475	1113
results	894	1177	case study	472	931
research	792	1050	applicable	444	998
development	603	829	knowledge	414	1022
analysis	518	690	relationship	356	801
One	494	574	competition	303	699
innovation	465	800	governance	248	517
knowledge	412	750	technology manager	241	526
process	400	506	literature	227	344
industry	399	637	implication	221	327

Table 2. Stages 1 & 2 – Top 10 MOT Phrases

Considering the MOT data first, Table 2 compares the ten most frequent terms or phrases as of Stages 1 and 2. As per Table 1, the clumping and, especially single-record term pruning, has reduced from 86014 to 10513 phrases – an 88% reduction. Table 2 lists the highest frequency terms and phrases based on record coverage. For instance, study appears in 1177 of the 5169 records (23%). The Table also shows instances, and we see that study appears more than once in some records to give a total of 1874 instances. MOT is Management of Technology. That said, the terms and phrases after clumping are somewhat more substantive. As one scans down the Stage 2 set of 10513 phrases, this is even more the case. Our sense is that a topical expert reviewing these to tag a set of themes to be analyzed (e.g., to track trends, or institutional emphases) would definitely prefer the clumped to the raw phrases.

In Tables 2-5, we show in how many of the full sample of MOT and DSSC records the particular terms appear. We also show instances (i.e., some terms appear more than once in a record). These just convey the changes in coverage resulting from the various clumping operations applied.

Table 3 shows the „Top 10" post-TFIDF terms and phrases, based on TFIDF scores. Recall that the 1999 terms and phrases at this Stage 3 are based on an arbitrary threshold – we sought about 2000. Note that term counts are unchanged for terms present in both Stages 2 & 3. TFIDF is not clumping, but rather screening based on occurrence patterns across the 5169 records.

Stage 3 - post-TFIDF			
Top 10	# Records	# Instances	SqRt TFIDF value
Knowledge	414	1022	35.05
technology	475	1113	34.59
applicable	444	998	33.68
relationship	356	801	32.89
competition	303	699	32.57
innovation technology	200	527	32.42
case study	472	931	31.72
technology manager	241	526	30.54
R&D	191	446	30.25
Governance	248	517	29.99
developed country	179	406	29.43

Table 3. Stage 3 – Top 10 MOT Phrases based on TFIDF

Table 4 presents another 10-term sample pair for Stages 1 and 2. Here, we alphabetically sort the phrase lists and arbitrarily take the ten phrases beginning with „knowledge" or „knowledg" --i.e., a stem version of the term. Notice that the big consolidation is for the stemmed version of „knowledg," for which the record count has gone up a tiny amount (2), whereas the instance count has increased by 272. In general, the term clumping increases term frequencies and consolidates related terms pretty well (but by no means completely).

Table 5 presents the top-tier PCA analysis results. The phrases appearing here tend to be more topically specific than those seen as most frequent at Stages 2 and 3. Only two terms -- „competition" and „knowledge" -- happen to be approximately in common. These nine factors pass a face validity check – they seem quite coherent and potentially meaningful to study of the MOT research arena. Naming of the factors is done by VantagePoint, using an algorithm that takes into account relative term loading on the factor and term commonalities among phrases.

Stage 1 Sample	#R	#I	Stage 2 Sample	#R	#I
knowledge	412	750	knowledge	414	1022

knowledge absorption ability KAA	1	1	knowledge acquisition	6	11
knowledge access	1	1	knowledge age	4	10
knowledge accumulated	1	1	knowledge asset	4	5
knowledge accumulation	4	8	knowledge base	14	17
knowledge accumulation model	1	2	knowledge based competencies	2	3
knowledge acquisition	6	11	knowledge based economy	21	28
knowledge acquisition KA	1	1	knowledge based organizational strategy	2	4
knowledge acquisition strategies	1	4	knowledge based perspective	3	4
knowledge across different sectors	1	1	Knowledge Based Product Models	2	2

Table 4. Stages 1 & 2 – 10 Sample MOT Phrases

Note: #R = # of Records; #I = # of Instances

As mentioned, we have done additional analyses of these data. In another PCA, starting with the 10513 terms (pre-TFIDF), we extracted a high frequency term set (112 terms or phrases appearing in 50-475 records). In addition we extracted a second-tier PCA based on 185 terms appearing in 25-49 records, and a third-tier PCA from 763 terms in 10-24 records. Each set was run using VantagePoint default settings for number of factors, yielding, respectively, 7, 9, and 16 factors. Of the present 9 top-tier factors, 3 show clear correspondence to either top or second-tier factors in the 10513-term based PCA; one shows partial correspondence; 5 are quite distinct. Which factor sets are better? Impressionalistically, the 9 post-TFIDF factors seem reasonable and somewhat superior, but lacking some of the specificity of (7 + 9 + 16 = 32) factors. As noted, we don't pursue the corresponding post-TFIDF PCA second and third tier factors because their record coverage is low.

Examination of DSSC phrase sets shows generally similar progressions as term clumping proceeds.In some respects, results are even more satisfactory with that more technical terminology.In the interest of space, we don't present tables like Tables 2-4 here.But here's a synopsis of one fruitful topical concentration within the DSSC phrase list:

Principle Component (Factor)	High Loading Phrases
Managing Supply Chain	Managing Supply Chain
	Supply Chain
Nanotechnology	Nanotechnology
	Commercial
Competing Technologies	Competition
	Capability

	Technology Capability
	Global Competition
	Competing Technologies
Technology Roadmap	Roadmap
	Technology Roadmap
Innovation Process	Innovation Process
	Innovation Activity
	Open Innovation
Knowledge	Knowledge
	Knowledge Manager
	Individual
	Knowledge Creation
	New Knowledge
	Share Knowledge
Project Success	Project Manager
	Project Success
Make Decisions	Make Decisions
	Decision Making Process
Communication Technology	ICT
	Communication Technology

Table 5. Stage 4 – Top Tier MOT PCA Factors and Constituent Phrases

- In the initial 90980 term list, there are 807 terms on "electron/electrons/electronic"

- In the 8181 term list, there are 119 terms on this

- In the 2008 term list, there are 40 terms remaining, such as "electron acceptor," "electron diffusion," "electron injection," "electron transfer," "electronic structure," etc.

Table 6 shows the twelve top-tier DSSC PCA factors and the phrases that load highly on those factors. These results pace a face validity test in that the grouping of terms seems generally sensible. These factors appear to be reasonable candidates for thematic analysis of this solar cell research & development activity.

Principle Component (Factor)	High Loading Phrases
Sol Gel Process	Sol Gel
	Sol Gel Process

Principle Component (Factor)	High Loading Phrases
	Gel-Sol Method
Polymer Electrolyte	Electrolyte
	Polym
	Ionic Liquid
	Polymer Electrolyte
	Gel Electrolyte
	Electrolyte Liquid
	Ionic Conduction
	Gel Polymer Electrolyte
	Electrolysis
	Gelator
	Poly electrolyte
	Temperature Molten-Salt
Conduction Band	Electron Injection
	Conduction Band
	Mobile Electrons
	Density Functional Theory
Coumarin Dye	Organic Dye
	Coumarin Dye
Solar Equipment	Photo Electrochemical cell
	Efficient Conversion
	Solar Energy
	Solar Equipment
Material Nanostructure	Material Nanostructure
	Redox Reaction
Electron Transport	Electron Transpot
	Back Reaction
ZnO	ZnO
	Nanowire
	Nanorod
	Semiconducting zinc compounds
Scanning Electron Microscopy	Scanning Electron Microscopy
	X-ray Diffraction
	Transmission Electron Microscopy
	Electron Microscopy
	X-ray Diffraction Analysis
	X-ray Photoelectron spectroscopy

Principle Component (Factor)	High Loading Phrases
Open Circuit Voltage	Open Circuit Voltage
	Fill Factor
Electrochemical Impedance Spectroscopy	Electrochemical Impedance Spectroscopy
	Electrochemical Corrosion
	Ion Exchange
Nanotube	Nanotube
	Anode
	Nanotube TiO2

Table 6. Stage 4 – Top Tier DSSC PCA Factors and Constituent Phrases

5. Discussion

Recent attention to themes like "Big Data" and "MoneyBall" draw attention to the potential in deriving usable intelligence from information resources. We have noted the potential for transformative gains, and some potential unintended consequences, of exploiting information resources [53]. Term clumping, as presented here, offers an important tool set to help move toward real improvements in identifying, tracking, and forecasting emerging technologies and their potential applications.

Desirable features in such text analytics include:

- Transparency of actions – not black box

- Evaluation opportunities – we see value in comparing routines on datasets to ascertain what works better; we recognize that no one sequence of operations will be ideal for all text analytics

Phrase consolidation advantages stand out in one DSSC example. Starting with some 2000 terms relating to variations of titanium dioxide (e.g., TiO2, TiO_2, TiO_2 film), we reduce to 4 such terms, with the "combine term networks" (Step f) particularly helpful.

We are pointing toward generation of a macro that would present the analyst with options as to which cleaning and clumping steps to run, in what order; however, we also hope to come up with a default routine that works well to consolidate topical terms and phrases for further analyses

Some future research interests have been noted in conjunction with the list of steps, of which we are actively working on Steps h, j, and k. We are particularly interested in processing unigrams, because of the potential in such approaches to work with multiple languages. On the other hand, we appreciate the value of phrases to convey thematic structure. Possibilities include processing single words, through a sequence of steps to Topic Modeling, and then trying to associate related phrases to help capture the thrust of each topic. We see potential use of clumped terms and phrases in various text analyses.To mention two relating to competitive technical intelligence (CTI) and Future-oriented Technology Analyses (FTA):

Combining empirical with expert analyses is highly desirable in CTI and FTA – clumped phrases can be further screened to provide digestible input for expert review to point out key topics and technologies for further scrutiny

Clumped phrases and/or PCA factors can provide appropriate level content for Technology RoadMapping (TRM) – for instance, to be located on a temporal plot.

We recognize considerable interplay among text content types as well.This poses various cleaning issues in conjunction with co-occurrence of topical terms with time periods, authors, organizations, and class codes.We look forward to exploring ways to use clumped terms and phrases to generate valuable CTI.

Key Acronyms:

CTI - Competitive Technical Intelligence

DSSCs - Dye-Sensitized Solar Cells [one of two topical test sets]

LSI - Latent Semantic Indexing

MOT - Management of Technology [the second of two topical test sets]

NLP - Natural Language Processing

PCA - Principal Components Analysis

ST&I - Science, Technology & Innovation

TM - Topic Modeling

WoS - Web of Science (including Science Citation Index)

6. Acknowledgements

We acknowledge support from the US National Science Foundation (Award #1064146 – "Revealing Innovation Pathways: Hybrid Science Maps for Technology Assessment and Foresight"). The findings and observations contained in this paper are those of the authors and do not necessarily reflect the views of the National Science Foundation.

We thank David J. Schoeneck for devising groundrules for a semi-automated, 3-tier PCA and Webb Myers for the macro to combine term networks.Nils Newman has contributed pivotal ideas as we build our term clumping capabilities and determine how to deploy them.

Author details

Alan L. Porter[1*] and Yi Zhang[2]

*Address all correspondence to: alan.porter@isye.gatech.edu

1 Search Technology, Inc., Norcross, Georgia, USA, and Technology Policy & Assessment Center, Georgia Tech, Atlanta, Georgia, USA

2 School of Management and Economics, Beijing Institute of Technology, Beijing, China

References

[1] VantagePoint. www.theVantagePoint.com, (accessed 20 May 2012).

[2] Porter, A.L., & Cunningham, S.W. (2005). *Tech Mining: Exploiting New Technologies for Competitive Advantage*, New York, Wiley.

[3] Kim, Y., Tian, Y., Jeong, Y., Ryu, J., & Myaeng, S. (2009). Automatic Discovery of Technology, Trends from Patent Text.In. *Proceedings of the 2009 ACM symposium on Applied Computing, ACMSAC2009, 9-12 March 2009,Hawaii, USA.*

[4] Verbitsky, M. Semantic TRIZ. *The TRIZ Journal2004; Feb.*, http://www.triz-journal.com/archives/2004/, (accessed 20 May 2012).

[5] Porter, A. L., Zhang, Y., & Newman, N. C. (2012). Tech Mining to Identify Topical Emergence in Management of Technology. *The International Conference on Innovative Methods for Innovation Management and Policy, IM2012, 23-26 May 2012. Beijing, China.*

[6] Newman, N. C., Porter, A. L., Newman, D., Courseault-Trumbach, C., & Bolan, S. D. (2012). Comparing Methods to Extract Technical Content for Technological Intelligence. *Portland International Conference on Management of Engineering and Technology, PICMET2012, 29 July-2 August, Vancouver, Canada.*

[7] Porter, A. L., Newman, D., & Newman, N. C. (2012). Text Mining to identify topical emergence: Case study on'Management of Technology. *The 17th International Conference on Science and Technology Indicators, STI2012, 5-8 September, Montreal, Canada.*

[8] Cunningham, S.W. (1996). The Content Evaluation of British Scientific Research. *D.Phil. Thesis, Science Policy Research Unit*, University of Sussex, Brighton, United Kingdom.

[9] Haywood, S. Academic Vocabulary. *Nottingham University*, http://www.nottingham.ac.uk/~alzsh3/acvocab/wordlists.htm, (accessed 26 May, 2012).

[10] Price, D.S. (1986). *Little science, big science and beyond*, New York, Columbia University Press.

[11] Garfield, E., Malin, M., & Small, H. (1978). Citation Data as Science Indicators. *Y. El-kana,et al, (Eds.), The Metric of Science: The Advent of Science Indicators,*, New York, Wiley.

[12] Van Raan, A. F. J. (1992). Advanced Bibliometric Methods to Assess Research Performance and Scientific Development: Basic Principles and Recent Practical Applications. *Research Evaluation,* 3(3), 151-166.

[13] De Bellis, N. (2009). *Bibliometrics and Citation Analysis,* Lanham, MD, The Scarecrow Press.

[14] Porter, A.L., & Detampel, M.J. (1995). Technology opportunity analysis. *Technol. Forecast. Soc. Change,* 49, 237-255.

[15] Watts, R.J., Porter, A.L., Cunningham, S.W., & Zhu, D. (1997). TOAS intelligence mining, an analysis of NLP and computational linguistics. *Lecture Notes in Computer Science,* 1263, 323-334.

[16] Zhu, D., & Porter, A.L. (2002). Automated extraction and visualization of information for technological intelligence and forecasting. *Technol. Forecast. Soc. Change,* 69495-506.

[17] Losiewicz, P., Oard, D.W., & Kostoff, R.N. (2000). Textual data mining to support science and technology management. *Journal of Intelligent Information Systems,* 15(2), 99-119.

[18] Robinson, D.K.R., HuangL., , Guo, Y., & Porter, A.L. Forecasting Innovation Pathways for New and Emerging Science & Technologies. *Technological Forecasting & Social Change.*

[19] Deerwester, S., Dumals, S., Furnas, G., Landauer, T., & Harshman, R. (1990). Indexing by latent semantic analysis. *Journal of the American Society for Information Science,* 41391-407.

[20] FodorI.K., . A survey of dimension reduction techniques. *U.S. Department of Energy, Lawrence Livermore National Lab.9 May 2002.https://e-reports-ext.llnl.gov/pdf/240921.pdf,* (accessed 22 May 2012).

[21] Watts, R. J., & Porter, A. L. (1999). Mining Foreign language Information Resources, Proceedings., *Portland International Conference on Management of Engineering and Technology, PICMET1999, July 1999, Portland, OR, USA;.*

[22] Watts, R. J., Porter, A. L., & Minsk, B. (2004). Automated text mining comparison of Japanese and USA multi-robot research, data mining 2004. *Fifth International Conference on Data Mining, Text Mining and their Business Applications,15-17Sep. 2004, Malaga, Spain;.*

[23] Bookstein, A., Klein, T., & Raita, T. (1998). Clumping properties of content-bearing words. *Journal of the American Society for Information Science,* 49(2), 102-114.

[24] Bookstein, A., & Raita, T. Discovering term occurrence structure in text. *Journal of the American Society for Information Science and Technology 2000*, 52(6), 476-486.

[25] Bookstein, A., Vladimir, K., Raita, T., & John, N. Adapting measures of clumping strength to assess term-term similarity. *Journal of the American Society for Information Science and Technology 2003*, 54(7), 611-620.

[26] Berry, M.W., & Castellanos, M. (2008). *Survey of text mining II : clustering, classification, and retrieval.*, New York:, Springer.

[27] Beil, F., Ester, M., & Xu, X. Frequent term-based text clustering. *Proceedings of the 8th International Conference on Knowledge Discovery and Data Mining, KDD2002*, http://dl.acm.org/citation.cfm?id=775110, (accessed 21 May 2012).

[28] Scime, A. (2005). *Web mining: applications and techniques.*, Hershey, PA, Idea Group Pub.

[29] Homayouni, R., Heinrich, K., Wei, L., & Berry, M.W. (2005). Gene clustering by latentsemantic indexing of MEDLINE abstracts. *Bioinformatics*, 21104-115.

[30] Xu, L., Furlotte, N., Lin, Y., Heinrich, K., & Berry, M.W. *Functional Cohesion of Gene Sets Determined byLatent Semantic Indexing of PubMedAbstracts.PLoS ONE 2011*, 6(4), e18851.

[31] Landauer, T.K., McNamara, D.S., Denis, S., & Kintsch, W. (2007). *Handbook of Latent Semantic Analysis*, Mahwah, NJ, Erlbaum Associates.

[32] Maletic, J. I., & Marcus, A. Supporting program comprehension using semantic and structural information. *Proceedings of the 23rd International Conference on Software Engineering, ICSE2001.*

[33] Blei, D., Ng, A., & Jordan, M. (2003). Latent Dirichlet allocation. *Journal of Machine Learning Research*, 3993-1022.

[34] Griffiths, T., & Steyvers, M. (2004). Finding Scientific Topics. *Proceedings of the National Academy of Sciences*, 101 (suppl.1), 5228-5235.

[35] Thomas, H. Probabilistic latent semantic indexing. *Proceedings of the 22nd annual international ACM SIGIR conference on Research and development in information retrieval, SIGIR1999.*

[36] Ando, R.K. Latent semantic space: iterative scaling improves precision of inter-document similarity measurement. *Proceedings of the 23rd annual international ACM SIGIR conference on Research and development in information retrieval, SIGIR2000.*

[37] Li, W., & McCallum, A. Pachinko allocation: DAG-structured mixture models of topic correlations. *Proceedings of the 23rd international conference on Machine learning, ICML2006.*

[38] David, M., Li, W., & Mc Callum, A. Mixtures of hierarchical topics with Pachinko allocation. *Proceedings of the 24th international conference on Machine learning, ICML 2007.*

[39] Wang, X., & McCallum, A. Topics over time: A non-Markov continuous-time model of topical trends. *Proceedings of the 12th ACM SIGKDD international conference on Knowledge discovery and data mining, KDD2006.*

[40] David, M. B., & John, D. H. Dynamic topic models. *Proceeding Proceedings of the 23rd international conference on Machine learning, ICML 2006.*

[41] Gruber, A., Rosen-Zvi, M., & Weiss, Y. *Hidden topic Markov models,* http://www.cs.huji.ac.il/~amitg/aistats07.pdf., Accessed March 20, 2012.

[42] Rosen-Zvi, M., Griffiths, T., Steyvers, M., & Smyth, P. The author-topic model for authors and documents. *Proceeding of the 20th conference on Uncertainty in artificial intelligence, UAI2004.*

[43] Mc Callum, A., Corrada-Emmanuel, A., & Wang, X. The Author-Recipient-Topic Model for Topic and Role Discovery. *Social Networks: Experiments with Enron and Academic Email.,* http://scholarworks.umass.edu/cgi/viewcontent.cgi?article=1024&context=cs_faculty_pubs., Accessed March 20, 2012.

[44] Mei, Q., Xu, L., Wondra, M., Su, H., & Zhai, C. Topic sentiment mixture: modeling facets and opinions in weblogs. *Proceedings of the 16th international conference on World Wide Web, WWW2007.*

[45] Ohsawa, Y., Benson, N.E., & Yachida, M. Keygraph: Automatic indexing by co-occurrence graph based on building construction metaphor. *Proceedings of the Advances in Digital Libraries Conference, ADL1998.*

[46] Tsuda, K., & Thawonmas, R. (2005). KeyGraph for Visualization of Discussions in Comments of a Blog Entry with Comment Scores. *World Scientific and Engineering Academy and Society (WSEAS) Trans. Computers, 12(4), 1794-1801.*

[47] Sayyadi, H., Hurst, M., & Maykov, A. Event Detection and Story Tracking in Social Streams. *Proceeding of 3rd Int'l AAAI Conference on Weblogs and Social Media, ICWSM09, May 17-20, 2009, San Jose, California, USA; 2009.*

[48] Kongthon, A. A. (2004). Text Mining Framework for Discovering Technological Intelligence to Support Science and Technology Management, Doctoral Dissertation,. *Georgia Institute of Technology,* http://smartech.gatech.edu/bitstream/handle/1853/5151/kongthon_alisa_200405_phd.pdf.txt?sequence=2, (accessed 20 May 2012).

[49] Kongthon, A., Haruechaiyasak, C., & Thaiprayoon, S. Constructing Term Thesaurus using Text Association Rule Mining. *Proceedings of the 2008 Electrical Engineering/Electronics, Computer, Telecommunications and Information Technology International Conference, ECTI2008.*

[50] Kongthon, A., & Angkawattanawit, N. Deriving Tree-Structured Network Relations in Bibliographic Databases. *Proceedings of the 10th International Conference on Asian Digital Libraries, ICADL 2007, December 10-13, Hanoi, Vietnam; 2007.*

[51] Courseault-Trumbach, C., & Payne, D. (2007). Identifying Synonymous Concepts in Preparation for Technology Mining. *Journal of Information Science*, 33(6).

[52] Watts, R.J., & Porter, A.L. (2003). R&D cluster quality measures and technology maturity. *Technological Forecasting and Social Change*, 70(8), 735-758.

[53] Porter, A.L., & Read, W. The Information Revolution: Current and Future Consequences. *Westport, CT: JAI/Ablex; 1998.*

[54] Zhang, Y., Porter, A. L., & Hu, Z. An Inductive Method for "Term Clumping": A Case Study on Dye-Sensitized Solar Cells. *The International Conference on Innovative Methods for Innovation Management and Policy, IM2012, 23-26May 2012, Beijing, China; 2012.*

[55] Porter, A.L., Schoeneck, D.J., & Anderson, T.R. (2012). PICMET Empirically: Tracking 14 Management of Technology Topics. *Portland International Conference on Management of Engineering and Technology, PICMET2012, 29 July-2 August, Vancouver, Canada.*

## Chapter 3

Analysis for Finding Innovative Concepts Based on Temporal Patterns of Terms in Documents

Hidenao Abe

Additional information is available at the end of the chapter

1. Introduction

In recent years, information systems in every field have developed rapidly, and the amount of electrically stored data has increased day after day. Electrical document data are also stored in such systems mainly for recording and for holding the facts. As for the medical field, documents are also accumulated not only in clinical situations, but also in worldwide repositories by various medical studies. Such data now provide valuable information to medical researchers, doctors, engineers, and related workers by retrieving the documents depending to their expertise. They want to know the up-to-date knowledge for providing better care to their patients. Hence, the detection of novel, important, and remarkable phrases and words has become very important to aware valuable evidences in the documents. However, the detection is greatly depending on their skills for finding the good evidences.

Besides, with respect to biomedical research documents, the MeSH [1] vocabulary provides overall concepts and terms for describing them in a simple and an accurate way. The structured vocabulary is maintained by NIH for reflecting some novel findings and interests on each specific field, considering amount of published documents and other factors based on the studies. Through such consideration, new concepts, which appear as new concepts every year, are usually added to the vocabulary if the concepts are useful. One criterion for adding new concepts is related to how attention paid to them by the researchers appears as an emergent pattern in published documents. As the fact, around few hundred of new concepts are added every year, and the maintenance of the concepts and their related structure has been done by manually. Thus, MeSH has another aspect as an important knowledge base for the biomedical research field. However, the relationships between particular data-driven trends and the newly added concepts did not be clarified.

By clarifying the relationship between such maintained vocabulary and the trends of term usages, readers in the field can detect the important terms for understanding the up-to-date trends in his/her field more clearly. Under the above-mentioned motivation, I developed a method for analyzing the similarity of terms on the structured taxonomy and the trend of a data-driven index of the terms [2]. In this chapter, I describe a result of the analysis by using the method for identifying similar terms based on the temporal behavior of usages of each term. The temporal pattern extraction method on the basis of term usage index consists of automatic term extraction methods, term importance indices, and temporal clustering in the next section. Then, in Section 4, a case study is carried out for showing the differences between similar terms detected by the temporal patterns of medical terms related to migraine drug therapy in MEDLINE documents. Finally, I conclude the analysis result in Section 6.

2. The method for analyzing distances on taxonomy and temporal patterns of term usage

In this section, I describe a method for detecting various trends of words and phrases in temporally published corpora. In order to analyze the relationships between usages of words and phrases in temporally published documents and the difference on a taxonomy, this trend detection method use a temporal pattern extraction method based on data-driven indices [2]. By using the similar terms identified on the basis of temporal patterns of the indices, the method measures their similarities between each term on the taxonomy that can be assumed as the sets of tree structures of concepts on a particular domain. One of the reasons why the method uses temporal patterns is for detecting various trends. The important aim of the method is not only detecting particular trend that a user set, but also detecting various trends based on the nature of the given corpora. The other reason is for finding representing terms, called as 'keywords' in each specific field, on the basis of the trends. Considering these two aims, the method uses the temporal pattern extraction process based on temporal behaviors of terms by measuring an importance index.

Then, on the basis on the temporal behavioral similarity of each index, the distances between the similar terms, which are the members of each temporal pattern, are measured. By using the distance on the structured vocabulary, the averages of the distances between the terms included in temporal patterns is compared for analyzing the relationship between the trends of temporal patterns and the similarities of terms on the vocabulary.

In the following sections, the method for detecting temporally similar terms based on each importance index is described firstly. Subsequently, the distance measure on the structured vocabulary is explained.

2.1. Obtaining temporal patterns of data-driven indices related to term usages

In order to discover various trends related to usages of the terms in temporally published corpus, the framework [2] is developed as a method for obtaining temporal patterns of an importance index. This framework obtains some temporal patterns based on the importance index from the given temporally published sets of documents. It consists of the following processes.

- Automatic term extraction in overall documents
- Calculation of importance indices
- Obtaining temporal clusters for each importance index
- Assignment of some meanings for the obtained temporal patterns

2.1.1. Automatic term extraction in a given corpus

Firstly, a system determines terms in a given corpus. Considering the difficulties of constructing particular dictionaries on each domain, term extraction without any dictionary is required. As for the representative method for extracting terms automatically, a term extraction method [3] based on the adjacent frequency of compound nouns is selected. This method involves the detection of technical terms by using the following values for a candidate compound noun CN:

$$FLR(CN) = f(CN) \times (\prod_{i=1}^{L}(FL(N_i) + 1)(FR(N_i) + 1))^{\frac{1}{2L}}$$

where $f(CN)$ means frequency of a candidate compound noun CN separately, and $FL(N_i)$ and $FR(N_i)$ indicate the frequencies of different words on the right and the left of each noun N_i in *bi*-grams included in each CN. Each compound noun CN is constructed $L(L \geq 1)$, one or more, nouns.

For example, there is a set of compound nouns $S = \{data\ mining, text\ mining, mining\ method\}$ from a corpus, and they appear just one time in the corpus. Then, we want to now the FLR score of *datamining*, $FLR(data\ mining)$. The left frequency of 'data' is 0, because of $FL(data) = 0$. The right frequency of 'data' is 1, because 'mining' appears just one time on the right of 'mining'. So $FR(data)$ is 1. As the same way, the frequencies of 'mining' are $FL(mining) = 2$ and $FR(mining) = 1$. Then, the $FLR(data\ mining)$ is calculated as follows.

$$FLR(data\ mining) = 1 \times \sqrt{(0+1)(1+1) \times (2+1)(1+1)} = 3.464\cdots$$

2.1.2. Calculation of data-driven indices for each term in each set of documents

After determining terms in the given corpus, the system calculates importance indices of these terms in the documents in each time period for representing the usages of the terms as the values. For the temporally published corpora, users can set up a period optionally. Most of the cases, the period is set up yearly, monthly, and daily, because the published documents are given timestamps. In this framework, each set of documents, that are published in each period, is denoted as D_{period}.

Some importance indices for words and phrases in a corpus are well known. Term frequency divided by inverse document frequency (tf-idf) is one of the popular indices used for measuring the importance of terms [4]. The tf-idf value for each term $term_i$ can be defined for the documents in each period, D_{period}, as follows:

$$TFIDF(term_i, D_{period}) =$$
$$tf(term_i, D_{period}) \times log\frac{|D_{period}|}{df(term_i, D_{period})}$$

where $tf(term_i, D_{period})$ is the frequency of each term $term_i$ in a corpus with $|D_{period}|$ documents. Here, $|D_{period}|$ is the number of documents included in each period, and $df(term_i, D_{period})$ is the frequency of documents containing term.

In the proposed framework, the method suggests treating these indices explicitly as a temporal dataset. This dataset consists of the values of the terms for each time point by using each index $Index(\cdot, D_{period})$ as the features. Figure 1 shows an example of such a dataset consisting of an importance index for each period. The value of the term $term_i$ is described as $Index(term_i, D_{period})$ in Figure 1.

Selecting m time periods as the features for the dataset

	...	$Index(\bullet, D_{2000})$	...	$Index(\bullet, D_{year})$	...
$term_1$	...	$Index(term_1, D_{2000})$	...	$Index(term_1, D_{year})$	...
$\vdots$		$\vdots$		$\vdots$	
$term_i$	...	$Index(term_i, D_{2000})$	...	$Index(term_i, D_{year})$	...
$\vdots$		$\vdots$		$\vdots$	
$term_n$	...	$Index(term_n, D_{2000})$	...	$Index(term_n, D_{year})$	...

Figure 1. Example of dataset consisting of an importance index.

2.1.3. Generating temporal patterns by using temporal clustering

After obtaining the dataset, the framework provides the choice of an adequate trend extraction method to the dataset. A survey of the literature shows that many conventional methods for extracting useful time-series patterns have been developed [5, 6]. Users can apply an adequate time-series analysis method and identify important patterns by processing the values in the rows of Figure 1. By considering these patterns with temporal information, users can understand the trends related to the terms such as transition of technological development with technical terms. The temporal patterns as the clusters also provide information about similarities between the terms at the same time. The system denotes the similar terms based on the temporal cluster assignments as $term_i \in c_k$.

2.1.4. Assigning meanings of the trends of the obtained temporal patterns

After obtaining the temporal patterns c_k, in order to identify the meanings of each pattern by using trends of the extracted terms for each importance index, the system applies linear regression analysis. The degree of the centroid of a temporal pattern c is calculated as follows:

$$Deg(c) = \frac{\sum_{j=1}^{M}(c_j - \bar{c})(x_j - \bar{x})}{\sum_{j=1}^{M}(x_j - \bar{x})^2}$$

where $\bar{x}$ is the average of $t_j - t_1$ for M time points and $\bar{y}$ is the average of the values c_j. Each value of the centroid, c_j, is a representative value of the importance index values of assigned terms in the pattern as $Index(term_i \in c_k, D_{period})$. Each time point t_j corresponds to each period, and the first period assigns to the first time point as t_1.

Simultaneously, the system calculates the intercept $Int(c)$ of each pattern c_k as follows:

$$Int(c) = \bar{y} - Deg(c)\bar{x}$$

Then, by using the two linear trend criteria, users assigne some meanings of the temporal patterns related to the usages of the terms.

2.2. Defining similarity of terms on a structured taxonomy

In this chapter, a tree structure of concepts that are defined with a relation such as is-a as 'structured taxonomy' is used. In the biomedical domain, MeSH (Medical Subjects Headings) [1] is one of the important structured taxonomy for representing key concepts of biomedical research articles. MeSH consists of 16 categories including not only proper categories for biomedicine but also general categories such as information science. It contains 25,588 concepts as 'Descriptor', and 464,282 terms as 'Entry Terms' in the version of 2001. Each concept has one or more entry terms and the tree numbers as the identifier in the hierarchy structure.

For this structure, the similarity of each pair of terms represented by using distance in the tree structure of MeSH is defined, as shown in Figure 2.

For example, when the distance between the two terms, $term_{i1}$ and $term_{i2}$, denotes as $Dist(term_{i1}, term_{i2})$, the distance between 'migraine' and 'sharp headache', $Dist(migraine, sharp headache)$, is calculated as 8 or 9. By using this distance, the similarity between each pair of terms is defined as the following:

$$Sim(term_{i1}, term_{i2}) = \frac{1}{1 + Dist(term_{i1}, term_{i2})}$$

where the similarity can be calculated when the both terms have tree numbers in MeSH.

For overall terms belonging to some group g, representative values are also defined their averaged similarity in the group as the following:

$$Avg.Sim(g) = \frac{1}{numPair} \sum_{term_i \in g} Sim(term_{i1}, term_{i2})$$

where $numPair$ is the number of matched pairs of the terms included in the group g. The definition is $numPair =_m C_2$, where the number of appeared terms m is $m = |term_i \in g \cap hasTreeNumber(term_i)|$.

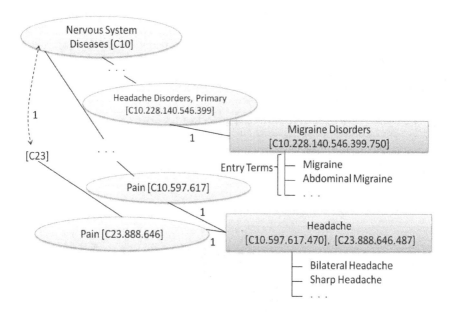

Figure 2. Example of MeSH hierarchy structure for migraine disorders and headache.

3. A case study for detecting trends of terms by obtaining temporal patterns

In this section, I describe a case study for analyzing similarity of terms detected some temporal patterns in medical research documents. For obtaining the temporal patterns, I used an importance index of the terms in each set of documents that ware published year by year. The medical research documents are retrieved from MEDLINE by using a search scenario over time. The scenario is related to migraine drug therapy similar to the first one in a previous paper on MeSHmap [7].

In this case study, I consider the search scenario and three meanings of trends as temporal clusters by using the degrees and intercepts of the trend lines for each term as follows. As for the meanings, the following two trends are assigned; "emergent" to ascending trend lines with negative intercepts, "subsiding" to decending trend lines with positive intercepts, and "popular" to ascending trend lines with positive intercepts.

3.1. Analysis of a disease over time

In this scenario, a user may be interested in exploring the progression of ideas in a particular domain, say, corresponding to a particular disease. By performing the search such that the disease is represented according to the year, one may obtain a temporal assessment of the changes in the field.

Let us assume that the user wants to explore the evolution of ideas about drugs used to treat chronic hepatitis. The user performs a search for abstracts of articles "chronic hepatitis/drug therapy [MH:NOEXP] AND YYYY [DP] AND clinical trial [PT] AND english [LA]" through PubMed. The string "YYYY" is replaced with the four digits necessary for retrieving articles published each year. The retrieval for PubMed can be performed trough their WebAPI written in Perl [8]. By iterating the query by updating the years, the script can retrieve the published research documents in the field depending on the query string. In this example, the temporal sets of documents year by year are gathered on the field related to the drug therapy for chronic hepatitis.

With this search query, we obtain articles published between 1982 and 2009 with the abstract mode of PubMed[1]. Figure 3 shows the numbers of article titles and abstracts retrieved by the query. In this study, each abstract is assumed as text to be one document.

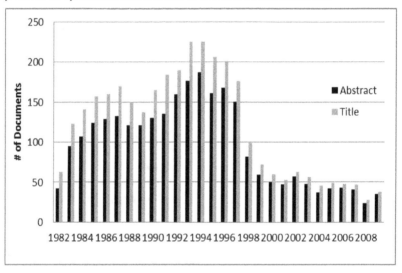

Figure 3. Numbers of documents with titles and abstracts related to hepatitis drug therapy published from 1982 to 2009.

From all of the retrieved abstracts, the automatic term extraction method identifies 12,194 terms. As for the titles, the method extracted 1,428 terms.

3.2. Obtaining temporal patterns of medical terms about chronic hepatitis drug therapy studies

By calculating the document frequency and the tf-idf values as the importance indices for each year on titles and abstracts respectively. By using the document sets and the index, the system obtained the dataset to obtain temporal clusters that consist of temporal behavior of each index year by year for each term.

As for the clustering algorithm, the k-means clustering algorithm implemented in Weka [9](Weka-3-6-2) are applied.   Since the implementation search better cluster

---

[1] The current heading of chronic hepatitis has introduced 1982.

assignments by minimizing the sum of squared errors (SSE), the upper limits of the number of clusters are set up 1% of the number s of terms. And the maximum iteration to search better assignment is set up 500 times.

Table 1 shows the result of the k-means clustering on the sets of documents.

Dataset		# of Clusters	SSE	Total trend		# of patterns		
				Avg.Deg	Avg.Int	Emergent	Popular	Subsiding
Abstrtacts	tf–idf	119	309.70	−0.04	2.65	1	47	71
	df	118	32.02	−0.01	0.64	0	32	86
Titles	tf–idf	14	136.58	−0.03	2.01	0	4	10
	df	14	15.03	−0.01	0.69	0	2	12

Table 1. Overall result of temporal clustering on titles and abstracts about chronic hepatitis drug therapy by using the three importance indices.

Figure 4 shows the centroid values of the temporal clusters and the representative terms of each temporal pattern on the title corpus based on the temporl tf-idf. The centroid values mean the averages of the yearly values of the terms in each cluster. The representative terms are selected with their FLR scores, that are the highest in each temporal custer. The cluster is selected with the following conditions: including phrases, highest linear degree with minimum intercepts to y-axis by sorting the average degrees and the average intercepts of the 14 clusters.

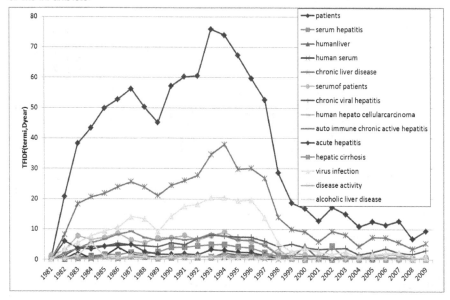

Figure 4. The representative terms and values of tf-idf temporal patterns on the titles of the chronic hepatitis articles.

As shown in Figure 4, the method can detect the trends based on the temporal behaviors of terms. Although the temporal patterns and the similar terms as the member of the clusters show the trends and the similar group at the same time, the meaning of each group indicates should be evaluated by medical experts.

4. Analyzing temporal trends of terms and the similarities on MeSH structure

In this example, the sets of documents published year by year on the field related to the drug therapy for migraine are gathered. Let us assume that the user wants to explore the evolution of ideas about drugs used to treat migraine[2]. The user performs a search for abstracts of articles "migraine/drug therapy [MH:NOEXP] AND YYYY [DP] AND clinical trial [PT] AND english [LA]" through PubMed. As same as the retrieval for chronic hepatitis in Section 3.

With this search query, articles published between 1980 and 2009 with the abstract mode of PubMed are retrieved. Figure 5 shows the numbers of article titles and abstracts retrieved by the query.

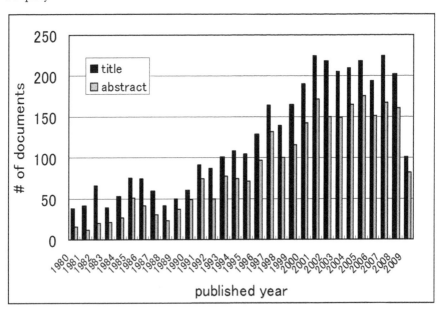

Figure 5. Numbers of documents with titles and abstracts related to migraine drug therapy published from 1980 to 2009.

By assuming the abstracts and the titles as each corpus, the automatic term extraction is applied. From all of the retrieved abstracts, the automatic term extraction method identifies 61,936 terms. Similarly, from all of the titles, the system extracts 6,470 terms.

---

[2] Migraine causes sharp and severe headaches to people. People who have migraine exist commonly in world-wide. The severe headaches give economical disadvantages not only to the patients, but also socially sometimes.

4.1. Obtaining temporal patterns of medical terms about migraine drug therapy studies

By calculating the document frequency and the tf-idf values as the importance indices for each year on titles and abstracts respectively. Then, the temporal clusters that consist of temporal behavior of each index year by year for each term are obtained. The clustering algorithm that is used in the following experiment is also the same as the setting in Section 3.

Table 2 shows the result of the k-means clustering on the sets of documents.

Dataset		# of Clusters	SSE	Total trend		# of patterns		
				Avg.Deg	Avg.Int	Emergent	Popular	Subsiding
Abstrtacts	tf-idf	129	216.81	0.17	−0.44	81	37	0
	df	129	36.67	0.04	−0.06	103	25	1
Titles	tf-idf	14	125.69	0.10	−0.03	5	9	0
	df	14	10.14	0.03	0.02	4	9	1

Table 2. Overall result of temporal clustering on titles and abstracts about migraine drug therapy by using the three importance indices.

Figure 6 shows the emergent cluster centroid and the top ten emergent terms on the abstracts on the basis of tf-idf. The cluster is selected with the following conditions: including phrases, highest linear degree with minimum intercepts to y-axis by sorting the average degrees and the average intercepts of the 14 clusters.

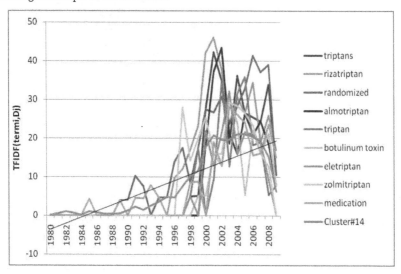

Figure 6. The detailed tf-idf temporal values included in the emergent temporal pattern (Cluster #14).

As shown in Figure 6, the method detected the emergent terms included in the emergent pattern that related to triptans drug therapy. The cluster also includes some terms related to the time for the therapy. The drugs including triptans, which are appeared in this pattern, are approved later 1990s in US and European countries, and early 2000s in Japan. Based on the result, the method obtained the temporal patterns related to the topics that attract interests of researchers in this field. In addition, the degree of the increasing and the shapes of the temporal patterns of each index show some aspects the movements of the research issue.

4.2. Similarity of the terms in obtained temporal patterns on MeSH

By using the similarity measure as described in Section 2, the averaged similarity of the medical terms included in each temporal pattern are calculated. In order to analyze the relationship between the trends and the similarities, a comparison is performed with the representative values of the averaged similarities of the term.

As shown in Table 3, the similarities for each temporal pattern are calculated. Smaller similarity value means that the terms included in the temporal pattern are defined separately on the MeSH structure. Besides, greater similarity value means that the similar terms on the temporal pattern are also defined similarly on the MeSH structure.

k	term_ck	Deg(ck)	Int(ck)	Meaning	AvgSim(ck)
2	clinical efficacy	0.063	−0.142	Emergent	0.133
3	placebo-controlled study	0.069	−0.299	Emergent	0.135
5	5-ht1 b/1 dagonists	0.044	−0.139	Emergent	0.131
8	migraine therapy	0.339	−1.870	Emergent	0.141
14	acute treatment of migraine	0.789	−3.566	Emergent	0.135
1	migraine patients	0.059	3.874	Popular	0.120
4	cluster headache	0.050	0.203	Popular	0.144
6	migraine	1.816	3.589	Popular	0.174
7	double-blind study	0.058	0.206	Popular	0.121
9	patients	0.748	1.363	Popular	0.138
10	management of migraine	0.025	0.816	Popular	0.133
11	tension-type headache	0.058	0.196	Popular	0.133
12	oral sumatriptan	0.255	0.955	Popular	0.131
13	migraine prophylaxis	0.025	0.523	Popular	0.160

Table 3. Temporal patterns obtained for the tf-idf dataset on the titles and the similarities of the terms in each temporal pattern.

Then, for clarifying the relationships between the temporal patterns and the similarity on the taxonomy, the difference of the similarity values by separating the meanings of the linear trends is compared on the two trends; emergent or not emergent. As for the first representative values, the two groups of the average values are tested by using t-test. Then, the representative values of the two groups of the similarity values are compared by using Wilcoxon rank sum test. Table 4 shows the averages and the medians of the similarity values.

The similarity values around 0.13 means that the pair of terms defined in each place with from 6 to 7 paths. By testing the difference between the two groups based on the linear trends, for the abstracts, the similarities of the terms included in the emergent temporal patterns are significantly smaller than the terms included in the popular patterns based on the tf-idf values. This result indicates that the tf-idf index detects new combinations

	Abstracts		Titles	
	Emergent	Not Emergent	Emergent	Not Emergent
tf-idf	0.126*	0.130*	0.134	0.139
df	0.129*	0.125*	0.134	0.141

(a) Averages

	Abstracts		Titles	
	Emergent	Not Emergent	Emergent	Not Emergent
tf-idf	0.126*	0.130*	0.132	0.138
df	0.131*	0.125*	0.133	0.139

(b) Medians

Table 4. Comparison of the representative values. (a)Averages, (b)Medians. * means significant difference on $\alpha = 0.05$.

of the concepts as its emergent trend. Besides, based on the temporal patterns by using the document frequency, the terms included in the emergent patterns are defined more similarly. More frequently used terms in the recently published documents are defined nearer than the other popular terms. This can be understandable by considering the process for maintaining the structure of the concepts manually.

5. Related work

Related to the method that I described, there are two separated research topics. One is to detect emergent trend in a given temporal corpora. The other is for learning structured taxonomy or ontology from a given corpus. They have not been combined as the method to analyze the relationship between the emergent terms and the place on the structure that the terms should be appeared. This work provides a novel idea not only as a text mining approach, but also for the two separated studies

5.1. Emergent Trend Detection (ETD) methods

In order to detect the emergent trend in a temporally published corpora, the method for detecting emergent trend have been developed [10, 11]. Most of these methods concentrated to find out just one trend at each setting. Moreover, they rather finding terms that represent emergent trends than the emergent trend itself. Thus, the user of these methods should interpret the meaning of the terms that are detected by the ETD method.

Conventional ETD methods are mostly based on the probabilistic transition of the term appearances as shown in the works such as [12, 13]. The method achieved for detecting emergent trend, which is actually a set of terms. However, they did not detect various trends as described in Section 3 and Section 4 at the same time. In addition to the difference, the proposed trend detection method has an availability to visualize both of the representing values of each temporal pattern and the detailed values for each term, using simple time-series charts.

5.2. Ontology Learning (OL) methods from domain corpora

In order to construct a taxonomy for each domain from a given corpus, the methods for leaning ontologies are proposed [14, 15]. However, they did not consider the difference over times of the structured taxonomy. The maintenances of the structure are majorly depending on the manual works of domain experts. Some support methods for the maintenance of the structured taxonomy are really required to the structured taxonomy useful and up-to-date. For this issue, the advanced method of the proposal of this chapter will provide the support with more objective evidences based on the temporal corpora of each particular domain.

6. Conclusion

In this chapter, I describe the method for detecting trends of terms in the published articles in MEDLINE as the case study on chronic hepatitis studies. With this case study, the result shows that the method can find various trends of terms and similar terms at the same time. In this case study, the similar terms detected by using their temporal behavior of the two importance indices; document frequency and tf-idf index. Then, the temporal patterns of the biomedical terms by using the two importance indices are obtained. The patterns indicate the similar usages of the terms on the biomedical research documents as the temporal corpus.

Subsequently, by using migraine drug therapy studies, a comparison of the similarity of the terms between the terms grouped up by our trend detection method and the terms in the structured vocabulary is shown. By using MeSH as the structured taxonomic definition of the medical terms, we compared the averaged similarity based on the distances on the tree structure between the terms included in each temporal pattern. By separating the trends of the temporal patterns based on the linear regression technique, the averaged similarities of the terms in each pattern show significant differences on the larger structured vocabulary. Based on the temporal patterns with the emergent trend of the tf-idf, the terms included in such patterns are not similar compared to the terms included in the popular patterns. This indicates that the novel concepts are obtained from new combination by using the existing concepts widely. Besides, the similarity of the different index detects the opposite relationship between its trend and the similarity on the taxonomic definition.

In the future, more indices for representing various aspects of term usages in a corpus will be introduced and compared. Then, based on the similarities on temporal behavior of each index as the temporal patterns, some predictive models such as numerical prediction models will be introduce for predicting adequate places of new concepts on a structured taxonomy.

Author details

Hidenao Abe

* Address all correspondence to: hidenao@shonan.bunkyo.ac.jp

Department of Information Systems, Faculty of Information and Communications, Bunkyo University, Japan

References

[1] Medical subject headings:. http://www.nlm.nih.gov/mesh/.

[2] Hidenao Abe and Shusaku Tsumoto. Trend detection from large text data. In *Proceedings of the 2010 IEEE International Conference on Systems, Man and Cybernetics*, pages 310–315. IEEE, 2010.

[3] Hiroshi Nakagawa. Automatic term recognition based on statistics of compound nouns. *Terminology*, 6(2):195–210, 2000.

[4] Karen Sparck Jones. A statistical interpretation of term specificity and its application in retrieval. *Document retrieval systems*, pages 132–142, 1988.

[5] Eamonn Keogh, Selina Chu, David Hart, and Michael Pazzani. Segmenting time series: A survey and novel approach. In *an Edited Volume, Data mining in Time Series Databases.*, pages 1–22. World Scientific, 2003.

[6] T. Warren Liao. Clustering of time series data: a survey. *Pattern Recognition*, 38:1857–1874, 2005.

[7] P. Srinivasan. Meshmap: a text mining tool for medline. In *Proc. of AMAI Symposium 2001*, pages 642–646, 2001.

[8] E-utilities:. http://www.ncbi.nlm.nih.gov/books/NBK25500/.

[9] I. H. Witten and E. Frank. *Data Mining: Practical Machine Learning Tools and Techniques with Java Implementations*. Morgan Kaufmann, 2000.

[10] Brian Lent, Rakesh Agrawal, and Ramakrishnan Srikant. Discovering trends in text databases. In *KDD '97: Proceedings of the third ACM SIGKDD international conference on Knowledge discovery in data mining*, pages 227–230. AAAI Press, 1997.

[11] April Kontostathis, Leon Galitsky, William M. Pottenger, Soma Roy, and Daniel J. Phelps. A survey of emerging trend detection in textual data mining. *A Comprehensive Survey of Text Mining*, 2003.

[12] Jon M. Kleinberg. Bursty and hierarchical structure in streams. *Data Min. Knowl. Discov.*, 7(4):373–397, 2003.

[13] Qiaozhu Mei and ChengXiang Zhai. Discovering evolutionary theme patterns from text: an exploration of temporal text mining. In *KDD '05: Proceedings of the eleventh ACM SIGKDD international conference on Knowledge discovery in data mining*, pages 198–207, New York, NY, USA, 2005. ACM.

[14] Philipp Cimiano, Johanna Völker and Rudi Studer. Ontologies on Demand? - A Description of the State-of-the-Art, Applications, Challenges and Trends for Ontology Learning from Text *Information, Wissenschaft und Praxis*, 57, 2006

[15] Hazman Maryam, Samhaa R. El-Beltagy and Ahmed Rafea A Survey of Ontology Learning Approaches *International Journal of Computer Applications*, 22, 8, 2011

## Chapter 4

Automatic Compilation of Travel Information from Texts: A Survey

Hidetsugu Nanba, Aya Ishino and
Toshiyuki Takezawa

Additional information is available at the end of the chapter

1. Introduction

Travel guidebooks and portal sites provided by tour companies and governmental tourist boards are useful sources of information about travel. However, it is costly and time-consuming to compile travel information for all tourist spots and to keep these data up-to-date manually. Recently, research about services for the automatic compilation and recommendation of travel information has been increasing in various research communities, such as natural language processing, image processing, Web mining, geographic information systems (GISs), and human interfaces. In this chapter, we overview the state of the art of the research and several related services in this field. We especially focus on research in natural language processing, including text mining.

The remainder of this chapter is organized as follows. Section 2 explains the automatic construction of databases for travel. Section 3 describes analysis of travelers' behavior. Section 4 introduces several studies about recommending travel information. Section 5 shows interfaces for travel information access. Section 6 lists several linguistic resources. Finally, we provide our conclusions and offer future directions in Section 7.

2. Automatic construction of databases for travel

In this section, we describe several studies about constructing databases for travel. In Section 2.1, we introduce a study that identified travel blog entries in a blog database. In Section 2.2, we describe several methods to construct databases for travel by extracting travel information, such as tourist spots or local products, from travel blog entries using information extraction techniques. In Section 2.3, we explain a method that constructs travel links automatically.

2.1. Automatic identification of travel blog entries

Travel blogs[1] are defined as travel journals written by bloggers in diary form. Travel blogs are considered useful for obtaining travel information, because many bloggers' travel experiences are written in this form.

There are various portal sites for travel blogs, which we will describe in Section 6. At these sites, travel blogs are manually registered by bloggers themselves, and the blogs are classified according to travel destination. However, there are many more travel blogs in the blogosphere, beyond these portal sites. In an attempt to construct an exhaustive database of travel blogs, Nanba et al. [25] identified travel blog entries written in Japanese in a blog database.[2]

Blog entries that contain cue phrases, such as "travel", "sightseeing", or "tour", have a high degree of probability of being travel blogs. However, not every travel blog contains such cue phrases. For example, if a blogger describes his/her journey to Norway in multiple blog entries, the blog might state "We traveled to Norway" in the first entry, while only writing "We ate wild sheep!" in the second entry. In this case, because the second entry does not contain any expressions related to travel, it is difficult to identify it as a travel blog entry. Therefore, Nanba et al. focused not only on each blog entry but also on the surrounding entries for the identification of travel blog entries. They formulated the identification of travel blog entries as a sequence-labeling problem, and solved it using machine learning. For the machine learning method, they examined the Conditional Random Fields (CRF) method [20]; its empirical success has been reported recently in the field of natural language processing. The CRF-based method identifies the tag [3] of each entry. Features and tags are given in the CRF method as follows: (1) k tags occur before a target entry; (2) k features occur before a target entry; and (3) k features follow a target entry (see Figure 1). They used the value of $k = 4$, which was determined in a pilot study. Here, they used the following features for machine learning: whether an entry contains any of 416 cue phrases, such as "旅行 (travel)", "ツアー (tour)", and "出発 (departure)", and the number of location names in each entry.

Using the above method, Nanba et al. identified 17,268 travel blog entries from 1,100,000 blog entries, and constructed a system that plotted travel blog entries on a Google map (see Figure 2).[4] In this figure, travel blog entries are shown as icons. If the user clicks an icon, the corresponding blog entry is shown in a pop-up window.

2.2. Automatic extraction of travel information from texts

Nakatoh et al. [24] proposed a method for extracting names of local culinary dishes from travel blogs written in Japanese, which were identified when the blog entry included both the name of a sightseeing destination and the word "tourism". They extracted local dishes by gathering nouns that are dependent on the verb "を食べる" (eat). Tsai and Chou [32] also proposed a method for extracting dish names from restaurant review blogs written in Chinese using a machine learning (CRF) technique.

---

[1] We use the term *travel blog*. Other studies use the term "Travelogues" [10], indicating social networking service (SNS) content, blogs, reviews, message boards, and so on, for travel.
[2] Although Nanba et al. identified Japanese travel blogs, their method can be applied to blogs written in other languages, if cue phrases for the language are prepared.
[3] In this case, the tag indicates whether each entry is a travel blog entry or not.
[4] http://www.ls.info.hiroshima-cu.ac.jp/test/travel-map/xml-travelmap.html

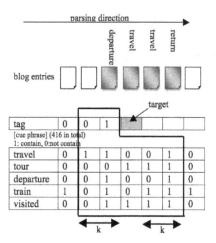

Figure 1. Features and tags used in CRF

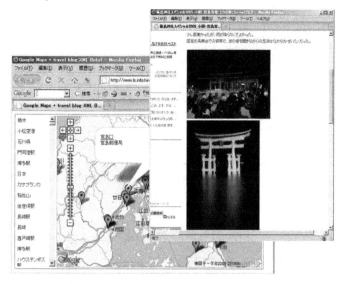

Figure 2. Travel blog entries plotted on a Google map

In the following, we explain the detail of the bootstrapping-based and machine learning-based information extraction approaches based on Nanba's work [25]. Nanba et al. extracted pairs comprising a location name and a local product from travel blogs written in Japanese, which were identified using the method described in Section 2.1. For the efficient extraction of travel information, they employed a bootstrapping method.

First, they prepared 482 pairs as seeds for the bootstrapping. These pairs were obtained automatically from a "Web Japanese N-gram" database provided by Google, Inc. The database comprises N-grams (N = 1–7) extracted from 20 billion Japanese sentences on the Web. They applied the pattern "[地名] 名物「[名物]」" ([slot of "location name"] local product 「[slot of "local product"]」) to the database, and extracted location names and local products from each corresponding slot, thereby obtaining the 482 pairs.

Second, they applied a machine learning-based information extraction technique to the travel blogs identified in the previous step, and obtained new pairs. In this step, they prepared training data for the machine learning in the following three steps.

1. Select 200 sentences that contain both a location name and a local product from the 482 pairs. Then automatically create 200 tagged sentences, to which both "location" and "product" tags are assigned.[5]

2. Prepare another 200 sentences that contain only a location name. Then create 200 tagged sentences, to which the "location" tag is assigned.

3. Apply machine learning to the 400 tagged sentences, and obtain a system that automatically allocates "location" and "product" tags to given sentences.

As a machine learning method, they used CRF. The CRF-based method identifies the class of each word in a given sentence. Features and tags are given in the CRF method as follows: (1) k tags occur before a target word; (2) k features occur before a target word; and (3) k features follow a target word. They used the value of $k = 2$, which was determined in a pilot study. They used the following six features for machine learning.

- Word.
- The part of speech to which the word belongs (noun, verb, adjective, etc.)
- Whether the word is a quotation mark.
- Whether the word is a cue word, such as "名物", "名産", "特産" (local product), "銘菓" (famous confection), or "土産" (souvenir).
- Whether the word is a surface case.
- Whether the word is frequently used in the names of local products or souvenirs, such as "cake" or "noodle".

2.3. Automatic compilation of travel links

Collections of Web links are usefel information sources. However, maintaining these collections manually is costly. Therefore, an automatic method for compiling collections of Web links is required. In this section, we introduce a method that compiles travel links automatically.

From travel blog entries, which were automatically identified using the method mentioned in Section 2.1, Ishino et al. [15] extracted the hyperlinks to useful Web sites for a tourist spot included by bloggers, and thereby constructed collections of hyperlinks for tourist spots. The procedure for classifying links in travel blog entries is as follows.

---

[5] Here, a location name corresponds to only a local product in each sentence.

1. Input a travel blog entry.
2. Extract a hyperlink and any surrounding sentences that mention the link (a citing area).
3. Classify the link by taking account of the information in the citing area.

They classified link types into the following four categories.

- S (Spot): The information is about tourist spots.
- H (Hotel): The information is about accommodation.
- R (Restaurant): The information is about restaurants.
- O (Other): Other than types S, H, and R.

A hyperlink may be classified as more than one type. For example, a hyperlink to "ラーメン博物館" (Chinese noodle museum, http://www.raumen.co.jp/home/) was classified as types S and R, because the visitors to this museum can learn the history of Chinese noodles in addition to eating them.

For the classification of link types, they employed a machine learning technique using the following features.

- A word.
- Whether the word is a cue phrase, detailed as follows, where the numbers in brackets shown for each feature represent the number of cues.

Cue phrase	The number of cues
A list of tourist spots, collected from Wikipedia.	17,371
Words frequently used in the name of tourist spots, such as "動物園" (zoo) or "博物館" (museum).	138
Words related to sightseeing, such as "見学" (sightseeing) or "散策" (stroll).	172
Other words.	131

Table 1. Cues for type S

Cue phrase	The number of cues
Words that are frequently used in the name of hotels, such as "ホテル" (hotel) or "旅館" (Japanese inn).	9
Component words for accommodations, such as "フロント" (front desk) or "客室" (guest room).	29
Words that are frequently used when tourists stay in accommodation, such as "泊る" (stay) or "チェックイン" (check in).	14
Other words.	21

Table 2. Cues for type H

Based on this method, Ishino et al. constructed a travel link search system.[6] The system generated a list of URLs for Web sites related to a location, and automatically identified link types and the context of citations ("citing areas"), where the blog authors described the sites. Figure 3 shows a list of links related to "大阪" (Osaka).

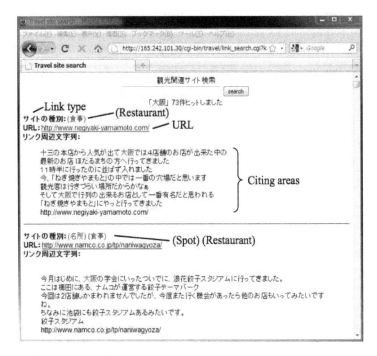

Figure 3. A list of Web sites for a travel spot

Cue phrase	The number of cues
Dish names such as "omelet", collected from Wikipedia.	2,779
Cooking styles such as "Italian cuisine", collected from Wikipedia.	114
Words that are frequently used in the name of restaurants, such as "レストラン" (restaurant) or "食堂" (dining room).	21
Words that are used when taking meals, such as "食べる" (eat) or "おいしい" (delicious).	52
General words that indicate food, such as "ご飯" (rice) or "料理" (cooking).	31
Other words.	31

Table 3. Cues for type R

---

[6] http://www.ls.info.hiroshima-cu.ac.jp/travel/

3. Travelers' behavior analysis

The analysis of people's transportation information is considered an important issue in various fields, such as city planning, architectural planning, car navigation, sightseeing administration, crime prevention, and tracing the spread of infection of epidemics. In this section, we focus on the analysis of travelers' behavior.

Ishino et al. [15] proposed a method to extract people's transportation information from automatically identified travel blogs written in Japanese [25]. They used machine learning to extract information, such as "departure place", "destination", or "transportation device", from travel blog entries. First, the tags used in their examination are defined.

- FROM tag indicates the departure place.
- TO tag indicates the destination.
- VIA tag indicates the route.
- METHOD tag indicates the transportation device.
- TIME tag indicates the time of transportation.

The following is a tagged example.

> It took <TIME>five hours</TIME> to travel from <FROM>Hiroshima</FROM> to<TO>Osaka</TO> by <METHOD>bus</METHOD>.

They formulated the task of identifying the class of each word in a given sentence and solved it using machine learning. For the machine learning method, they used CRF [20], in the same way as Nanba et al. [25], which we mentioned in Section 2.2. The CRF-based method identifies the class of each entry. Features and tags are used in the CRF method as follows: (1) k tags occur before a target entry; (2) k features occur before a target entry; and (3) k features follow a target entry. They used the value $k = 4$ [7], which was determined via a pilot study. They used the following features for machine learning.

- A word.
- The part of speech to which the word belongs (noun, verb, adjective, etc.).
- Whether the word is a quotation mark.
- Whether the word is a cue phrase.

The details of cue phrases, together with the number of cue phrases of the given type, are shown as follows.

1. **FROM**: The word is a cue that often appears immediately after the "FROM" tag, such as "から" (from) or "を出発" (left): 40.

---

[7] Nanba et al.[25] used the smaller value $k = 2$ in the extraction of pairs comprising a location name and a local product (Section 2.2), because the tags are determined by a word itself or its adjacent words in most cases in Nanba's task.

2. **FROM & TO**: The word is frequently used in the name of a tourist spot, such as "博物館" (museum) or "遊園地" (amusement park): 45.
   The word is frequently used in the name of a destination, such as "観光" (sightseeing tour) or "駅" (station): 11.
   The word is the name of a tourist spot: 13,779.
   The word is the name of a station or airport: 9437.

3. **TO**: The word is a cue that often appears immediately after the "TO" tag, such as "まで" (to) or "に到着" (arrival): 271.

4. **VIA**: The word is a cue that often appears immediately after the "via" tag, such as "経由" (via) or "通って" (through): 43.
   The word is the name of a highway: 101.

5. **METHOD**: The word is the name of a transportation device, such as "飛行機" (airplane) or "自動車" (car): 148.
   The word is the name of a vehicle: 128.
   The word is the name of a train or bus: 2033.

6. **(TIME)**: The word is an expression related to time, such as "分" (minute) or "時間" (hour): 77.

They also constructed a visualization of transportation information, which is shown in Figure 4. In this figure, each arrow indicates a link from a departure place to a destination. In addition to arrows, transportation methods, such as trains or buses, are shown as icons.

Transportation information can also be extracted from texts written in English. Davidov [6] presented an algorithm framework that enables automated acquisition of map-link information from the Web, based on linguistic patterns such as "from X to". Given a set of locations as initial seeds, he retrieved an extended set of locations from the Web, and produced a map-link network that connected these locations using edges showing the transportation type.

4. Recommending travel information

Recommendation systems provide a promising approach to ranking commercial products or documents according to a user's interests. In this section, we describe several studies and services that recommend travel information. We describe the recommendation of tourist spots, landmarks, travel products, accomodation, and photos.

4.1. Recommending tourist spots

Recommending tourist spots[8] has been well studied in the multimedia field. Movies and images are used as information sources in addition to texts. In this section, we describe two multimedia studies.

Hao et al. [10] proposed a method for mining location-representative knowledge from travel blogs based on a probabilistic topic model (the Location–Topic model). Using this model,

---

[8] Here, we use the terms "tourist spot" and "landmark" for a region, such as "Paris" or "New York", and also for a location or building, such as "the Eiffel Tower" or "Statue of Liberty".

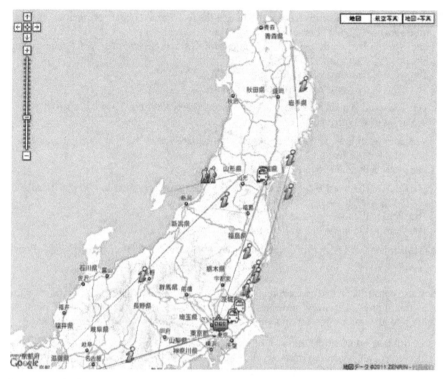

Figure 4. Example of transportation information automatically extracted from travel blogs

they developed three modules: (1) destination recommendation for flexible queries; (2) characteristics summarization for a given destination, with representative tags and snippets; and (3) identification of informative parts of a travel blog and enriching recommendations with related images.

Figure 5 shows an example of the system output. In this figure, a travel blog segment[9] is enriched with three images that depict its most informative parts. Each image's original tags and the words in the text to which it corresponds are also presented.

Wu et al. [34] proposed a system that summarized tourism-related information. When a user (traveler) entered a query, such as "What is the historical background of Tian Tan?", the system searched for and obtained information from Wikipedia, Flickr, YouTube, and official tourism Web sites using the tourist spot name as a query. The system also classified the query as belonging to one of five categories—"general", "history", "landscape", "indoor scenery", and "outdoor scenery"—in order to provide users with more relevant information. For example, when a query is classified as belonging to the "history" category, the information is obtained from texts, while for a query regarding "outdoor scenery", the information is obtained from photos and videos.

---

[9] A segment of a Maui travel blog entitled "Our Maiden Journey to Magical Maui", http://www.igougo.com/journal-j23321-Maui-Our_Maiden_Journey_to_Magical_Maui.html

| This was our first trip to Hawaii, let alone Maui. The *beaches*, activities, types of accommodations, and restaurants make it a great choice for a first visit to the *islands*. 1) The *beaches*! There are so many all over the *island*, and all different types: white, black, even red. Large, busy, and with amenities and activities, or small, private, and rustic (no facilities). 2) The activities! Go *snorkeling*, *diving*, *surfing*, parasailing, *fishing*, golfing, hiking up an old *volcano*, biking down the *volcano*, four-wheeling on unpaved, virtually vacant dirt roads through old *lava* flows, driving on narrow, curvy, crowded roads through *tropical* forests, and helicopter rides around the *island*. 3) The restaurants! There are so many fine-dining choices with all types of menus, as well as sandwich shops and the more familiar chains. | *ocean*, life, blue, sea, brown, green, *beach*, *water*, animal, *coral*, hawaii, sand, marine, *underwater*, *turtle*, shell, *diving*, maui, *snorkeling*, *reef*, creature, flipper | travel, vacation, mountain, cold, tourism, *island*, *volcano*, hawaii, *islands*, nationalpark, paradise, pacific, horizon, maui, haleakala, *crater*, summit, ... | sky, *beach*, water, clouds, hawaii, *sand*, *surf*, maui, palmtrees |

Figure 5. Example of travel blog segment visually enriched with related images

4.2. Recommending landmarks

Finding and recommending landmarks is considered an important research topic in the multimedia field, along with recommending tourist spots. Abbasi et al. [1] focused on the photo-sharing system Flickr, and proposed a method to identify landmark photos using tags and social Flickr groups. Gao et al. [7] also proposed a method to identify landmarks using Flickr and the Yahoo Travel Guide.

Ji et al. [17] proposed another method for finding landmarks. They adopted the method of clustering blog photos relating to a particular tourist site, such as Louvre Museum in Paris.[10] Then they represented these photos as a graph based on the clustering results, and detected landmarks using link analysis methods, such as the PageRank [3] and HITS [19] algorithms.

4.3. Recommending travel products

Ishino et al. [14] proposed a method that added links to advertisements for travel products to the travel information links that were described in Section 2.3.[11] The procedure for providing ad links is as follows.

1. Input a link type and the citing areas of a travel information link.
2. Extract keywords from the citing areas.
3. Extract product data containing all keywords, and calculate the similarity between the citing areas of a travel information link and the product data.
4. Provide the ad link to the product data having the highest similarity to the travel information link.

They extracted keywords for travel products corresponding to the link type. They used the same cues to classify travel information links [15] (see Section 2.3), and then extracted keywords from the citing areas of links of types S (Spot) and R (Restaurant).

---

[10] For calculating the similarity between two photos, they used the Bag-of-Visual-Words representation [18, 26], which represents an image as a set of salient regions (visual words), called Bag-of-Visual-Words vectors. Then the similarity between photos is measured based on the cosine distance between their Bag-of-Visual-Words vectors. In addition to the features in each image, they also used textual information for each photo, such as the title, description, and surrounding text.

[11] http://www.ls.info.hiroshima-cu.ac.jp/travel/

First, the method for extracting keywords from the citing areas of links of type S is described. The cues for type S, such as tourist spots collected from Wikipedia and words frequently used in the names of tourist spots, tend to become keywords. Therefore, they registered these cues as candidate keywords for links of type S. If the citing areas of these links contained candidate keywords, they extracted the candidates as keywords. In addition, if citing areas contained names of places, they extracted the names as keywords.

The cues for type R, such as dish names and cooking styles, also tend to become keywords. Therefore, they registered these cues as candidate keywords for links of type R. If the citing areas for links of type R contained candidate keywords, they extracted them as keywords.

4.4. Recommending accommodation

Titov and McDonald [31] proposed an aspect-based summarization system, and applied the method to the summarization of hotel reviews. The system took as input a set of user reviews for a specific product or service with a numeric rating (left side in Figure 6), and produced a set of relevant aspects, which they called an aspect-based summary (right side in Figure 6). To extract all relevant mentions in each review for each aspect, they introduced a topic model. They applied their method to hotel reviews on the TripAdvisor Web site[12], and obtained aspect-based summaries for each hotel.

Food: 5; Decor: 5; Service: 5; Value: 5
The chicken was great. On top of that our service was excellent and the price was right. Can't wait to go back!

Food: 2; Decor: 1; Service: 3; Value: 2
We went there for our anniversary. My soup was cold and expensive plus it felt like they hadn't painted since 1980.

Food: 3; Decor: 5; Service: 4; Value: 5
The food is only mediocre, but well worth the cost. Wait staff was friendly. Lot's of fun decorations.

→

Food	"The chicken was great", "My soup was cold", "The food is only mediocre"
Decor	"it felt like they hadn't painted since 1980", "Lots of fun decorations"
Service	"service was excellent", "Wait staff was friendly"
Value	"the price was right", "My soup was cold and expensive", "well worth the cost"

Figure 6. Producing aspect mentions from a corpus of aspect rated reviews

To obtain more reliable hotel reviews, opinion spams should be detected and eliminated. Opinion spams are fictitious opinions that have been deliberately written to sound authentic. Ott et al. [27] proposed a method to detect opinion spam among consumer reviews of hotels. They created 400 deceptive opinions using the Amazon Mechanical Turk (AMT) crowdsourcing service[13] by asking anonymous online workers (Turkers) to create the opinion spam for 20 chosen hotels. In addition to these spam messages, they selected 6,977 truthful opinions from TripAdvisor, and used both groups for their task.

4.5. Recommending photos

Bressan et al. [2] proposed a travel blog assistant system that facilitated the travel blog writing by selecting for each blog paragraph the most relevant images from an image set. The procedure is as follows.

---

[12] http://www.tripadvisor.com
[13] https://www.mturk.com/

1. The system adds metadata to the traveler's photos based on a generic visual categorizer, which provides annotations (short textual keywords) related to some generic visual aspects of and objects in the image.[14]

2. Textual information (tags) was obtained using a cross-content information retrieval system using a repository of multimedia objects.

3. For a given paragraph, the system ranked the uploaded images according to the similarity between the extracted metadata and the paragraph.

5. Interfaces for travel information access

In this section, we describe two studies that focused on interfaces for travel information access.

5.1. Providing travel information along streetcar lines

Ishino et al. [13] proposed a method for collecting blog entries about the Hiroshima Electric Railway (Hiroden) from a blog database.[15] Hiroden blog entries were defined as travel journals that provide regional information for streetcar stations in Hiroshima. The task of collecting Hiroden blog entries was divided into two steps: (1) collection of blog entries; and (2) identification of Hiroden blog entries.

Figure 7 shows a route map used by the system for providing travel information along the Hiroden streetcar lines. The route map shows Hiroden streetcar stations and major tourist spots. The steps in the search procedure are as follows.

- (Step 1) Click the Hiroden streetcar station, such as "原爆ドーム前" (Atomic Bomb Dome), in Figure 7 to generate a list of links to Hiroden blog entries (Figure 8).

- (Step 2) Click the link to a Hiroden blog entry to display it.

5.2. Natural language interface for accessing databases

Several ontologies for e-tourism have been developed (see Section 6). Unfortunately, the gap between human users who want to retrieve information and the Semantic Web is yet to be cloased. Ruiz-Martínez et al. [30] proposed a method for querying ontological knowledge bases using natural language sentences. For example, when the user inputted the query "I want to visit the most important tourist attractions in Paris", the system conducted part-of-speech tagging, lemmatizing, and modification of query terms by synonyms, and finally searched the ontology.

---

[14] Bressan et al. used images that were categorized into 44 classes as training data for visual categorization. Each class was given a short text name, such as "clouds and sky" or "beach". When an image was categorized as belonging to classes A and B using the visual categorizer, the short texts given to each class were assigned as keywords of the image.

[15] http://165.242.101.30/travel/hiroden/

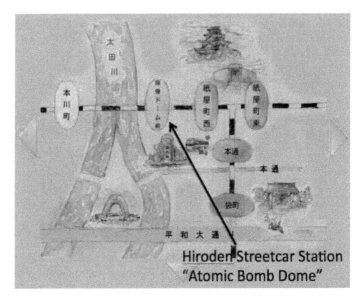

Figure 7. A route map of the Hiroden system

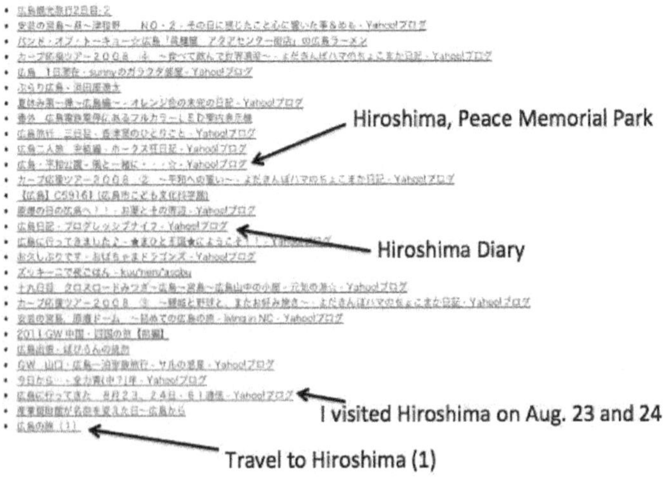

Figure 8. A list of links to Hiroden blog entries

6. Linguistic resources for studies of automatic compilation of travel information from texts

Text Corpora

- TripAdvisor: http://tripadvisor.com
  This site provides fifty million reviews written in various languages.
- Footstops: http://footstops.com
  This site provides more than 8,000 blog entries written in English.
- IgoUgo: http://www.igougo.com
  This site provides 530,000 reviews and 62,000 blog entries written in English.
- Travbuddy: http://www.travbuddy.com
  This site provides more than 90,000 reviews and 180,000 blog entries written in English.
- TravelBlog: http://www.travelblog.org
  This site provides more than 600,000 blog entries written in English. Each entry is classified at city level in a geographic hierarchy.
- Travellerspoint: http://www.travellerspoint.com
  This site provides more than 180,000 blog entries written in English.
- TravelPod: http://www.travelpod.com
  This site is one of the oldest travel portal, started since 1997, and provides blog entries written in English.
- 4travel: http://4travel.jp
  This site provides approximately 300,000 reviews and 600,000 blog entries written in Japanese. Each review is classified at city level in a geographic hierarchy.

Databases for Travel

- Rakuten travel data: http://www.nii.ac.jp/cscenter/idr/datalist.html (Japanese)
  Basic information about 11,468 properties and 350,000 reviews
- Travel product data in Rakuten Shopping Mall (Rakuten Ichiba): http://www.nii.ac.jp/cscenter/idr/datalist.html (Japanese)
  The data comprise 50 million items. Each item has name, code, price, URL, picture, shop code, category ID, and descriptive text and registration data.

Useful Sites or Services for Travel

- Yahoo Travel Guide: http://travel.yahoo.com/
  This site provides an area-based recommendation service. For each country, several main cities are listed.
- WikiTravel: http://wikitravel.org
  The travel recommendation system contributed by "WikiTravellers". For each destination, the articles in WikiTravel generally include all or parts of the following information: history, climate, landmarks, work information, shopping information, food, and how to get there.

Ontologies for Travel

- The World Tourism Organization (WTO) provides a multilingual thesaurus in English, French, and Spanish that provides a standard terminology for tourism [33].

- DERI's e-Tourism Working group has created a tourism ontology called "OnTour" [28]. This ontology describes the main conventional concepts for tourism such as accommodation or activities, together with other supplementary concepts such as GPS coordinates or a postal address.

- LA_DMS is an ontology for tourism destinations that was developed for the Destination Management System (DMS). This system adapts information requests about tourist destinations to users' needs [16].

Many other ontologies for travel were introduced by Ruiz-Martínez et al. [30].

Evaluation Workshop

GeoCLEF: Geographic Information Retrieval

GeoCLEF (http://ir.shef.ac.uk/geoclef/) was the cross-language geographic retrieval track run as part of the Cross-Language Evaluation Forum (CLEF). It operated from 2005 to 2008 [11, 12, 21, 22]. The goal of this task was to retrieve news articles relevant to particular aspects of geographic information.

NTCIR GeoTime

NTCIR GeoTime was another cross-language geographic retrieval track run as part of the NTCIR. It operated from 2008 to 2011 [8, 9]. The focus of this task was searching with geographic and temporal constraints using Japanese and English news articles as target documents.

7. Conclusions and future directions

In this chapter, we have introduced the state of the art of research and services related to travel information. There are several future directions for this research field.

- We mentioned in Section 2 that several natural language processing technologies are useful for creating databases for travel. These technologies may also be applied to maintain manually created databases or ontologies for travel, such as those discussed in Section 6.

- Multilingualization of the ontologies for travel using machine translation techniques [4] is also considered an important task for encouraging further studies in this research field.

- There are many different locations that have the same name (place name polysemy), and there may be multiple names for a given location (place name synonymy). To eliminate this geo-ambiguity problem, Ji et al. [17] proposed the Hierarchical-comparison Geo-Disambiguation (HGD) algorithm, which distinguished the city-level location using a combination of its lower-level locations, derived from the hierarchical location relationships. In addition to this method, several natural language processing technologies, such as automatic acquisition of synonyms [5, 29, 35, 36] and word sense disambiguation [23], are available.

• Recommending landmarks (landmark finding) is a standard research topic in image processing using Flickr. In this chapter, we mentioned three studies [1, 7, 17] that relied mainly on image processing and tag-based recommendation techniques rather than natural language processing. The authors believe that there is still room to improve the methods of recommending landmarks by natural language processing, because sentiment analysis techniques, such as those used for recommending accommodation, have not yet been used for recommending landmarks.

Author details

Hidetsugu Nanba*,
Aya Ishino and Toshiyuki Takezawa

* Address all correspondence to: nanba@hiroshima-cu.ac.jp

Graduate School of Information Sciences, Hiroshima City University, Japan

References

[1] Abbasi, R., Chernov, S., Nejdl, W., Paiu, R., Staab, S. (2009) Exploiting Flickr Tags and Groups for Finding Landmark Photos. Proceedings of ECIR 2009, pp.654–661.

[2] Bressan, M., Csurka, G., Hoppenot, Y., and Renders, J.M. (2008) Travel Blog Assistant System (TBAS) - An Example Scenario of How to Enrich Text with Images and Images with Text using Online Multimedia Repositories. Proceedings of VISAPP Workshop on Metadata Mining for Image Understanding.

[3] Brin, S. and Page, L. (1998) The Anatomy of a Large-scale Hypertextual Web Search Engine. Proceedings of World Wide Web Conference 1998.

[4] Brown, P.F., Pietra, S.A.D., Pietra, V.J.D., and Mercer, R.L. (1993) The Mathematics of Statistical Machine Translation: Parameter Estimation, Computational Linguistics, Vol.19, No.2, pp.263–311.

[5] Callison-Burch, C., Koehn, P., and Osborne, M. (2006) Improved Statistical Machine Translation Using Paraphrases. Proceedings of NAACL 2006, pp.17–24.

[6] Davidov, D. (2009). Geo-mining: Discovery of Road and Transport Networks Using Directional Patterns. Proceedings of the 2009 Conference on Empirical Methods in Natural Language Processing, pp.267–275.

[7] Gao, Y., Tang, J, Hong, R., Dai, Q., Chua, T.-S., and Jain, R. (2010) W2Go: A Travel Guidance System by Automatic Landmark Ranking. Proceedings of ACM Multimedia'10.

[8] Gey, F., Larson, R., Machado, J., and Yoshioka, M. (2011) NTCIR9-GeoTime Overview: Evaluating Geographic and Temporal Search: Round 2. Proceedings of NTCIR-9 Workshop Meeting.

[9] Gey, F., Larson, R., Kando, N., Machado, J., and Sakai, T. (2010) NTCIR-GeoTime Overview: Evaluating Geographic and Temporal Search. Proceedings of NTCIR-8 Workshop Meeting.

[10] Hao, Q., Cai, R., Wang, C., Xiao, R., Yang, J.-M., Pang, Y., and Zhang, L. (2010) Equip Tourists with Knowledge Mined from Travelogues. Proceedings of World Wide Web Conference 2010.

[11] Gey, F., Larson, R.R., Sanderson, M., Bischoff, K., Mandl, T., Womser-Hacker, C., Santos, D., Rocha, P., Nunzio, G.M.D., Ferro, N. (2006) GeoCLEF 2006: The CLEF 2006 Cross-Language Geographic Information Retrieval Track Overview. Proceedings of CLEF 2006, pp.852–876.

[12] Gey, F. Larson, R.R., Sanderson, M., Joho, H., Clough, P., and Petras, V. (2005) GeoCLEF: The CLEF 2005 Cross-Language Geographic Information Retrieval Track Overview. Lecture Notes in Computer Science, LNCS4022, pp.908–919.

[13] Ishino, A., Nanba, H., and Takezawa, T. (2012) Construction of a System for Providing Travel Information along Hiroden Streetcar Lines. Proceedings of the 3rd IIAI International Conference on e-Services and Knowledge Management.

[14] Ishino, A., Nanba, H., and Takezawa, T. (2011) Providing Ad Links to Travel Blog Entries Based on Link Types. Proceedings of the 9th Workshop on Asian Language Resources, collocated with IJCNLP 2011, pp.63–70.

[15] Ishino, A., Nanba, H., and Takezawa, T. (2011) Automatic Compilation of an Online Travel Portal from Automatically Extracted Travel Blog Entries. Proceedings of ENTER 2011.

[16] Jakkilinki, R., Ceorgievski, M., and Sharda, N. (2007) Connecting Destinations with an Ontology-Based e-Tourism Planner. Information and Communication Technologies in Tourism, pp.21–32.

[17] Ji, R., Xie, X., Yao, H., and Ma, W.-Y. (2009) Mining City Landmarks from Blogs by Graph Modeling. Proceedings of ACM Multimedia'09, pp.105–114.

[18] Jia, M.-L., Fan, X., Xie, X., Li, M.-J., and Ma, W.-Y. (2006) Photo-to-search: Using Camera Phones to Inquire of the Surrounding World. Mobile Data Management.

[19] Kleinberg, J. (1999) Authoritative Sources in a Hyperlinked Environment, Journal of the ACM, Vol.46, No.5, pp.604–622.

[20] Lafferty, J., McCallum, A., and Pereira, F. (2001) Conditional Random Field: Probabilistic Models for Segmenting and Labeling Sequence Data. Proceedings of the 18th Conference on Machine Learning: pp.282–289.

[21] Mandl, T., Carvalho, P., Nunzio, G.M.D., Gey, F., Larson, R.R., Santos, D., Womser-Hacker, C. (2008) GeoCLEF 2008: The CLEF 2008 Cross-Language Geographic Information Retrieval Track Overview. Proceedings of CLEF 2008, pp.808–821.

[22] Mandl, T., Gey, F., Nunzio, G.M.D., Ferro, N., Larson, R.R., Sanderson, M., Santos, D., Womser-Hacker, C., Xie, X. (2007) GeoCLEF 2007: The CLEF 2007

Cross-Language Geographic Information Retrieval Track Overview. Proceedings of CLEF 2007, pp.745–772.

[23] Manning, C. D. and Schu   tze, H (2000) Foundations of Statistical Natural Language Processing, chapter 7, MIT Press.

[24] Nakatoh, T., Yin, C., and Hirokawa, S. (2011) Characteristic Grammatical Context of Tourism Information,ICIC Express Letters, Vol.4, No.5.

[25] Nanba, H., Taguma, H., Ozaki, T., Kobayashi, D., Ishino, A., and Takezawa, T. (2009) Automatic Compilation of Travel Information from Automatically Identified Travel Blogs. Proceedings of the Joint Conference of the 47th Annual Meeting of the Association for Computational Linguistics and the 4th International Joint Conference on Natural Language Processing, pp.205–208.

[26] Nister, D. and Stewenius, H. (2006) Scalable Recognition with a Vocabulary Tree. Proceedings of CVPR 2006.

[27] Ott, M., Choi, Y. Cardie, C., and Hancock, J.T. (2011) Finding Deceptive Opinion Spam by Any Stretch of the Imagination. Proceedings of the 49th Annual Meeting of the Association for Computational Linguistics, pp.309–319.

[28] Prantner, K. (2004) OnTour -The Ontology-, DERI Innsbruck.

[29] Quirk, C., Brockett, C., and Dolan, W. (2004) Monolingual Machine Translation for Paraphrase Generation. Proceedings of EMNLP 2004, pp.142–149.

[30] Ruiz-Martínez, J.M., Castellanos-Nieves, D., Valencia-García, R., Fernández-Breis, J.T., García-Sánchez, F., Vivancos-Vicente, P.J., Castejón-Garrido, J.S., Camõn, J.B., and Martínez-Bëjar, R. (2009) Accessing Touristic Knowledge Bases through a Natural Language Interface, Proceedings of PKAW 2008, LNAI 5465, pp.147–160.

[31] Titov, I. and McDonald, R. (2008) A Joint Model of Text and Aspect Ratings for Sentiment Summarization. Proceedings of Annual Meeting of the Association for Computational Linguistics & Human Language Technology, pp.308–316.

[32] Tsai, R.T.-H. and Chou, C.-H. (2011) Extracting Dish Names from Chinese Blog Reviews Using Suffix Arrays and a Multi-Modal CRF Model, Proceedings of ACM SIGIR 2011.

[33] World Tourism Organization (2001) Thesaurus on Tourism and Leisure Activities of the World Tourism Organization.

[34] Wu, X., Li, J., and Neo, S.-Y. (2008) Personalized Multimedia Web Summarization for Tourist. Proceedings of World Wide Web Conference 2008.

[35] Zhao, S., Niu, C., Zhou, M., Liu, T., and Li, S. (2008) Combining Multiple Resources to Improve SMT-based Paraphrasing Model. Proceedings of ACL-HLT 2008, pp.1021–1029.

[36] Zhou, L., Lin, C.-Y., Munteanu, D.S., and Hovy, E. (2006) ParaEval: Using Paraphrases to Evaluate Summaries Automatically. Proceedings of HLT-NAACL 2006, pp.447–454.

## Chapter 5

A Semantic-Based Framework for Summarization and Page Segmentation in Web Mining

Alessio Leoncini, Fabio Sangiacomo,
Paolo Gastaldo and Rodolfo Zunino

Additional information is available at the end of the chapter

1. Introduction

The World Wide Web has become a fundamental resource of information for an increasing number of activities, and a huge information flow is exchanged today through the Internet for the widest range of purposes. Although large-bandwidth communications yield fast access to virtually any kind of contents by both human users and machines, the unstructured nature of most available information may pose a crucial issue. In principle, humans can best extract relevant information from posted documents and texts; on the other hand, the over-whelming amount of raw data to be processed call for computer-supported approaches. Thus, in recent years, *Web mining* research tackled this issue by applying data mining techniques to Web resources [1].

This chapter deals with the predominant portion of the web-based information, i.e., documents embedding natural-language text. The huge amount of textual digital data [2, 3] and the dynamicity of natural language actually can make it difficult for an Internet user (either human or automated) to extract the desired information effectively: thus people every day face the problem of information overloading [4], whereas search engines often return too many results or biased/inadequate entries [5]. This in turn proves that: 1) treating web-based textual data effectively is a challenging task, and 2) further improvements are needed in the area of Web mining. In other words, algorithms are required to speed up human browsing or to support the actual crawling process [4]. Application areas that can benefit from the use of these algorithms include marketing, CV retrieval, laws and regulations exploration, competitive intelligence [6], web reputation, business intelligence [7], news articles search [1], topic tracking [8], and innovative technologies search. Focused crawlers represent another potential, crucial area of application of these technologies in the security domain [7, 9].

The research described in this chapter tackles two challenging problems in Web mining techniques for extracting relevant information. The first problem concerns the acquisition of useful knowledge from textual data; this is a central issue for *Web content mining* research, which mostly approached this task by exploiting text-mining technologies [1]. The second problem relates to the fact that a web page often proposes a considerable amount of information that can be regarded as 'noise' with respect to the truly informative sections for the purposes at hand [10]. According to [10], uninformative web page contents can be divided into navigation units, decoration items, and user interaction parts. On one hand, these elements drain the user's attention, who has to spend his/her time to collect truly informative portions; on the other hand, they can affect the performances of algorithms that should extract the informative content of a web page [10]. This problem is partially addressed by the research area of *semantic Web*, which aims to enrich web pages with semantic information accessible from humans and machines [5]. Thus *semantic Web mining* aims to combine the outcomes of semantic Web [11] and Web mining to attain more powerful tools that can reliably address the two problems described above [5].

The approach adopted in this work, however, does not rely on semantic information already embedded into the Web resources, and the semantic characterization of words and sentences plays a crucial role to reach two outcomes:

- to work out from a Web resource a concise summary, which outlines the relevant topics addressed by the textual data, thus discarding uninformative, irrelevant contents;

- to generate a web page segmentation that points out the relevant text parts of the resource.

Semantic characterization is obtained by applying semantic networks to the considered Web resource. As a result, natural language text maps into an abstract representation, that eventually supports the identification of the topics addressed in the Web resource itself. A heuristic algorithm attains the latter task by using the abstract representation to work out the relevant segments of text in the original document. Page segmentation is then obtained by properly exploiting the information obtained on the relevant topics and the topics covered by the different sections of the Web page.

The novelty contribution of this work lies in a framework that can tackle two tasks at the same time: text summarization and page segmentation. This result is obtained by applying an approach that extracts semantic information from the Web resource and does not rely on external information that may not be available. Combining effective page segmentation with text summarization can eventually support advanced web content mining systems that address the discovery of patterns, the tracking of selected topics and the efficient resource finding.

Experimental results involved the well-know DUC 2002 dataset [12]. Such dataset has been used to evaluate the ability of the proposed framework to consistently identify the topics addressed by a document and eventually generate the corresponding summary. The ROUGE tool [13] has been used to measure the performance of the summarization algorithm exploited by the present framework. Numerical results proved that the research described in this chapter compares positively with state-of-the-art approaches published in the literature.

The rest of the chapter is organized as follows. Section 2 gives an overview of the state of the art in the different research areas involved. Section 3 introduces the overall approach proposed in this research, while Section 4 discusses the actual implementation of the framework. Section 5 presents the experimental results. Some concluding remarks are made in Section 6.

2. Related work

The current research proposes a web mining algorithm that exploits knowledge-based semantic information to integrate text-summarization and web page-segmentation technologies, thus improving the overall approach effectiveness. The following sections overview the state of the art in the different research areas involved: web content mining, text summarization, and web page segmentation. The Section also highlights the points of novelty introduced by the present research with respect to previous works.

2.1. Web content mining

Web mining is the use of data mining techniques to automatically discover and extract information from web documents and services; the applicative areas include resource finding, information selection, generalization and data analysis [14]. Incidentally, machine-learning methods usually address the last two tasks. Web mining includes three main sub-areas: web content mining, web structure mining, and web usage mining [15]. The former area covers the analysis of the contents of web resources, which in general comprise different data sources: texts, images, videos and audio; metadata and hyperlinks are often classified as text content. It has been proved that unstructured text represents the prevailing part of web resources [14, 16] this in turn motivates the large use of text mining technologies.

A wide variety of works in the literature focused on text mining for web content mining [17]. Some web content mining techniques for web search, topic extraction and web opinion mining were explored in [18]. In [19], Liu et al. showed that web content mining could address applicative areas such as sentiment classification, analysis and summarization of consumer reviews, template detection and page segmentation. In [20], web content mining tackled business applications by developing a framework for competitive intelligence. In [21], an advanced search engine supported web-content categorization based on word-level summarization techniques. A web-page analyzer for detecting undesired advertisement was presented in [22]. The work described in [23] proposed a web-page recommendation system, where learning methods and collaborative filtering techniques cooperated to produce a web filter for efficient user navigation.

The approach presented in this research differs from those related works in two main aspects: first, it exploits semantic-based techniques to select and rank single sentences extracted from text; secondly, it combines summarization with web page segmentation. The proposed approach does not belong to the semantic web mining area, which refers to methodologies that address the development of specific ontologies that enrich original web page contents in a structured format [11, 24]. To the best of the authors' knowledge, the literature provides only two works that used semantic information for web content mining. The research described in [25] addressed personalized multimedia management systems, and used semantic, ontology-based contextual information to attain a personalized behavior in content access and retrieval. An investigation of semantic-based feature extraction for web mining is proposed in [26], where the WordNet [27] semantic network supported a novel metrics for semantic similarity.

2.2. Text summarization

A summary is a text produced by one or more other texts, expressing important information of original texts, and no longer than half of the original texts [28]. Actually, text summarization techniques aim to minimize the reading effort by maximizing the information density that is prompted to the reader [29]. Summarization techniques can be categorized into two approaches: in extractive methods, summaries stem from the verbatim extraction of words or sentences, whereas abstractive methods create original summaries by using natural language generators [30].

The works of Das et al. [30] and Gupta et al. [31] provided extensive surveys on extractive summarization techniques. Several methods relied on word frequency analysis, cue words extraction, or selection of sentences according to their position in the text [32]. More recent works used tf-idf metrics (term frequency - inverse document frequency) [33], graphs analysis, latent semantic analysis [34], machine learning techniques [35], and fuzzy systems [36, 37]. Other approaches exploited semantic processing: [38] adopted lexicon analysis, whereas concepts extraction supported the research presented in [39]. Abstractive summarization was addressed in [40], where the goal was to understand the main concepts of a document, and then to express those concepts in a natural-language form.

The present work actually relies on a hybrid extractive-abstractive approach. First, most informative sentences are selected by using co-occurrence of semantic domains [41], thus involving an extractive summarization. Then, abstractive information is produced by working out the most representative domains for every document.

2.3. Web page segmentation

Website pages are designed for visual interaction, and typically include a number of visual segments conveying heterogeneous contents. Web page segmentation aims to grasp the page structure and split contents according to visual segments. This is a challenging task that brings about a considerable number of issues. Different techniques were applied to web page segmentation in the past years: PageRank [42], graphs exploration [43], rules [10, 44, 45], heuristics [46, 47, 48, 49], text processing [50], image processing [51], machine learning [52, 53], and semantic processing [54].

Web page segmentation methods apply heuristic algorithms, and mainly rely on the Document Object Model (DOM) tree structure that is associated to a web resource. Therefore, segmentation algorithms may not operate properly when those ancillary features are not available or when they do not reflect the actual semantic structure of the web page. Conversely, the approach presented in this chapter only relies on the processing of the textual information that can be retrieved in the web resource.

3. A Framework for Text Summarization and Segmentation

The processing of textual data in a Web page yields two outcomes: a text summary, that identifies the most relevant topics addressed in the Web page, and the set of sentences that are most correlated with those topics. The latter indirectly supports the segmentation of the web page, as one can identify the substructures that deal with the relevant topics. Several advanced applications for Web mining can benefit from this approach: intelligent crawlers that explore links only related to most informative content, focused robots that follow specific content evolution, and web browsers with advertising filters or specific content- highlighting capabilities. This Section presents the overall approach, and introduces the various elements that compose the whole framework. Then, Section 4 will discuss the actual implementation of the framework used in this work.

3.1. Overall system description

The approach relies on a two-level abstraction of the original textual information that is extracted from the web page (Figure 1); semantic networks are the tools mainly exploited to accomplish this task. First, raw text is processed to work out *concepts*. Then, concepts are grouped into domains; here, a domain represents a list of related words describing a particular subject or area of interest. According to Gliozzo et al [55], domain information corresponds to a paradigmatic relationship, i.e., two words with meanings that are closely related (e.g., synonyms and hyponyms).

Semantic networks allow to characterize the content of a textual resource according to semantic domains, as opposed to a conventional bag of words. The ultimate objective is to exploit a coarse-grained level of sense distinctions, which in turn can lead to identify the topics actually addressed in the Web page. Toward that end, suitable algorithms must process the domain-based representation and recognize the relevant information in the possibly noisy environment of a Web page. Indeed, careful attention should be paid to the fact that many Web pages often address multiple, heterogeneous domains. Section 4 presents in detail the procedure implementation to identify specific domains in a Web page.

Text summarization is obtained after the identification of the set, Θ, of domains that characterize the informative content of the Web page. The summary is obtained by detecting in the original textual source the sentences that are mostly correlated to the domains included in Θ. To complete this task sentences are ranked according to the single terms they involve, since the proposed approach only sets links between terms and concepts (domains). The process can generate the eventual summary according to two criteria: the first criterion yields a summary that describes the overall content of the Web page, and therefore does not distinguish the various domains included in Θ; the second criterion prompts a multiplicity of summaries, one for each domain addressed in Θ.

That approach to text summarization supports an unsupervised procedure for page segmentation, too. Indeed, the described method can 1) identify within a Web page the sentences that are most related to the main topics addressed in the page itself, and 2) label each sentence with its specific topic. Thus text summarization can help assess the structure of the Web page, and the resulting information can be combined with that provided by specific structure-oriented tools (e.g., those used for tag analysis in html source code).

Figure 2 shows the two alternative strategies that can be included in the Web mining system. The first strategy uses the text summarization abilities to find relevant information in a Web page, and possibly to categorize the contents addressed. The second strategy targets a selective search, which is driven by a query prompted by the user. In the latter case, text summarization and the eventual segmentation allow the mining tool to identify the information that is relevant for the user in the considered Web page.

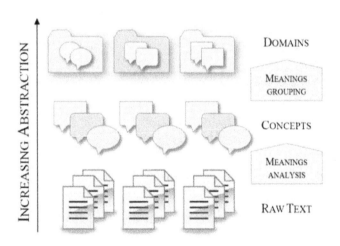

Figure 1. The two abstraction layers exploited to extract contents from textual data.

3.2. Overall system description

The overall framework can be schematized according to the following steps (Figure 3):

From the Web page to textual data:

a. get a Web page;

b. iextract textual data from the source code of the Web page.

Text preprocessing:

a. identify words and sentences terminators to split text into words (tokens) and sentences;

b. erase stop words;

c. lemmatization.

Abstraction:

a. first abstraction level: a semantic network is used to extract a set of concepts from every token; eventually, a list of concepts is obtained;

b. second abstraction level: the concepts are grouped in homogeneous sets (domains).

Content analysis:

a. strategy: automatic selection of domain

b. identify the informative contents addressed by processing the list of domains obtained after Step 3 (Abstraction);

c. strategy: user-driven domain

process the list of domains obtained after Step 3 (Abstraction) to search for the topics indicated by the user.

Outputs:

Summarization:

a. use the output of Step 4 (Content Analysis) to rank the sentences included in the textual source;

b. build a summary by using the most significant sentences according to the rank.

Page Segmentation:

a. use the sentences ranking to select the portions of the web page that deal with the main topics.

Step 4 (Content Analysis) and Step 5 (Outputs) can be supported by different approaches. Section 4 will discusses the approaches adopted in this research.

4. Implementation

The processing starts by feeding the system with the download of a web page. Raw text is extracted by applying the 'libxml' parsing library [56] to the html source code.

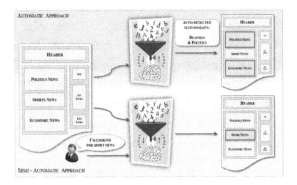

Figure 2. The proposed system can automatically detect the most relevant topics, or alternatively can select single text sections according to the user requests

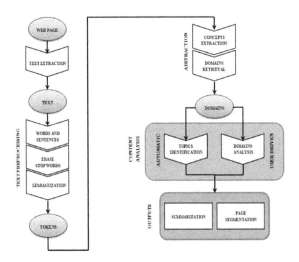

Figure 3. The data flow of the proposed framework

4.1. Text preprocessing

This phase receives as input the raw text and completes two tasks: 1) it identifies the beginning and the end of each sentence; 2) it extracts the tokens from each sentence, i.e., the terms that compose the sentence. Additional subtasks are in fact involved for optimal text processing: after parsing raw text into sentences and tokens, idiom is identified and stop-words are removed accordingly; this operation removes frequent and semantically non-selective expressions from text. Then, *lemmatization* simplifies the inflectional forms of a term (sometimes derivationally related forms) down to a common radix form (e.g., by simplifying plurals or verb persons). These subtasks are quite conventional in natural language processing systems [57], and aim to work out a set of representative tokens.

The process that extracts sentence and tokens from text is driven by a finite-state machine (FSM), which parses the characters in the text sequentially. The formalism requires the definition of the following quantities:

- state *STARTT*: a token begins;

- state *ENDT*: end of token achieved;

- state *STARTS*: a sentence begins (hence, also a token begins);

- state *ENDS*: end of sentence achieved (hence, end of token also achieved);

- set *tdelim*, which includes space, tab and newline codes, plus the following characters: "\',/:;.!?[]{}()*^-~_=

- set *sdelim*, which includes common sentence delimiter characters, such as :;!?'"

- set *number*, which includes all the numbers;

- set *lower*, which includes all the lower case alphabet characters;

- set *upper*, which includes all the upper case alphabet characters;

- set character, which is obtained as the union of set *lower* and set *upper*;

- set *dot*, which only include the dot character.

A detailed description of the complete procedure implemented by the FSM is provided in Figure 4. Actually, Figure 4(a) refers to the core procedure, which includes the initial state STARTS; Figure 4(b) refers to the sub-procedure that starts when the state NUMBER is reached in the procedure of Figure 4(a); Figure 4(c) refers to the sub-procedure that starts when the state ALPHA is reached in the procedure of Figure 4(a). In all the schemes the elements with circular shape represent the links between the three procedures: the light-grey elements refer to links that transfer the control to a different procedure; the dark-grey elements refer to links that receive the control from a different procedure.

The process implemented by the FSM yields a list of tokens, a list of sentences and the position of each token within the associated sentence. Stop-word removal takes out those tokens that either are shorter than three characters or appear in a language-specific list of terms (conjunctions, articles, etc). This effectively shrinks the list of tokens. Finally, a lemmatization process reduces each token to its root term. Different algorithms can perform the lemmatization step, depending on the document language. WordNet morphing features [27] support best lemmatization in the English idiom, and has been adopted in this research.

In the following, the symbol Ω will define the list of tokens extracted after text preprocessing: $\Omega = \{t_i; i = 1,..,N_t\}$, where t_i is a token and N_t is the number of tokens.

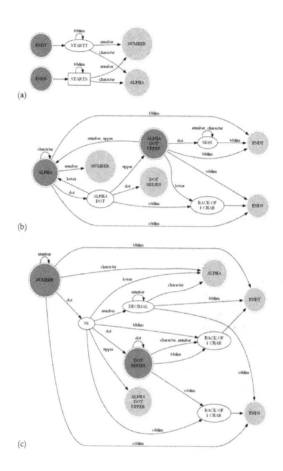

Figure 4. The Finite State Machine that extracts sentences and tokens from text. The three scheme refers to as many sub-procedures

4.2. The abstraction process: from words to domains

The framework uses a semantic network to map tokens into an abstract representation, which can characterize the informative content of the basic textual resource on a cognitive basis. The underlying hypothesis is that to work out the topics addressed in a text, one cannot just depend on the mentioned terms, since each term can in principle convey different senses. On the other hand, the semantic relations that exist between concepts can help understand whether the terms can connect to a single subject or area of interest.

The present approach implements such an abstraction process by mapping tokens into domains. An intermediate step, from tokens to concepts, supports the whole procedure. Two well-known semantic networks have been used to complete this task: EuroWordNet [58], i.e the multilanguage version of WordNet [27], and its extension WordNet Domains [41]. Both EuroWordNet and WordNet Domains are ontologies designed to decorate words or sets of words with semantic relations. The overall structure of EuroWordNet and WordNet Domains are based on the conceptual structures theory [59] which describes the different types of relations that can tie together different concepts.

4.2.1. From tokens to concepts

The abstraction from tokens to concepts is accomplished by using EuroWordNet. Euro-WordNet is an extension of WordNet semantic knowledge base for English, inspired by the current sycholinguistic theory of human lexical memory [27]. Nouns, verbs, adjectives and adverbs are organized in sets of synonyms (*synsets*), each of which represents a lexical concept. Actually, the same word can participate in several synsets, as a single word can have different senses (polysemy). Synonym sets are connected to other synsets via a number of semantic relations, which vary based on the type of word (noun, verb, adjective, and adverb); for example, synsets of noun can be characterized by relations such as hyponymy and meronymy. Words can also be connected to other words through lexical relations (e.g., antinomy). EuroWordNet supports different languages; thus, in principle, the approach proposed in this chapter can be easily extended to documents written in Italian, Spanish, French, and German. Table 1 gives, for each language, the number of terms and the number of concepts provided by EuroWordNet [58].

In the present research, the list of concepts that characterize a text is obtained as follows:

a.   For each token $t_i \in \Omega$, extract the list of concepts (i.e., synsets) X_i that EuroWordNet associate to the token: $X_i = \{c_k; k = 1,..,N_{c,i}\}$, where $N_{c,i}$ is the number of different concepts in X_i.

b.   Assemble the overall list of concepts: $\Sigma = X_1 \cup X_2 \cup X_3 \cup .... \cup X_{Nt}$

To not inflate the list of concepts, in this work the tokens that connect to more than eight concepts are discarded. Such threshold has been set empirically by exploiting preliminary experiments. The list of concepts, Σ, represents an intermediate step to work out the domains; this step will be discussed in the next subsection.

The use of synsets to identify concepts possibly brings about the drawback of word disambiguation. The problem of determining which one, out of a set of senses, are invoked in a textual context for a single term is not trivial, and specific techniques [55, 60, 61] have been developed to that purpose. Word disambiguation techniques usually rely on the analysis of the words that lie close to the token itself [61, 62]. Other approaches exploit queries on a knowledge base. A notable example of this approach exploits WordNet Domains and is discussed in [63]. As a matter of fact, word disambiguation methods suffer from both high computational complexity [60, 64] and the dependency on dedicated knowledge bases [65]. In this work, word disambiguation is implicitly obtained by completing the abstraction from concepts to domains.

Language	Number of terms	Number of concepts
English	120160	112641
Italian	37194	44866
Spanish	32166	30350
French	18798	22745
German	17099	15132

Table 1. EuroWordNet: supported languages and corresponding elements

4.2.2. From concepts to domains

WordNet Domains [41] supports the abstraction from concepts to domains. A domain is a structure that gathers different synsets belonging to a common area of interest; thus a domain can connect to synsets that pertain to different syntactic categories. Conversely, one synset can be linked to multiple domains. Each domain groups meanings into homogenous clusters; therefore, one can use the abstraction from concepts to domains to work out the topics that are actually addressed in the underlying set of tokens Ω. This can be done as follows:

a. identify the domains that can be associated to the concepts included in Σ;

b. For each concept $c_i \in \Sigma$, extract the list of domains Θ_i that WordNet Domains associate to that concept: $\Theta_i = \{d_j; j = 1, ..., N_{d,i}\}$, where $N_{d,i}$ is the number of different domains in Θ_i.

c. Obtain the overall list of domains Θ as $\Theta_1 \cup \Theta_2 \cup \Theta_3 \cup .... \cup \Theta_{N_c}$, where N_c is the cardinality of Σ.

design a criterion to work out the foremost domains from Θ.

Different approaches can support the latter step. The implicit goal is to attain word disambiguation, i.e. to remove the ambiguity that may characterize single tokens when they are viewed individually. Thus, one should take advantage of the information obtained from a global analysis; the underlying hypothesis is that the actual topics can be worked out only correlating the information provided by the single tokens. In the present work, that information is conveyed by the list of domains, Θ. The domain-selection algorithm picks out the domains that occur most frequently within the text. The procedure can be formalized as follows:

a.   Create an array F with N_d elements, where is the cardinality $|\Theta|$ of set $\Theta = \{d_j; j = 1, .., N_d\}$

b.   Set each element of F to 0: $f_j = 0, j = 1, .., N_d$

c.   For each $t_i \in \Omega$

a.   Identify the list of domains to which t_i is linked: $J = \{j \mid d_j$ linked to $t_i\}$

b.   If $|J| = 1$

$f_j = f_j + 1; \bullet j \in J$

else if $|J| > 1$

$f_j = f_j + 0.5;$ $\cdot$ $j \in J$

The array F eventually measures the relevance of each domain d_j. The algorithm evaluates the relevance of a domain by taking into account the intrinsic semantic properties of a token. Thus, the relative increment in the relevance of a domain is higher when a token can only be linked to one domain. The rationale behind this approach is that these special cases are not affected by ambiguities.

The array of relevancies, F, provides the input to the task designed to work out the most relevant topics and eventually generate the summary.

4.3. Text Summarization

The framework is designed to generate a summary by identifying, in the original text, the textual portions that most correlate with the topics addressed by the document. Two tasks should be completed to attain that goal: first, identifying the topics and, secondly, correlating sentences with the set of topics themselves.

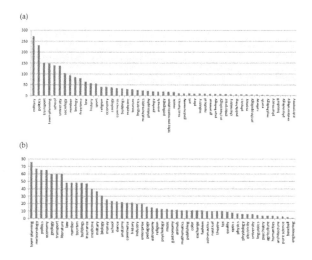

Figure 5. Two examples of array of domains relevancies

The first subtask is accomplished by scanning the array of relevancies, F. In principle, the relevant topics should correspond to the domains having the highest scores in F. However, the distribution of relevancies in the array can play a crucial role, too. Figure 5 illustrates this aspect with two examples. Figure 5(a) refers to a case in which a fairly large gap separates a subset of (highly relevant) domains from the remaining domains. Conversely, Figure 5(b) depicts a case in which the most relevant domains cannot be sharply separated from the remaining domains. The latter case is more challenging as it may correspond either to a text that deals with heterogeneous contents (e.g., the home page of an online newspaper) or to an ineffective characterization of the domains.

To overcome this potential issue, the proposed algorithm operates under the hypothesis that only a limited number of domains compose the subset of relevant topics. The rationale behind this approach is that a tool for content mining is expected to provide a concise description of the Web page, whereas a lengthy list of topics would not help meet such a conciseness constraint. The objective of the algorithm therefore becomes to verify if the array F can highlight a limited subset of domains that are actually outstanding.

The algorithm operates as follows. First, a threshold α is used to set a reference value for the relevance score of a domain; as a result, all the domains in F that did not achieve the reference value are discarded, i.e., they are considered not relevant. Then, a heuristic pruning procedure is used to further shrink the subset of candidate domains; the eventual goal –as anticipated above- is to work out a limited number of topics.

The selection procedure can be formalized as follows:

a. Sort F in descending order, so that f_1 gives the score r_1 of the most relevant domain

b. Obtain F^* by removing from F all the domains with relevance smaller than αr_1

a. If the cardinality of F^* is smaller or equal to θ

b. Else

1. Find the largest gap g_{mn} between consecutive domains in F^*

2. If g_{mn} is larger than χ and m is smaller or equal to θ

select as relevant all the domains from d_1 to d_m

3. Else

it is not possible to select relevant domains

The heuristic pruning procedure is applied only if the number of selected domains (i.e., the domains included in F^*) is larger than a threshold θ, which set an upper limit to the list of relevant topics. The heuristic procedure is designed to identify a cluster of relevant domains within the set F^*; to achieve this goal, the gap between consecutive domains is evaluated (the domains in F^* are provided in descending order according to the relevance score). The parameter χ sets the threshold over which a gap is considered significant. As anticipated, the latter procedure may also provide a void subset of relevant topics.

The eventual summary is obtained by picking out the sentences of the original text that most correlate with the relevant topics. To do so, the list of available sentences is sorted in order of relevance scores. Score values are worked out by considering the tokens that form each sentence: if a token can be related to any selected topic, then the relevance of the associate sentence increases. The eventual score of a sentence, finally, stems from normalizing the number of tokens linked to the relevant topics with respect to the total number of tokens that compose the sentence. The procedure can be outlined as follows:

a. Inputs:

The list of selected domains $\Phi = \{d_j; j = 1,..,N_w\}$, where N_w is the cardinality of Φ.

The list of sentences $\Sigma = \{s_l; l = 1,..,N_s\}$, where N_s is the cardinality of Σ.

The list of tokens included in a sentence s_l, $\Omega_l = \{t_{lq}; q = 1,..,N_{tl}\}$, where N_{tl} is the cardinality of Ω_l.

b. Create an array R with N_s elements; each element registers the relevance of the l-th sentence

c. For each sentence $s_l \in \Sigma$

For each token $t_{lq} \in \Omega_l$

If the token can be linked to a domain in Φ

$r_l = r_l + 1$

d. Normalize the elements of R: $r_l = r_l / |\Omega_l|$

The most relevant sentences are obtained by ranking the array R. Actually the selection removes the sentences that are too short to be consistently evaluated. The eventual rank of the sentences is used to build the summary. In general, the summary will include all the sentences that achieved a relevance greater than a threshold.

5. Experimental Results

The DUC 2002 dataset [12] provided the experimental basis for the proposed framework. The dataset has been designed to test methodologies that address fully automatic multi-document summarization. It is organized as follows:

• 59 subjects;

• for each subject, from 5 to 10 different news about that event;

• for each subject, an extractive summary (400 word) created by involving human participants.

Thus, a summarization technique can be evaluated by comparing the outcome of the computer-driven process with that provided by the dataset (the ground truth).

In this work, the DUC 2002 dataset supported two experimental sessions. The first session aimed at evaluating the ability of the proposed framework to generate an effective summary from the documents included in the dataset. The second session was designed to analyze the behavior of the framework in a typical scenario of Web mining: a text source obtained from a Web page that includes different contributions possibly addressing heterogeneous topics.

5.1. The first experimental session: summarization effectiveness

To evaluate the method's ability at effective summarization, this session adopted the ROUGE software [13]. This made it possible to measure the performances of the proposed approach (as per Section 4) on the DUC 2002 dataset.

ROUGE is a software package for automatic evaluation of summaries that has been widely used in recent years to assess the performance of summarization algorithms. The ROUGE tool actually supports different parameterizations; in the present work, ROUGE-1 has been implemented, thus involving 1-gram co-occurrences between the reference and the candidate summarization results. Using DUC 2002 as a benchmark and ROUGE as the evaluation tool allowed a fair comparison between the present approach and other works already published in the literature.

Table 2 gives the results obtained by the proposed framework on the DUC 2002 dataset. The Table compares experiments tested under different configurations of the summarization algorithm; in particular, experimental set-ups differ in the number of sentences used to generate the summary. The first column gives the number of most informative sentences extracted from the original text; the second, third, and fourth columns report on recall, precision, and f-measure, respectively, as measured by ROUGE.

Number of sentences	Recall	Precision	F-measure
10	0.3297	0.5523	0.4028
15	0.4421	0.5747	0.4884
20	0.5317	0.5563	0.5319
25	0.5917	0.5126	0.5382
30	0.6406	0.4765	0.5363

Table 2. The performance achieved by the proposed framework on the DUC 2002 dataset as assessed by ROUGE

Table 2 shows that the methodology presented in this chapter attained results that compared favorably with those achieved by state-of-the-art algorithms [66] on DUC 2002. In this regard, one should consider that the best performance obtained on DUC 2002 is characterized by the following values [66]: recall = 0.47813, precision = 0.45779, F-measure = 0.46729. This confirmed the effectiveness of the underlying cognitive approach, mapping raw text into an abstract representation, where semantic domains identified the main topics addressed within each document. Numerical results point out that the highest F-measure was attained when the summarization algorithm picked out at least the most 20 relevant sentences in a text.

An additional set of experiments further analyzed the outcomes of the proposed approach. In this case, the goal was to understand whether the topic-selection criterion actually fit the criterion implicitly applied by human subjects when summarizing the texts. This involved

the array, *F*, measuring the relevance of a set of domains (as per section 4.2.2); for each subject included in DUC 2002, the array *F* was computed with respect to:

- the news linked to that subject;

- the corresponding summary provided by the dataset.

Figure 6 gives a sample of the pair of arrays associated with one of the subjects in the DUC
2002 dataset; in the graph, light-grey lines are associated with the actual reference scores in
the benchmark, whereas dark-grey lines refer to the relevance values worked out by the proposed method.

Statistical tools measured the consistency of the domain-selection process: chi-square test
runs compared, for each subject, the pair of distributions obtained; the goal was to verify the
null hypothesis, namely, that the two distributions came from the same population. The
standard value of 0.05 was selected for the confidence level.

The results obtained with the chi-square tests showed that the null hypothesis could *not* be
rejected in any of the 49 experiments involved (each subject in DUC 2002 corresponded to
one experiment). This confirmed that the distributions of the relevant domains obtained
from the whole text could not be distinguished from those obtained from the (human generated) summaries in the DUC 2002 dataset.

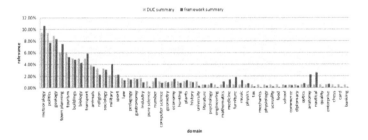

Figure 6. Comparison between the relevance of domains –for the same subject of DUC 2002- in the DUC summary
and in the summary provided by the proposed algorithm

5.2. The second experimental session: web mining

The first experimental session proved that the framework can effectively tackle this task
(and eventually generate a proper summary) when the input was a news-text, which mainly
dealt with a single event. A web page, however, often collects different textual resources,
each addressing a specific, homogenous set of topics. Hence, the second experimental session was designed to evaluate the ability of the proposed framework to identify the most
informative subsections of a web page.

The experiments involved the DUC 2002 dataset and were organized as follows. A set of new documents were generated by assembling the news originally provided by DUC 2002. Each new document eventually included four news articles and covered four different topics. Then, the list of documents was processed by the proposed framework, which was expected – for each document – to select as the most relevant topics those that were chosen in the set up. Table 3 reports on the results of this experiment; each row represents a single document: the first column gives the topics actually addressed by the document, while the second column gives the topics proposed by the framework. The table reports in boldface the topics that the framework was not able to pinpoint.

Experimental evidence confirmed that the proposed framework yielded satisfactory results in this experiment, too. In this regard, one should also take into account that

- the relative length of the single news somewhat influenced the overall distribution of the topics relevance;

- in several cases the real topics not identified by the framework as the most relevant (i.e., the topics in bold) had relevance scores very close to those characterizing the selected ones.

Actual Topics	Topics Proposed by the Framework
Literature / Military / Music / Politics	History / Military / Music / Politics
Literature / **Military** / Music / Politics	Buildings / Literature / Music / Politics
Literature / Military / **Music** / Politics	Literature / Military / Politics / Sociology
Literature / Military / Music / Politics	Biology / Military / Music / Politics
Literature / Military / **Music** / Politics	Military / Politics / School / Sociology
Astronomy / Economy / Music / **Sport**	Astronomy / Biology / Economy / Music
Astronomy / Music / Politics / **Sport**	Biology / Music / Politics / Town Planning
Economy / **Music** / Physics / **Sport**	Economy / Law / Physics / Transport
Music / Physics / Politics / **Sport**	Law / Physics / Politics / Transport
Music / Physics / Politics / Sport	Physics / Politics / Sport / Transport

Table 3. Comparison between actual document topics and topics proposed by the framework

The dataset involved in the experiment was artificially generated to evaluate the effectiveness of the proposed framework in a scenario that resembles a "real word" case. Hence, a fair comparison with other methodologies cannot be proposed. However, Table 3 provides a solid experimental evidence of the efficiency of the approach introduced in this research, as the 'artificial' web pages were composed by using the original news included in the DUC 2002 dataset. As a result, one can conclude that the performances attained by the framework in terms of ability to identify the relevant topics in an heterogeneous document are very promising.

5.3. Web Page Segmentation

The framework can analyze a web page according to two different strategies. The first strategy, identifying the most relevant topics, typically triggers further actions in advanced web-content mining systems: gathering a short summary of the web page (possibly a short summary for each main topic), page segmentation, graphic editing of the web page to favor readability.

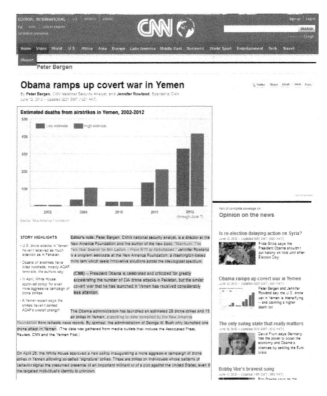

Figure 7. An example of web page analysis supported by the proposed framework

Figure 7 and Figure 8 provide examples of this kind of application. In both cases, the web page included a main section that actually defined the addressed contents, together with other textual parts that did not convey relevant information. The framework supported web content mining by identifying the sentences that actually linked to the relevant topics. These sentences have been highlighted in Figure 7 and Figure 8.

The second strategy typically aims to support users that want to track selected topics. In this case, the goal is to identify the web-page sections that actually deals with the topics of interest. Figure 9 provides an example: the selected topic was 'pharmacy/medicine,' and the web page was the 'News' section of the publisher *InTech*. The figure shows that an advanced web content mining system could exploit the information provided by the framework to high-light the text parts that were considered correlated with the topic of interest.

Figure 8. A second example of web page analysis supported by the proposed framework

6. Conclusions

The research presented in this chapter introduces a framework that can effectively support advanced Web mining tools. The proposed system addresses the analysis of the textual data provided by a web page and exploits semantic networks to achieve multiple goals: 1) the identification of the most relevant topics; 2) the selection of the sentences that better corre-lates with a given topic; 3) the automatic summarization of a textual resource. The eventual framework exploits those functionalities to tackle two tasks at the same time: text summari-zation and page segmentation.

The semantic characterization of text is indeed a core aspect of the proposed methodology, which takes advantage of an abstract representation that expresses the informative content of the basic textual resource on a cognitive basis. The present approach, though, cannot be categorized under the Semantic Web area, as it does not rely on semantic information already embedded into the Web resources.

In the proposed methodology, semantic networks are used to characterize the content of a textual resource according to semantic domains, as opposed to a conventional bag of words. Experimental evidences proved that such an approach can yield a coarse-grained level of sense distinctions, which in turn favors the identification of the topics actually addressed in the Web page. In this regard, experimental results also showed that the system can emulate human assessors in evaluating the relevance of the single sentences that compose a text.

An interesting feature of the present work is that the page segmentation technique is based only on the analysis of the textual part of the Web resource. A future direction of this research can be the integration of the content-driven segmentation approach with conventional segmentation engines, which are more oriented toward the analysis of the inherent structure of the Web page. The resulting framework should be able to combine the outcomes of the two modules to improve the performance of the segmentation procedure.

Figure 9. Tracking a selected topic by using the proposed framework

Future works may indeed be focused on the integration of semantic orientation approaches into the proposed framework. These techniques are becoming more and more important in the Web 2.0 scenario, where one may need the automatic analysis of fast-changing web elements like customer reviews and web reputation data. In this regard, the present framework may provide content-filtering features that support the selection of the data to be analyzed.

Author details

Alessio Leoncini, Fabio Sangiacomo, Paolo Gastaldo and Rodolfo Zunino

Department of naval, electric, electronic and telecommunications engineering (DITEN), University of Genoa, Genoa, Italy

References

[1] Kosala, R., & Blockeel, H. (2000). Web mining research: A survey. *SIGKDD Explorations*, 2(1), 1-15.

[2] Gantz, J. F., Reinsel, D., Chute, C., Schlichting, W., Mcarthur, J., Minton, S., Xheneti, I., Toncheva, A., & Manfrediz, A. (2010). The Expanding Digital Universe: A Forecast of Worldwide Information Growth Through. *Information and Data 2007.*, 1-21.

[3] Naghavi, M., & Sharifi, M. (2012). A Proposed Architecture for Continuous Web Monitoring Through Online Crawling of Blogs. *International Journal of UbiComp*, 3(1), 11-20.

[4] Maes, P. (1994). Agents that reduce work and information overload. *Communications of the ACM*, 37(7), 30-40.

[5] Stumme, G., Hotho, A., & Berendt, B. (2006). Semantic Web Mining: State of the art and future directions. *Journal of Web Semantics*, 4(2), 124-143.

[6] Dai, Y., Kakkonen, T., & Sutinen, E. (2011). MinEDec: a Decision-Support Model That Combines Text-Mining Technologies with Two Competitive Intelligence Analysis Methods. *International Journal of Computer Information Systems and Industrial Management Applications*, 3-165.

[7] Thuraisingham, B.M. (2003). Web Data Mining: Technologies and their Applications in Business Intelligence and Counter-terrorism. *Boca Raton: CRC Press*.

[8] Allan, J. (2002). Topic Detection and Tracking: Event-based Information Organization. *Norwell: Kluwer Academic Publisher*.

[9] Chen, H. Discovery of improvised explosive device content in the Dark Web. Proceedings of IEEE International Conference on Intelligence and Security Informatics, ISI ' June (2008). Taipei, Taiwan. 2008. , 08, 17-20.

[10] Yu, S., Cai, D., Wen, J. R., & Ma, W. Y. (2003). Improving pseudo-relevance feedback in web information retrieval using web page segmentation. *Proceedings of the 12th International Conference on World Wide Web, WWW'03,New York, USA*.

[11] Berners-Lee, T., Hendler, J., & Lassila, O. (2001). The semantic web. *Scientific American*.

[12] Document understanding conference. (2002). http://www-nlpir.nist.gov/projects/ duc/, (accessed 14 May 2012).

[13] Lin, C.Y. Rouge: A package for automatic evaluation of summaries. *Proceedings of the ACL-04 Workshop: Text Summarization Branches Out, Barcelona, Spain. 2004.*

[14] Etzioni, O. (1996). The world wide web: Quagmire or gold mine. *Communications of the ACM*, 39(11), 65-68.

[15] Madria, S. K., Bhowmick, S. S., Ng, W. K., & Lim, E. P. (1999). Research issues in web data mining. *Proceedings of First International Conference on Data Warehousing and Knowledge Discovery, DaWaK'99, Florence, Italy.*

[16] Chakrabarti, S. (2000). Data mining for hypertext. *A tutorial survey*, 1.

[17] Singh, B., & Singh, H. K. Web data mining research: a survey. *Proceedings of 2010 IEEE International Conference on Computational Intelligence and Computing Research, IC-CIC'10. 2010.*

[18] Xu, G., Zhang, Y., & Li, L. (2011). Web Content Mining. *Web Mining and Social Networking*, 6-71.

[19] Liu, B. (2005). Web content mining. *Proceedings of 14th International World Wide Web Conference, WWW'05,May 2005, Chiba, Japan.*

[20] Baumgartner, R., Gottlob, G., & Herzog, M. (2009). Scalable web data extraction for online market intelligence. *Proceedings of the VLDB Endowment*, 2(2), 1512-1523.

[21] Manne, S. (2011). A Novel Approach for Text Categorization of Unorganized data based with Information Extraction. *International Journal on Computer Science and Engineering*, 2846-2854.

[22] Ntoulas, A., Najork, M., Manasse, M., & Fetterly, D. (2006). Detecting spam web pages through content analysis. *Proceedings of the 15th international conference on World Wide Web, WWW'06,Edinburgh, Scotland.*

[23] Khribi, M. K., Jemni, M., & Nasraoui, O. (2009). Automatic Recommendations for E-Learning Personalization Based on Web Usage Mining Techniques and Information Retrieval. *Educational Technology & Society*, 12(4), 30-42.

[24] Maedche, A., & Staab, S. (2001). Ontology Learning for the Semantic Web. *IEEE Intelligent Systems*, 16(2), 72-79.

[25] Vallet, D., Castells, P., Fernandez, M., Mylonas, P., & Avrithis, Y. (2007). Personalized content retrieval. *context using ontological knowledge. IEEE Transactions on Circuits and Systems for Video Technology 2007*, 17(3), 336-346.

[26] Hliaoutakis, A., Varelas, G., Voutsakis, E., Petrakis, E. G. M., & Milios, E. (2006). Information retrieval by semantic similarity. *International Journal on Semantic Web and Information Systems*, 3(3), 55-73.

[27] Miller, G.A. (1995). WordNet: A Lexical Database for English. *Communications of the ACM*, 38(11), 39-41.

[28] Radev, D. R., Hovy, E., & Mc Keown, K. (2002). Introduction to the special issue on summarization. *Computational Linguistics*, 28(4), 399-408.

[29] Zipf, G. (1949). Human Behaviour and the Principle of Least-Effort. *Cambridge: Addison-Wesley*.

[30] Das, D., & Martins, A. F. T. (2007). A Survey on Automatic Text Summarization. *Engineering and Technology*, 4-192.

[31] Gupta, V., & Lehal, G. S. (2010). A Survey of Text Summarization Extractive Techniques. *Journal of Emerging Technologies in Web Intelligence*, 2(3), 258-268.

[32] Nenkova, A. (2005). Automatic text summarization of newswire: lessons learned from the document understanding conference. *Proceedings of the 20th national conference on Artificial intelligence, AAAI'05, Pittsburgh, USA.*

[33] García-Hernández, R. A., & Ledeneva, Y. (2009). Word Sequence Models for Single Text Summarization. *Proceedings of the Second International Conferences on Advances in Computer-Human Interactions, ACHI', 09, 1-7, Cancun, Mexico. Washington: IEEE Computer Society; 2009.*

[34] Hennig, L. (2009). Topic-based multi-document summarization with probabilistic latent semantic analysis. *Proceedings of the Recent Advances in Natural Language Processing Conference, RANLP-2009.*

[35] Svore, K., Vanderwende, L., & Burges, C. (2007). Enhancing Single-Document Summarization by Combining RankNet and Third-Party Sources. *Proceedings of the Joint Conference on Empirical Methods in Natural Language Processing and Computational Natural Language Learning, EMNLP-CoNLL.*

[36] Hannah, M. E., Geetha, T. V., & Mukherjee, S. (2011). Automatic extractive text summarization based on fuzzy logic: a sentence oriented approach. *Proceedings of the Second international conference on Swarm, Evolutionary, and Memetic Computing, SEMCCO'11, Visakhapatnam, India. Berlin: Springer-Verlag.*

[37] Suanmali, L., Salim, N., & Binwahlan, M. S. (2009). Fuzzy Logic Based Method for Improving Text Summarization. *International Journal of Computer Science and Information Security*, 2(1), 65-70.

[38] Barzilay, R., & Elhadad, M. (1997). Using Lexical Chains for Text Summarization. *Proceedings of the ACL Workshop on Intelligent Scalable Text Summarization.*

[39] Zamanifar, A., Minaei-Bidgoli, B., & Sharifi, M. (2008). A New Hybrid Farsi Text Summarization Technique Based on Term Co-Occurrence and Conceptual Property of Text. *Proceedings of Ninth ACIS International Conference on Software Engineering, Artificial Intelligence, Networking and Parallel/Distributed Computing, SNPD'08, Phuket, Thailand.*

[40] Erkan, G., & Radev, D.R. (2004). LexRank: graph-based lexical centrality as salience in text summarization. *Journal of Artificial Intelligence Research*, 22(1), 457-479.

[41] Magnini, B., & Cavaglià, G. Integrating Subject Field Codes into WordNet. *Gavrilidou M, Crayannis G, Markantonatu S, Piperidis S, Stainhaouer G. (eds.) Proceedings of the Second International Conference on Language Resources and Evaluation, LREC-2000, 31 May-2 June 2000Athens, Greece.*

[42] Yin, X., & Lee, W. S. (2004). Using link analysis to improve layout on mobile devices. *Proceedings of the Thirteenth International World Wide Web Conference, WWW'04,New York, USA.*

[43] Yin, X., & Lee, W. S. (2005). Understanding the function of web elements for mobile content delivery using random walk models. *Special interest tracks and posters of the 14th international conference on World Wide Web, WWW'05,Chiba, Japan.*

[44] Cai, D., Yu, S., Wen, J. R., & Ma, W. Y. (2003). Extracting Content Structure for Web Pages based on Visual Representation. *Proceedings of the 5th Asia-Pacific web conference on Web technologies and applications, APWeb'03, Xian, China. Berlin: Springer-Verlag.*

[45] Cai, D., Yu, S., Wen, J. R., & Ma, W. Y. (2004). Block-based web search. *Proceedings of the 27th annual international ACM SIGIR conference on Research and development in information retrieval, SIGIR'04, Sheffield, UK.*

[46] Ahmadi, H., & Kong, J. (2008). Efficient web browsing on small screens. *Proceedings of the working conference on Advanced visual interfaces, AVI'08, Napoli, Italy.*

[47] Burget, R. (2007). Automatic document structure detection for data integration. *Proceedings of the 10th international conference on Business information systems, BIS'07, Poznan, Poland.*

[48] Burget, R., & Rudolfova, I. (2009). Web page element classification based visual features. *Proceedings of First Asian conference on Intelligent Information and Database Systems, ACIIDS'09, Dong hoi, Quang binh, Vietnam.*

[49] Milic-Frayling, N., & Sommerer, R. (2002). Smartview: Flexible viewing of web page contents. *Poster Proceedings of the Eleventh International World Wide Web Conference, WWW'02,Honolulu, USA.*

[50] Kohlschütter, C., & Nejdl, W. (2008). A densitometric approach to web page segmentation. *Proceeding of the 17th ACM conference on Information and knowledge management, CIKM'08, Napa Valley, USA.*

[51] Cao, J., Mao, B., & Luo, J. (2010). A segmentation method for web page analysis using shrinking and dividing. *International Journal of Parallel, Emergent and Distributed Systems*, 25(2), 93-104.

[52] Borodin, Y., Mahmud, J., Ramakrishnan, I. V., & Stent, A. (2007). The hearsay nonvisual web browser. *Proceedings of the 2007 international cross-disciplinary conference on Web accessibility, W4A'07, Banff, Canada.*

[53] Mahmud, J. U., Borodin, Y., & Ramakrishnan, I. V. (2007). Csurf: a context-driven non-visual web-browser. *Proceedings of the 16th international conference on World Wide Web, WWW'07,Banff, Canada.*

[54] Mehta, R. R., Mitra, P., & Karnick, H. (2005). Extracting semantic structure of web documents using content and visual information. *Special interest tracks and posters of the 14th international conference on World Wide Web, WWW'05,Chiba, Japan.*

[55] Gliozzo, A., Strapparava, C., & Dagan, I. (2009). Unsupervised and Supervised Exploitation of Semantic Domains in Lexical Disambiguation. *Computer Speech and Language,* 18(3), 275-299.

[56] libxml: The XML C parser and toolkit of Gnome. http://xmlsoft.org , (accessed 16 May 2012).

[57] Decherchi, S., Gastaldo, P., & Zunino, S. (2009). K-means clustering for content-based document management in intelligence. *Solanas A, Martinez A. (ed.) Advances in Artificial Intelligence for Privacy, Protection, and Security. Singapore: World Scientific,* 287-324.

[58] Vossen, P. (1998). Eurowordnet: A Multilingual Database with Lexical Semantic Networks. *Kluwer Academic Publishers.*

[59] Sowa, J.F. (1992). Conceptual Graphs Summary. *Nagle TE, Nagle JA, Gerholz LL, Eklund PW. (ed.) Conceptual structures. Upper Saddle River: Ellis Horwood,* 3-51.

[60] Navigli, R. (2009). Word Sense Disambiguation: A Survey. *ACM Computing Surveys,* 41(2), 10:1-10:69.

[61] Karov, Y., & Edelman, S. (1998). Similarity-based word sense disambiguation. *Computational Linguistics,* 24(1), 41-60.

[62] Schütze, H. (1998). Automatic Word Sense Discrimination. *Computational Linguistics,* 24(1), 99-123.

[63] Magnini, B., Strapparava, C., Pezzulo, G., & Gliozzo, A. (2002). The role of domain information in Word Sense Disambiguation. *Natural Language Engineering,* 8(4), 359-373.

[64] Mallery, J.C. (1988). Thinking about foreign policy: Finding an appropriate role for artificial intelligence computers. *PhD thesis. MIT Political Science Department Cambridge.*

[65] Gale, W. A., Church, K., & Andyarowsky, D. (1992). A method for disambiguating word senses in a corpus. *Computers and the Humanities,* 26-415.

[66] Barrera, A., & Verma, R. (2011). Automated extractive single-document summarization: beating the baselines with a new approach. *Proceedings of the 2011 ACM Symposium on Applied Computing, SAC'11, TaiChung, Taiwan.*

## Chapter 6

Ontology Learning Using Word Net Lexical Expansion and Text Mining

Hiep Luong, Susan Gauch and Qiang Wang

Additional information is available at the end of the chapter

1. Introduction

In knowledge management systems, ontologies play an important role as a backbone for providing and accessing knowledge sources. They are largely used in the next generation of the Semantic Web that focuses on supporting a better cooperation between humans and machines [2]. Since manual ontology construction is costly, time-consuming, error-prone, and inflexible to change, it is hoped that an automated ontology learning process will result in more effective and more efficient ontology construction and also be able to create ontologies that better match a specific application [20]. Ontology learning has recently become a major focus for research whose goal is to facilitate the construction of ontologies by decreasing the amount of effort required to produce an ontology for a new domain. However, most current approaches deal with narrowly-defined specific tasks or a single part of the ontology learning process rather than providing complete support to users. There are few studies that attempt to automate the entire ontology learning process from the collection of domain-specific literature and filtering out documents irrelevant to the domain, to text mining to build new ontologies or enrich existing ones.

The World Wide Web is a rich source of documents that is useful for ontology learning. However, because there is so much information of varying quality covering a huge range of topics, it is important to develop document discovery mechanisms based on intelligent techniques such as focused crawling [7] to make the collection process easier for a new domain. However, due to the huge number of retrieved documents, we still require an automatic mechanism rather than domain experts in order to separate out the documents that are truly relevant to the domain of interest. Text classification techniques can be used to perform this task.

In order to enrich an ontology's vocabulary, several ontology learning approaches attempt to extract relevant information from WordNet, a semantic network database for the English language developed by Princeton University [23]. WordNet provides a rich knowledge base in which concepts, called synonymy sets or synsets, are linked by semantic relations. However, a main barrier to exploiting the word relationships in WordNet is that most words have multiple senses. Due to this ambiguity, not all senses for a given word can be used as a source of vocabulary. Expanding a concept's vocabulary based on an incorrect word sense would add many unrelated words to that concept and degrade the quality of the overall ontology. Thus, candidate word senses must be filtered very carefully. Most existing approaches have had mixed results with sense disambiguation, so the vocabulary for a specific domain mined from WordNet typically requires further manual filtering to be useful.

In our work, we employ a general ontology learning framework extracts new relevant vocabulary words from two main sources, i.e., Web documents and WordNet. This framework can be used for ontologies in any domain. We demonstrate our approach to a biological domain, specifically the domain of amphibian anatomy and morphology. In this work, we are exploring two techniques for expanding the vocabulary in an ontology: 1) lexical expansion using WordNet; and 2) lexical expansion using text mining. The lexical expansion from WordNet approach accurately extracts new vocabulary for an ontology for any domain covered by WordNet. We start with a manually-created ontology on amphibian morphology. The words associated with each concept in the ontology, the concept-words, are mapped onto WordNet and we employ a similarity computation method to identify the most relevant sense from multiple senses returned by WordNetfor a given concept-word. We then enrich the vocabulary for that original concept in the amphibian ontology by including the correct sense's associated synonyms and hypernyms.

Our text mining approach uses a focused crawler to retrieve documents related to the ontology's domain, i.e., amphibian, anatomy and morphology, from a combination of general search engines, scholarly search engines, and online digital libraries. We use text classification to identify, from the set of all collected documents, those most likely to be relevant to the ontology's domain. Because it has been shown to be highly accurate, we use a SVM (Support Vector Machine) classifier for this task [6] [40]. Finally, we implemented and evaluatedseveral text mining techniques to extract relevant information for the ontology enrichment from the surviving documents.

In this paper, we describe our work on the ontology learning process and present experimental results for each of the two approaches. In section 2, we present a brief survey of current research on ontology learning, focused crawlers, document classification, information extraction, and the use of WordNet for learning new vocabulary and disambiguating word senses. In section 3, we present our ontology learning framework and our two approaches, i.e., lexical expansion using WordNet and text mining. Sections 4 and 5 describe these approaches in more detail and report the results of our evaluation experiments. The final section presents conclusions and discusses our ongoing and future work in this area.

2. Related Work

An ontology is an explicit, formal specification of a shared conceptualization of a domain of interest [11], where formal implies that the ontology should be machine-readable and the domain can be any that is shared by a group or community. Much of current research into ontologies focuses on issues related to ontology construction and updating. In our view, there are two main approaches to ontology building: (i) manual construction of an ontology from scratch, and (ii) semi-automatic construction using tools or software with human intervention. It is hoped that semi-automatic generation of ontologies will substantially decrease the amount of human effort required in the process [12][18][24]. Because of the difficulty of the task, entirely automated approaches to ontology construction are currently not feasible.

Ontology learning has recently been studied to facilitate the semi-automatic construction of ontologies by ontology engineers or domain experts. Ontology learning uses methods from a diverse spectrum of fields such as machine learning, knowledge acquisition, natural language processing, information retrieval, artificial intelligence, reasoning, and database management [29]. Gómez-Pérez et al [10] present a thorough summary of several ontology learning projects that are concerned with knowledge acquisition from a variety of sources such as text documents, dictionaries, knowledge bases, relational schemas, semi-structured data, etc. Omelayenko [24] discusses the applicability of machine learning algorithms to learning of ontologies from Web documents and also surveys the current ontology learning and other closely related approaches. Similar to our approach, authors in [20] introduces an ontology learning framework for the Semantic Web thatincluded ontology importation, extraction, pruning, refinement, and evaluation giving the ontology engineers a wealth of coordinated tools for ontology modeling. In addition to a general framework and architecture, they have implemented Text-To-Onto system supporting ontology learning from free text, from dictionaries, or from legacy ontologies. However, they do not mention any automated support to collect the domain documents from the Web or how to automatically identify domain-relevant documents needed by the ontology learning process. Maedche et al. have presented in another paper [21] a comprehensive approach for bootstrapping an ontology-based information extraction system with the help of machine learning. They also presented an ontology learning framework which is one important step in their overall bootstrapping approach but it has still been described as a theoretic model and did not deal with the specific techniques used in their learning framework. Agirre et al., [1] have presented an automatic method to enrich very large ontologies, e.g., WordNet, that uses documents retrieved from the Web. However, in their approach, the query strategy is not entirely satisfactory in retrieving relevant documents which affects the quality and performance of the topic signatures and clusters. Moreover, they do not apply any filtering techniques to verify that the retrieved documents are truly on-topic. Inspiring the idea of using WordNet to enrich vocabulary for ontology domain, we have presented the lexical expansion from WordNet approach [18] providing a method of accurately extract new vocabulary for an ontology for any domain covered by WordNet.

Many ontology learning approaches require a large collection of input documents in order to enrich the existing ontology [20]. Although most employ text documents [4], only a few deal with ontology enrichment from documents collected from the Web rather than a manually created, domain-relevant corpus. To create a corpus from the Web, one can use general purpose crawlers and search engines, but this approach faces problems with scalability due to the rapid growth of the Web. Focused crawlers, on the other hand, overcome this drawback, i.e., they yield good recall as well as good precision, by restricting themselves to a limited domain [7]. Ester et al [7] introduce a generic framework for focused crawling consisting of two major components: (i) specification of the user interest and measuring the resulting relevance of a given Web page; and (ii) a crawling strategy.

Rather than working with domain-relevant documents from which vocabulary can be extracted, some ontology construction techniques exploit specific online vocabulary resources. WordNet is an online semantic dictionary, partitioning the lexicon into nouns, verbs, adjectives, and adverbs [23]. Some current researchers extract words from WordNet's lexical database to enrich ontology vocabularies [8][16][31]. In [27], Reiter et al describe an approach that combines the Foundational Model of Anatomy with WordNet by using an algorithm for domain-specific word sense disambiguation. In another approach similar to ours, Speretta et al exploit semantics by applying existing WordNet-based algorithms [31]. They calculate the relatedness between the two words by applying a similarity algorithm, and evaluated the effect of adding a variable number of the highest-ranked candidate words to each concept. A Perl package called Word-Net::Similarity [25] is a widely-used tool for measuring semantic similarity that contains implementations of eight algorithms for measuring semantic similarity. In our work, we evaluate the WordNet-based similarity algorithms by using the JSWL package developed by [26] that implements some of the most commons similarity and relatedness measures between words by exploiting the hyponymy relations among synsets.

Semantic similarity word sense disambiguation approaches in WordNet can be divided into two broad categories based on (i) path length and (ii) information content. Warinet al [37] describe a method of disambiguating an ontology and WordNet using five different measures. These approaches disambiguate semantic similarity based on the information content, (e.g., Lin [16], Jiang-Conrath [13], and Resnik [28]) and path length method (e.g., Leacock-Chodorow [15], and Wu-Palmer [38]). They present a new method that disambiguatesthe words in their ontology, the Common Procurement Vocabulary. Semantic similarity can also be calculated using edge-counting techniques. Yang and Powers [39] present a new path-weighting model to measure semantic similarity in WordNet. They compare their model to a benchmark set by human similarity judgments and found that their geometric model simulates human judgments well. Varelas et al [35] propose the Semantic Similarity Retrieval Model (SSRM), a general document similarity and information retrieval method suitable for retrieval in conventional document collections and the Web. This approach is based on the term-based Vector Space Model by computing TF-IDF weights to term representations of documents. These representations are then augmented by semantically similar terms (which are discovered from WordNet by applying a semantic query in the neighborhood of each term) and by re-computing weights to all new and pre-existing terms.

Text mining, also known as text data mining or knowledge discovery from textual databases, refers generally to the process of extracting interesting and non-trivial patterns or knowledge from unstructured text documents [3][12]. Tan [33] presents a good survey of text mining products/applications and aligns them based on the *text refining* and *knowledge distillation* functions as well as the *intermediate form* that they adopt. In terms of using text mining for the ontology learning task, Spasic et al. [30] summarizes different approaches in which ontologies have been used for text-mining applications in biomedicine. In another work, Velardi et al. [36] presents OntoLearn, a set of text-mining techniques to extract relevant concepts and concept instances from existing documents in a Tourism domain. Authors have devised several techniques to (i) identify concept and (ii) concept instances, (iii) organize such concepts in sub-hierarchies, and iv) detect relatedness links among such concepts.

In order to improve accuracy of the learned ontologies, the documents retrieved by focused crawlers may need to be automatically filtered by using some text classification technique such as Support Vector Machines (SVM), k-Nearest Neighbors (kNN), Linear Least-Squares Fit, TF-IDF, etc. A thorough survey and comparison of such methods and their complexity is presented in [40] and the authors in [6] conclude that SVM to be most accurate for text classification and it is also quick to train. SVM [34] is a machine learning model that finds an optimal hyper plane to separate two then classifies data into one of two classes based on the side on which they are located [5] [14].The k-nearest neighbors (kNN) algorithm is among the simplest of all machine learning algorithms: an object is classified by a majority vote of its neighbors, with the object being assigned to the class most common amongst its k nearest neighbors. In pattern recognition, the kNN is a method for classifying objects based on closest training examples in the feature space. It is a type of instance-based learning where the function is only approximated locally and all computation is deferred until classification. This algorithm has also been used successfully in many text categorization applications [41].

3. Ontology Learning Framework

3.1. Architecture

In this section, we present the architecture of our ontology learning process framework (c.f. Figure 1) that incorporates two approaches, i.e., lexical expansion and text mining, to identify new domain-relevant vocabulary for ontology enrichment. These approaches are presented in detail in sections 4 and 5.

3.1.1. Lexical expansion approach

This approach starts from a small manually constructed ontology, then tries to mine relevant words from WordNet in order to enrich the vocabulary associated with ontology concepts. It contains main following steps:

1. Extract all single concept-words from the seed ontology. Filter these words by removing stop-words; locate each remaining word's senses within WordNet.

2. Build a reference hypernym tree for each word sense as a reference source for semantic similarity disambiguation.

3. If a concept-word has multiple senses, identify the correct word sense usinga similarity computation algorithm on reference hypernym tree.

4. Select the most similar sense and add its synonyms and hypernyms to the corresponding concept in the ontology.

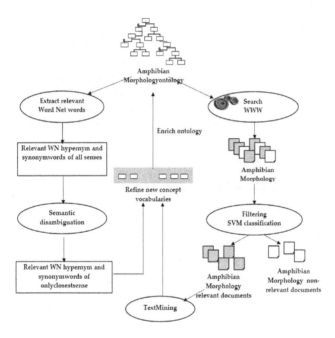

Figure 1. Architecture of ontology learning framework.

3.1.2. Text mining approach

The main processes are as following:

1. We begin with an existing small, manually-created amphibian morphology ontology [22]. From this, we automatically generate queries for each concept in the hierarchically-structured ontology.

2. We submit these queries to a variety of Web search engines and digital libraries. The program downloads the potentially relevant documents listed on the first page (top-ranked 10) results.

3. Next, we apply SVM classification to filter out documents in the search results that match the query well but are less relevant to the domain of our ontology. For example,

a document contains the word "cell" but it is in the context of cellphone, telecommuni-
cation... will be filtered out. Other documents containing that word "cell" with the context of amphibian, embryo structure or biological... will be kept.

After the above process, we have created a collection of documents relevant to amphibian
morphology. These are input to an information extraction (IE) system to mine information
from documents that can be used to enrich the ontology.

3.2. Domain and Ontology Application

The need for terminological standardization of anatomy is pressing in amphibian morphological research [22]. A long-term NSF-sponsored project, AmphibAnat, aims to integrate
the amphibian anatomical ontology knowledge base with systematic, biodiversity, embryo-
logical and genomic resources. However, another important goal of this project is to semi-
automatically construct and enrich the amphibian anatomical ontology. An amphibian
ontology will facilitate the integration of anatomical data representing all orders of amphibians, thus enhancing knowledge representation of amphibian biology and diversity.

```
⊟  ● amphibian anatomical entity
    ⊟  ● material anatomical entity
        ⊟  ● anatomical structure
            ⊞  ● multi-tissue structure
            ⊞  ● tissue
            ⊞  ● embryonic structure
            ⊞  ● cell
            ▪   ● organism subdivision
```

Figure 2. A part of the amphibian ontology

Based on information in a manually constructed seed ontology, we use a focused crawler
and data-mining software in order to mine electronic resources for instances of concepts and
properties to be added to the existing ontologies [17][19]. We also use concept-words of this
ontology to match the corresponding relevant words and senses in WordNet. The current
amphibian ontology created by this project consists of 1986 semantic concepts (with the
highest depth level is 9) and 570 properties. Figure 2 presents a part of this ontology which
is available in two main formats: (i) OWL and (ii) OBO - Open Biomedical Ontology.

4. Extracting New Vocabulary

In this section, we introduce our two main vocabulary-extraction approaches, one based on
identifying information from an already-existing vocabulary resource (WordNet) and one

based on extracting vocabulary directly from the domain literature.The advantages of using WordNet is that it contains words and relationships that are, because it was manually constructed, highly accurate.However, the drawbacks are that the vocabulary it contains is broad and thus ambiguous.Also, for specialized domains, appropriate words and/or word senses are likely to be missing. Thus, we contrast this approach with one that works directlyon the domain literature.In this case, the appropriate words and word senses are present and ambiguity is less of a factor. However, the relationships between the word senses are implicit in how they are used in the text rather than explicitly represented.

4.1. Lexical Expansion Approach

This approach attempts to identify the correct WordNet sense for each concept-word and then add that sense's synsets and hypernyms as new vocabulary for the associated concept. We base our concept-word sense disambiguation on comparing the various candidate senses to those in a reference source of senses for the domain of the ontology. To provide this standard reference, we manually disambiguate the WordNet senses for the concept-words in the top two levels of the amphibian ontology. We then create a reference hypernym tree that contains the WordNethypernyms of these disambiguated WordNet senses. The problem of solving the lexical ambiguity that occurs whenever a given concept-word has several different meanings is now simplified to comparing the hypernym tree for each candidate word sense with the reference hypernym tree. We then compute a tree similarity metric between each candidate hypernym tree and the reference hypernym tree to identify the most similar hypernym tree and, by association, the word sense most closely related to the ontology domain.

4.1.1. WordNet Synonym and Hypernym

WordNet has become a broad coverage thesaurus that is now widely used in natural language processing and information retrieval [32]. Words in WordNet are organized into synonym sets, called *synsets*, representing a concept by a set of words with similar meanings. For example, frog, toad frog, and batrachian are all words in the same synset. Hypernyms, or the IS-A relation, is the main relation type in WordNet. In a simple way, we can define "*Y is a hypernym of X if every X is a (kind of) Y*". All hypernym levels of a word can be structured in a hierarchy in which the meanings are arranged from the most specific at the lower levels up to the most general meaning at the top, for example "amphibian" is a hypernym of "frog", "vertebrate, craniate" is a hypernym of "amphibian", and so on.

For a given word, we can build a hypernym tree including all hypernyms in their hierarchy returned by WordNet. When a word has multiple senses, we get a set of hypernym trees, one per sense. In order to find the hypernyms of a given word in WordNet, we must provide the word and the syntactic class in which we are interested. In our approach, since ontologies generally represent information about objects, we are restricting the word senses considered to only the noun senses for a candidate word.

4.1.2. Reference Hypernym Tree

Because WordNet organizes nouns into IS-A hypernym hierarchies that provide taxonomic information, it is useful for identifying semantic similarity between words [25]. Our approach constructs a reference hypernym tree (or standard hypernym tree) from a few manually disambiguated words. When a word has multiple senses, we construct the hypernym tree for each sense. Then, we calculate how close each candidate sense's hypernym tree is to this reference source. We argue that the more similar a hypernym tree is to the reference tree, the closer the word sense is to the key concepts in the ontology.

```
|- entity
 |- physical_entity
  |- object, physical_object
   |- whole, unit
    |- living_thing, animate_thing
     |- organism, being
      |- animal, animate_being, beast, brute,
       creature, fauna
      |- chordate
       |- vertebrate, craniate
        |- amphibian
         |- urodele, caudate
   ...
   |- abstraction, abstract_entity
    |- psychological_feature
     |- cognition, knowledge, noesis
      |- knowledge_domain, knowledge_base, domain
       |- discipline, subject, subject_area,
        subject_field, field, field_of_study
        |- science, scientific_discipline
         |- natural_science
```

Figure 3. A part of the reference hypernym tree.

To build the reference hypernym tree, we consider only the top two levels of concepts of the amphibian ontology since they cover many vocabularies appearing at lower levels. In addition, since the concepts are also related using the "IS A" relation, the hypernyms of the concepts in top two levels of the ontology are also hypernyms of the concepts in the lower levels. The main steps of this process are as following: first, we convert each concept in top two level into concept-words that can be submitted to WordNet, for instance the concept "anatomical_structure" is divided into two concept-words "anatomical" and "structure". The top two levels of our ontology contain 15 concepts and 19 concept-words. Then, we use WordNet to collect all the hypernyms for each concept-word. We manually choose the hypernym that best matches the meaning in our domain and then add to the reference hypernym tree. Figure 3 presents a part of our reference hypernym tree that contains 110 hypernyms covering 12 hierarchical levels. This reference tree will be used as truth to evaluate the correct sense extracted from WordNet for each experiment word.

4.1.3. Similarity Computation Algorithm

In this section, we present our tree-based similarity measurement technique that is used to compare hypernym trees corresponding to different senses of a concept-word with the reference hypernym tree. Our similarity measure is based on two factors:

- *Matched Tree Depth (D):* Since all hypernym trees are represented from the most general (top level) to the more specific meanings (lower levels), matches between hypernyms in the lower levels of the two trees should be ranked higher. For example, matching on "frog" is more important than matching on "vertebrate". We calculate the depth (D) as the distance from the most general hypernym (i.e., "entity") until the first hypernym that occurs in both the reference hypernym tree and a candidate hypernym tree. The higher valued matched tree depth indicates that the meaning of the matched word is more specific, thus it would be more relevant to the domain.

- *Number of common elements (CE):* Normally, if two trees contain many of the same entities, they are judged more similar. Once we determine the depth (D), we count the number of common elements between the reference hypernym tree and a candidate tree. If two candidate trees have the same match depth, then the tree with more elements in common with the reference hypernym tree would be considered the more similar one.

Once the hypernym tree is constructed for each sense, we are able to apply the similarity computation algorithm to calculate these two above factors (i.e. D and CE) for each case. Then, we weight these two factors to get the highest value.

Figure 4 shows an example of how the reference hypernym tree can be used to disambiguate word senses and select the most relevant one. Suppose that the hypernym trees in this example, i.e., HTree1, HTree2 and HTree3, each correspond to one sense of a given concept-word. We compare each hypernym tree to the reference hypernym tree by calculating the matched tree depth and the number of common elements between two trees. Results show that the first tree HTree1 is closest to the standard tree with the depth (D=6) and number of common elements (CE=13) are greater than others.

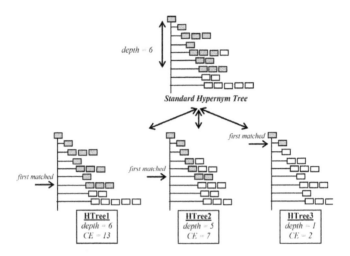

Figure 4. Similarity computation using the Reference (Standard) HypernymTree.

4.1.4. Experiments

a. Dataset and Experiments

As discussed in Section 3.2, we use the amphibian morphology ontology developed by the AmphibAnat project [22] for our experiments. We used WordNet (3.0) as the lexical source and the API library of MIT Java WordNet Interface (JWI 2.1.5) to locate the synsets and hypernyms for a given concept-word.

We begin by processing names for the concepts in the top two levels of the amphibian ontology and manually disambiguating them to create the reference hypernym tree. We then process the names for the 1971 concepts in levels 3 and below. Since many concepts are named with phrases of two or more wordsm and WordNet only contains single words, we need to convert these words into single words, i.e., the concept-words. After removing duplicate concept-words, e.g., concepts "anatomical_structure" and "multi-tissue_structure" have a duplicate concept-word, "structure", stopwords (e.g., of, to, for) and numbers, we end up with a set of 877 unique concept-words. However, because the ontology is very domain specific, many of these concept-words do not appear in WordNet at all. Very specific terms in the amphibian domain, e.g., premaxilla, dorsalis, adjectives, e.g., nervous, embryonic, hermaphroditic, and incomplete words added during the ontology creation process, e.g., sp, aa, do not appear in WordNet. Therefore, we report results using only the 308 concept-words that were contained in WordNet.

We matched these 308 words to WordNet to identify all their corresponding senses, synonyms and hypernyms. However, not all of the senses for a given word are relevant so we need to disambiguate the semantic similarity of these senses to choose the closest and most correct one for our amphibian domain. We applied each of three similarity computation algorithms, to determine the closest sense for each word and evaluated them: 1) based on the number of matched tree depth (#Depth); 2) based on the number of common elements (#CE); and 3) based on the sum of both factors (#Depth+CE). For each method, we got a list of word senses selected by the algorithm and compared these senses to the truth-list provided by our human expert to evaluate the effectiveness of our algorithm.

b. Evaluation Measures

In order to evaluate the results of our both approaches, i.e., Lexical Expansion and Text Mining, we needed to know the correct word sense (if any) for each word. An expert in the amphibian domain helped us by independently judging the words and senses identified by each technique and identifying which were correct. These judgments formed the truth lists against which the words extracted by text mining and the senses chosen by the lexical expansion were compared.

Information extraction effectiveness is measured in terms of the classic Information Retrieval metrics of Precision, Recall and F-measure. We used these measures for both approaches, but with some different definitions of measure for each approach. In the lexical expansion approach, since each word in WordNet may have different senses and we have to find the correct one, we define:

- *Precision (P):* measures the percentage of the words having correct sense identified by our algorithm that matched the sense judged correct by the human expert.

$$P = \frac{\#\_words\_having\_correct\_sense\_identified}{\#\_words\_returned} \tag{1}$$

- *Recall (R):* measures the percentage of the correct words identified by our algorithm that matched those from the truth-list words.

$$R = \frac{\#\_words\_having\_correct\_sense\_identified}{\#\_truth-list\_words} \tag{2}$$

We use F-measure which is calculated as following for both approaches.

$$F_\beta = \frac{(1+\beta^2)*P*R}{\beta^2*P+R} \tag{3}$$

Because we want to enhance the ontology with only truly relevant words, we want a metric that is biased towards high precision versus high recall. We chose to use the F-measure with a β value that weights precision four times higher than recall.

4.1.5. Result Evaluation

Among 308 word returned from WordNet, human expert judged that 252 of the extracted words were correct. Of the 56 incorrect words returned, there were no senses in WordNet relevant to the amphibian domain. Since each of above 252 returned words may have some correct senses judged by the human expert, we got finally 285 correct senses.In order to see how well each algorithm performed, we implemented different thresholds to see how results are varied as we increased our selectivity based on level of match and/or number of common elements matched. We varied the depth from 1 to 10, the common elements from 2 to 20, and the sum of the two from 3 to 30. For example with the #Depth+CE method, the range of threshold t is from 3 to 30; the value t=15 means that we take only senses having the number #Depth+CE is greater than 15. Figures 5, 6 and 7 show the F-measures achieved by three methods of #Depth, #CE and #Depth+CE respectively using various threshold values.

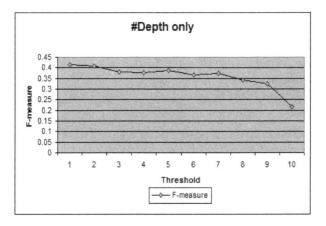

Figure 5. F-measure of the #Depth only method (β=0.25).

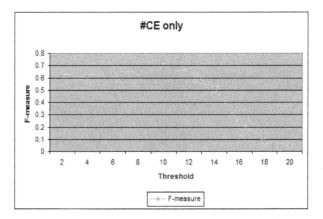

Figure 6. F-measure of the #CE only method (β=0.25).

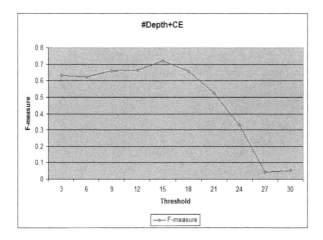

Figure 7. F-measure of the #Depth+CE method (β=0.25).

We found that we got poor results when using depth only, i.e., a maximum F-measure of 0.42 with a threshold of 1, but the common elements approach performed better with a maximum F-measure of 0.67 with a threshold of 10. However, the best result was achieved when we used the sum of depth and common element using a threshold t=15. This produced a precision of 74% and recall of 50% and an F-measure of 0.72. In this case, 155 words were found by the algorithm of which 115 were correct. Table 1 presents the number of unique synonym and hypernym words we could add to the ontology from WordNet based on our disambiguated senses.

Threshold	3	6	9	12	15	18	21	24	27	30
#words returned	308	291	271	225	155	98	62	17	8	4
# words correct	190	178	176	149	115	70	38	10	1	1
#SYN	417	352	346	308	231	140	78	26	1	1
#HYN	164	156	151	123	80	48	42	12	2	2

Table 1. Number of retrieved synonyms and hypernyms words.

To better understand this approach, we present an example based on the concept-word "cavity." WordNet contains 4 different senses for this word: 1) pit, cavity, 2) cavity, enclosed space; 3) cavity, caries, dental caries, tooth decay; and 4) cavity, bodily cavity, cavum. Based on the total value of #Depth+CE, our algorithm correctly selects the fourth sense as the most relevant for the amphibian ontology (c.f., Table 2). Based on this sense, we then consider the synonyms [*cavity, bodily_cavity, cavum*] and hypernyms [*structure, anatomical_structure, complex_body_part, bodily_structure, body_structure*] as words to enrich the vocabulary for the concept "cavity". This process is applied for all concept-words in the seed amphibian ontology and new mined vocabularies will be used to enrich the corresponding concepts of the ontology.

	# Depth	#CE	#Depth+CE
1st sense	5	7	12
2nd sense	4	7	11
3rd sense	10	7	17
4th sense	**15**	**7**	**22**

Table 2. Example of semantic similarity computation for the concept-word "cavity".

4.2. Text Mining Approach

4.2.1. Searching and Collecting Documents

In order to collect a corpus of documents from which ontological enrichments can be mined, we use the seed ontology as input to our focused search. For each concept in a selected subset of ontology, we generate a query that is then submitted to two main sources, i.e., search engines and digital libraries. To aid in query generation strategies, we created an interactive system that enables us to create queries from existing concepts in the ontology and allows us to change parameters such as the Website address, the number of returned results, the format of returned documents, etc.

We next automatically submit the ontology-generated queries to multiple search engines and digital libraries related to the domain (e.g., Google, Yahoo, Google Scholar, http://www.amphibanat.org). For each query, we process the top 10 results from each search site using an HTML parser to extract the hyperlinks for collecting documents.

4.2.2. Classifying and Filtering Documents

Although documents are retrieved selectively through restricted queries and by focused search, the results can contain some documents that are less relevant or not relevant at all. Therefore, we still need a mechanism to evaluate and verify the relevance of these documents to the predefined domain of the ontology. To remove unexpected documents, first we automatically remove those that are blank or too short, are duplicated documents, or those that are in a format that is not suitable for text processing. We then use LIBSVMclassification tool [5] to separate the remaining documents into two main categories: (i) relevant and (ii) non-relevant to the domain of ontology. We have also varied different parameters of LIBSVM such as kernel type (-t), degree (-d), weight (-wi)... in order to select the best parameters for our classification. Only those documents that are deemed truly relevant are input to the pattern extraction process.

The SVM classification algorithm must first be trained, based on labeled examples, so that it can accurately predict unknown data (i.e., testing data). The training phase consists of finding a hyper plane that separates the elements belonging to two different classes. Our topic focused search combining with the SVM classification as described in [17] is 77.5% accurate, in order to evaluate our text mining approach in the absence of noise, we report in this paper our results based on the labeled relevant training examples. In future, the topic focused crawler will be used to feed directly into the text mining process.

4.2.3. Information Extraction using Text Mining

After the topic-specific searching produces a set of documents related to the amphibian morphology domain, this phase information mines important vocabulary from the text of the documents. Specifically, our goal is to extract a set of words that are most related to the domain ontology concept-words. We have implemented and evaluated a vector space approach using two methods to calculate the *tf*idf* weights. Since most ontology concept-words are nouns, we also explored the effect of restricting our extracted words to nouns only. The weight calculation methods compared were the *document-based selection* and *corpus-based selection*. In both approaches, in order to give high weights to words important to the domain, we pre-calculated the *idf* (inverse document frequency) from a collection of 10,000 documents that were randomly downloaded from a broad selection of categories in the ODP[1] collection.

a. Document-based selection (L1)

This method, *L1*, first calculates weights of words in each document using *tf*idf* as follows:

$$W(i, j) = rtf_{(i, j)} * idf_i \tag{4}$$

$$rtf_{(i, j)} = \frac{tf_{(i, j)}}{N(j)} \tag{5}$$

$$idf_i = \log \frac{|D|}{|\{d : t_i \in d\}|} \tag{6}$$

where

$W(i,j)$ is the weight of term i in document j

$rtf_{(i,j)}$ is the relative term frequency of term i in document j

idf_i is the inverse document frequency of term i, which is pre-calculated across 10,000 ODP documents

$tf_{(i,j)}$ is the term frequency of term i in document j

$N(j)$ means the number of words in document j

$|D|$ is the total number of documents in the corpus

---

1 Open Directory Project http://www.dmoz.org/

$|\{d:t_i d\}|$ is number of documents in which t_i appears.

A word list sorted by weights is generated for each document from which the top k words are selected. These word lists are then merged in sorted order these words to only one list ranked by their weight. We performed some preliminary experiments, not reported here, which varied k from 1 to 110. The results reported here use k = 30, a value that was found to perform best.

b. Corpus-based selection (L2)

This method, L2, calculates weights of words by using *sum(tf)*idf*. Thus, the collection based frequency is used to identify a single word list rather than selecting a word list for each document based on the within-document frequency and then merging, as is done in method L1. The formula is thus:

$$W(i) = \sum_{j=1}^{n} rt f_{(i, j)} * id f_i \qquad (7)$$

where

W(i) is the weight of term i in the corpus

The other factors are calculated as in L1 method.

c. Part-of-speech restriction (L1N, L2N)

For each of the previous approaches, we implemented a version that removed all non-nouns from the final word list. We call the word lists, *L1N* and *L2N*, corresponding to the subset of words in lists *L1* and *L2* respectively that are tagged as nouns using the WordNet library [25] using JWI(the MIT Java WordNet Interface).

4.2.4. Experiments

a. Dataset and Experiments

The current amphibian ontology is large and our goal is to develop techniques that can minimize manual effort by growing the ontology from a small, seed ontology. Thus, rather than using the whole ontology as input to the system, for our experiments we used a subset of only the five top-level concepts from the ontology whose meaning broadly covered the amphibian domain. Ultimately, we hope to compare the larger ontology we build to the full ontology built by domain expert.

We found that when we expand the query containing the concept name with keywords describing the ontology domain overall, we get a larger number of relevant results. Based on these explorations, we created an automated module that, given a concept in the ontology, currently generates 3 queries with the expansion added, e.g., "amphibian" "morphology" "pdf". From each of the five concepts, we generate three queries, for a total of 15 automatically generated queries. Each query is then submitted to each of the four search sites from which the top ten results are requested. This results in a maximum of 600 documents to process. However, because some search sites return fewer than ten results for some queries, we perform syntactic filtering, and duplicate documents are returned by search engines, in practice this number was somewhat smaller.

It is crucial to have a filtering stage to remove irrelevant and slightly relevant documents to the amphibian ontology. We have adopted an SVM-based classification technique trained on 60 relevant and 60 irrelevant documents collected from the Web. In earlier experiments, our focused search combining with the SVM classification was able to collect new documents and correctly identify those related to the domain with an average accuracy 77.5% [17][19].

Ultimately, the papers collected and filtered by the topic-specific spider will be automatically fed into the text mining software (with an optional human review in between). However, to evaluate the effectiveness of the text mining independently, without noise introduced by some potentially irrelevant documents, we ran our experiments using 60 documents manually judged as relevant, separated into two groups of 30, i.e., *Group_A* and *Group_B*. All these documents were preprocessed to remove HTML code, stop words and punctuation. We ran experiments to tune our algorithms using *Group_A* and then validated our results using *Group_B*.

For the document-based approach, we took the top 30 words from each document and merged them. This created a list of 623 unique words (*L1*). To be consistent, we also selected the top 623 words produced by the corpus based approach (*L2*). We merged these two lists and removed duplicates, which resulted in a list of 866 unique words that were submitted for human judgment. Based on our expert judgment, 507 of the total words were domain-relevant and 359 were considered irrelevant. These judgments were then used to evaluate the 6 techniques, i.e., *L1*, *L2*, *L1+L2*, *L1N*, *L2N* and *L1N+L2N*.

When we selected only the nouns from L1 and L2, this resulted in lists L1N and L2N that contained 277 and 300 words, respectively. When these were merged and duplicates were removed, 375 words were submitted for judgment of which 253 were judged relevant and 122 were judged irrelevant to the amphibian morphology domain

b. Evaluation Measures

In the text mining approach, we define:

- *Precision (P):* measures the percentage of the correct words identified by our algorithm that matched those from the candidate words.

$$P = \frac{\#\_correct\_words\_identified}{\#\_candidate\_words} \tag{8}$$

- *Recall (R):* measures the percentage of the correct words identified by our algorithm that matched those from the truth-list words.

$$R = \frac{\#\_correct\_words\_identified}{\#\_truth - list\_words} \tag{9}$$

Based on these two measures, we also calculate the F-measure as the equation (3) to evaluate methods' performances.

4.2.5. Results

We evaluated our results by comparing the candidate word lists that were extracted from the relevant documents using our algorithms with the judgments submitted by our human domain expert. Since not all words on the word lists are likely to be relevant, we varied how many of the top weighted words were used. We chose threshold values t from 0.1 to 1.0 corresponding to the percentage of top candidate words that are extracted (e.g., t=0.1 means that top 10% words are selected). We carried out 6 different tests corresponding to the four candidate lists, i.e., L1, L2, L1N, L2N and two more cases L1+L2 (average of L1 and L2) and L1N+L2N (average of L1N and L2N) as input to our algorithm. These tests are named by their list names L1, L2, L1+L2, L1N, L2N and L1N+L2N. Figure 8 presents the F-measures achieved by these tests using various threshold values.

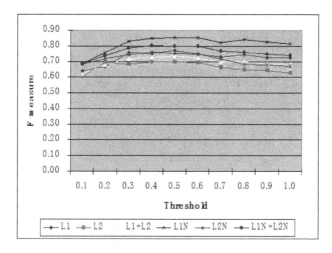

Figure 8. F-measure of the tests in Group_A (β=0.25).

The best result was achieved in the test L1N, using the highest weighted nouns extracted from individual documents. By analyzing results, we find that the best performance is achieved with a threshold t=0.6, i.e., the top 60% of the words (277 words total) in the candidate list are used. This threshold produced precision of 88% and recall of 58% meaning that 167 words were added to the ontology of which 147 were correct.

To confirm our results, we validated the best performing algorithm, *L1N* with a threshold of 0.6, using the 30 previously unused relevant documents in *Group_B*. We applied the document-based selection algorithm using nouns only with a threshold value 0.6. In this case, the achieved results are P = 77%, R = 58% and F-measure = 0.7. This shows that, although precision is a bit lower, overall the results are reproducible on a different document collection. In this case 183 words were added to the ontology of which 141 were correct.

Threshold	0.1	0.2	0.3	0.4	0.5	0.6	0.7	0.8	0.9	1.0
#candidatewords	28	55	83	110	139	167	194	222	249	277
# words added	22	50	77	101	124	147	162	188	206	225

Table 3. Number of words can be added.

Table 3 reports in more detail on the number of candidate words and how many correct words can be added to the ontology through the text mining process with the document-based selection and restricting our words to nouns only, i.e. the L1N test with threshold 0.6 on the validation documents, *Group_B*. We also observe that the top words extracted using this technique are very relevant to the domain of amphibian ontology, for example, the top 10 words are: frog, amphibian, yolk, medline, muscle, embryo, abstract, pallium, nerve, membrane.

4.3. Discussions

The experimental results show that the ontology enrichment process can be used with new relevant vocabularies extracted from both of our approaches of text mining and lexical expansion. Overall, the text mining approach achieved a better result than the WordNet approach. Table 4 shows the performance comparison of these two approaches in their best case.

Measures	Lexical Expansion Approach	Text Mining Approach
Precision	0.74	0.88
Recall	0.50	0.58
F-Measure	0.72	0.85
#Candidate Words	155	167
#Words mined correctly	115	147
#Words mined incorrectly	40	20

Table 4. Comparison of two approaches in the best case.

In the text mining approach, we got the best results using a vector space approach with the document-based selection and restricting our words to nouns only. Overall, our algorithm produced good accuracy, over than 81% for all cases. If we restrict our candidates to only the top-weighted candidates extracted from the documents, the precision is higher but the recall decreases. In the best case, where the F-measure is maximized, the precision is 88% on the test collection. Our algorithm was also validated with another dataset (i.e. documents in Group_B), the precision in this case decreases to 77% which is still acceptable and does not affect significantly to the number and quality of relevant words extracted.

The results in the lexical analysis approach also show that our similarity computation method can provide an effective way to identify the correct sense for words in a given ontology. These senses then provide a source of new vocabulary that can be used to enrich the ontology. Our algorithm was best with the precision of 74% in the method of #Depth+CE. If we consider words with fewer senses, the accuracy of detection of correct words is higher. This level of accuracy was achieved using a reference hypernym tree with 110 hypernyms, built from only 14 manually disambiguated concept-words from the top two levels of our amphibian morphology ontology. From these words, we are able to identify a large collection of synonyms and hypernyms that are a good potential source for the ontology enrichment process.

5. Ontology Enrichment

In previous sections, we have presented our main approaches to mine new relevant vocabularies to enrich a domain ontology from two main sources: (i) the WordNet database; and (ii) domain-relevant documents collected from the Internet. In this section we describe how we enrich the domain ontology by adding these newly-mined words to the appropriate concepts. Our main task in this phase is finding a method to add correctly a new candidate word to the best appropriate ontology concept vocabulary.

5.1. Lexical Expansion Approach

As presented in the section 4.1, our lexical expansion approach has identifies the correct WordNet sense for each concept-word and then considering that sense's synsets and hypernyms as new vocabulary for the associated concept.In the previous phase, we used the hypernyms trees to identify the correct sense for each concept-word. For each correct sense, we add the synonym words (synsets) of that sense to the ontology concept vocabulary. Because we know which concept the synset is associated with, an advantage of this approach is that it is trivial to attach the new vocabulary to the correct concept.

From the 285 correct senses mined in the first phase, our lexical expansion mineda total of 352 new synonym words over 155 concept words that were returned. Many synonym words were duplicates, so we refined the candidate vocabulary by removing redundant words, leaving 321 new words to add to the ontology.

To evaluate the accuracy of this approach, we presented each of these 155 word-concept pairings to a human domain expert and asked them to validate whether or not the pairing is accurate. In their judgment, 115 words were relevant to the amphibian morphology domain, and their 260 synonyms words were considered. We then refined these synonym words by removing duplicates. Thus, we ultimately added 231 words to the appropriate concepts, almost entirely automatically. The precision of adding correct synonym words to the ontology was 71.9%. The only manual step in this process is the filtering out of the incorrect word-senses extracted from WordNet.

5.2. Text Mining Approach

5.2.1. Overview

To reiterate our task, given a list of potential synonyms to be added to an ontology, we want to develop an algorithm to automatically identify the best matching concept for each candidate. Unlike the WordNet approach, this is a much more difficult task for words mined from the literature. The candidate words are domain relevant, but exactly where in the ontology do they belong?We again turn to thedomain-relevant corpus of documents to determine the concept in the ontology to which these newly mined candidate words should be attached. The main differences between our approach and that of others are:

- The documents are used as the knowledge base of word relationships as well as the source of domain-specific vocabulary. Specifically, for each concept (and each candidate word), chunks of text are extracted around the word occurrences to create concept-word contexts and candidate word contexts. The words around each concept and/or candidate word occurrence thus contain words related to the semantics of the concept/candidate word.

- Word phrases can be handled. Instead of handling each word in a word phrase separately and then trying to combine the results, as we did with WordNet, we can process the word phrase as a whole. For each word phrase, we extract text chunks in which all of the words occur. Thus, the contexts are related to the concept-word as a whole, not just the individual component words.

The four main steps of our approach are:

1. Extract text chunks surrounding the concept-word(s) from each input document. Combine the text chunks extracted to create context files that represent the concept. Using the same method, create context files for each candidate word (i.e., potential synonym).

2. For each candidate, calculate the context-based similarity between the candidate context and each concept context.

3. Identify the most similar concepts using kNN (k nearest neighbors).

4. Assign the candidate words to the concept(s) with the highest similarity.

5.2.2. Extracting concept-word contexts

This process begins with a set of domain-related documents that are used as a knowledge base. From each preprocessed text file, we locate all candidate word occurrences and then created windows of plus/minus N words around each occurrence. Overlapping windows are then combined to create non-overlapping text chunks. Because varying numbers of overlapping windows may be combined to create the text chunks, the text chunks vary in size and in the number of word occurrences they contain. In order to illustrate the text chunks selection process, consider a single document representing the concept name "neural_canal" with the query keywords are "neural" and "canal".

a. Step 1: Identify windows around each query keyword

In one part of the document under consideration with the window size of +-10, there are three occurrences of both terms "neural" and "canal" and thus three windows of size 21 with a word in the middle. We can see that Windows 1, 2, and 3 all contain keywords and they are overlapping.

Window 1: (middle keyword is "neural")

morphy pronounced reduction process boulengerella lateristriga maculata hypothesized synapomorphic species neural synapomorphy laterosensory canal system body majority characiforms completely developed posterior

Window 2: (middle keyword is "canal")

process boulengerella lateristriga maculata hypothesized synapomorphic species neural synapomorphy laterosensory canal system body majority characiforms completely developed posterior neural laterosensory canal

Window 3: (middle keyword is "neural")

synapomorphy laterosensory canal system body majority characiforms completely developed posterior neural laterosensory canalsystem body nearly lateral line scales minimally pore

b. Step 2: Combine overlapping chunks of text

In this step, we combine all overlapping windows to create the text chunks as following.

morphy pronounced reduction process boulengerella lateristriga maculata hypothesized synapomorphic species neural synapomorphy laterosensory canal system body majority characiforms completely developed posterior neural laterosensory canal system body nearly lateral line scales minimally pore

c. Step 3: Combining chunks of text across document

In this step, we simply combine the text chunks extracted for a given context from a document by appending them together.

5.2.3. Generating Vectors for the Extracted Contexts

After having extracted text chunks surrounding to keyword instances (i.e., concepts or synonyms), we have two sets of contexts: (1) **S** representing candidate synonyms; and (2) **C** representing concepts. In this step, we transform the contexts to vectors representing the keywords. We adopted *tf**idf approach to index tokens from the context files and assign weight values to these tokens. Thus, all keywords can be represented by a series of features (i.e., weighted tokens) extracted from the relevant chunks. We have generated two types of vectors for each keyword, i.e., *individual vectors* and a *centroid vector*. An *individual vector* summarizes the contexts around a keyword within a single document while a centroid vector combines the individual vectors to summarize all contexts in which a keyword appears.

a. Individual Vector

Let's take an example of a concept keyword C_k represented by 5 context files extracted from 5 relevant documents (i.e., N=5). This keyword will have 5 individual vectorsrepresenting for each individual context file. We used the KeyConcept package [9] to index features and calculate their weights; each individual vector has the following format:

$$IN D_{i\_}C_k = (feature_{i1}:weigh\, t_{i1}, feature_{i2}:weigh\, t_{i2}, ..., feature_{im}:weigh\, t_{im}) \qquad (10)$$

in which weight$_{ij}$ = rtf$_{ij}$ * idf$_j$, the relative term frequency rtf$_{ij}$ and the inverse document frequency idf$_{ij}$ are respectively calculated by the following formulas

$$rt f_{ij} = \frac{\# feature_j\_in\_context_i}{\# features\_in\_context_i} \qquad (11)$$

$$id f_j = \log\left(\frac{\# documents\_in\_collection}{\# documents\_containing\_feature_j}\right) \qquad (12)$$

In our experiments, the document collection we used is very specific to the amphibian morphology domain. In order to make the idf value more fair and accurate, we adopt the idf dataset based on the ODP that we had used in the previous paper [19].

b. Centroid Vectors

The centroid vector of the concept keyword C_k is calculated based on the individual vectors over N relevant documents.

$$CEN\_C_k = \sum_{i=1}^{N} IN D_{i\_}C_k \qquad (13)$$

5.2.4. Similarity Computation and Ranking

In the next sections, we present our methods to calculate the similarity between two sets, i.e., (1) S representing candidate synonyms; and (2) C representing concepts, to create and rank a list of synonym-concept assignments.

Since each context is essentially a collection of text, we use the classic cosine similarity metric from the vector space model to measure the semantic relatedness of two contexts. For each context S_m representing a candidate synonym and C_n representing a concept, the similarity of each pair (S_m, C_n) is the weight of cosine similarity value calculated by the following formula:

$$sim(S_m, C_n) = \frac{\sum_{i=1}^{t} w_{i,m} \times w_{i,n}}{\sqrt{\sum_{i=1}^{t} w^2_{i,m}} \times \sqrt{\sum_{i=1}^{t} w^2_{i,n}}} \tag{14}$$

where

$w_{i,m}$: weight of the feature i in the vector representing S_m

$w_{i,n}$: weight of the feature i in the vector representing C_n

t: total number of features

Note that these similarity values are normalized by the size of the context.

Since each keyword is presented either by N individual vectors (i.e., N context files) or a centroid vector over N context files, we propose to conduct four different methods to calculate the similarities between candidate synonym vectors and concept vectors:

- *Indi2Indi*: calculates the similarity value between each individual vector of a synonym keyword in S_m and each individual vector of the concept keyword in C_n.

- *Cent2Indi*: calculates the similarity value between the centroid vector of a synonym keyword in S_m and each individual vector of the concept keyword in C_n.

- *Indi2Cent*: calculates the similarity value between each individual vector of a synonym keyword in S_m and a centroid vector of the concept keyword in C_n.

- *Cent2Cent*: calculates the similarity value between the centroid vector of a synonym keyword in S_m and a centroid vector of the concept keyword in C_n.

Finally, for each candidate synonym it is assigned to the top concepts whose context C_n has the highest similarity values to the context for S_m.

Once the similarity between each word pair in (S_m, C_n) is calculated, we use the kNN method to rank the similarity computation results. The higher the similarity means the candidate synonym would be closer to the target concept. For each candidate word, we take top k items from the similarity sorted list. Then, we accumulate the weights of pairs having the same concept names. The final ranked matching list is determined by the accumulated weights. We then pick the pairs having highest weights value between S_m and C_n as the potential concepts to which the candidate synonym is added.

5.2.5. Experiments

a. Baseline: Existing WordNet-Based Algorithms

We evaluated four WordNet-based algorithms that had produced high accuracy as reported, i.e., Resnik [27], Jiang and Conrath [13], Lin [16], and Pirro and Seco [26], using all 191 test synonyms in our dataset.

Precision   # Correct pairs identified

Algos	Top1	Top2	Top3	Top4	Top5	Top6	Top7	Top8	Top9	Top10
LIN	1	4	4	9	11	12	13	13	15	15
JIANG	1	2	3	7	7	9	10	11	11	11
RESNIK	2	9	9	10	15	16	16	16	17	17
PIRRO	1	3	4	5	9	10	10	12	13	13
LIN	0.52%	2.09%	2.09%	4.71%	5.76%	6.28%	6.81%	6.81%	7.85%	7.85%
JIANG	0.52%	1.05%	1.57%	3.66%	3.66%	4.71%	5.24%	5.76%	5.76%	5.76%
RESNIK	**1.05%**	**4.71%**	**4.71%**	**5.24%**	**7.85%**	**8.38%**	**8.38%**	**8.38%**	**8.90%**	**8.90%**
PIRRO	0.52%	1.57%	2.09%	2.62%	4.71%	5.24%	5.24%	6.28%	6.81%	6.81%

Table 5. Evaluation of WordNet-based algorithms.

Our baseline approach using WordNet was complicated by the fact that it does not contain word phrases, which are very common in the concepts and synonyms in our ontology. We separate each word phrase (e.g., neural_canal) into single words, e.g., neural and canal, then submit each to WordNet to calculate the similarity. Then, we add together the individual word similarity score to produce the total similarity value for each phrase. For each of the 191 synonyms in the test set, the similarity between that synonym and each of the 530 concept names pairs was calculated, and then the concepts were ranked in decreasing order by similarity. Table 5 presents the accuracy for each method at different cutoff points in the list.

From the Table 5, we can see that Resnik's algorithm works best with this test set, although is only 1.05% accurate at the rank 1 location and 8.9% the correct concept appeared within the top 10 ranked concepts. The other approaches are not as accurate.

b. Context-Based Algorithms

We evaluated results by comparing the list of top ranked concepts for each synonym produced using our context-based method with the truth list we extracted from the ontology. The performance is reported over varying text chunk sizes (or text window sizes - *wsize*), from 4 to 40 tokens. Due to space limits, we only report here the best case achieved for each method (c.f. Figure 9). We also evaluated different values of k from 5 to 30 in the kNN methods to determine the k value that returned the best result. The numbers of k reported in each chart were different since the number or results generated depend on the number of vectors compared by each method. For example, when we measure the similarity between a synonym and a concept name, the *Indi2Indi* method used 5 individual vectors for each synonym and concept; but we have only one vector for each keyword in the *Cent2Cent* method.

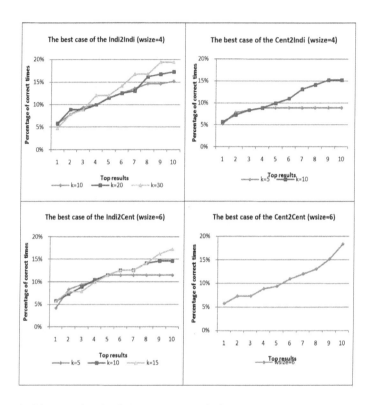

Figure 9. Result of the context-based similarity computation methods

By analyzing results, we find that the best performance is achieved in the Indi2Indi method with the window size (wsize) 4 and the k value 30 (c.f. Figure 9). Other methods slightly performed less well than the Indi2Ind. When the window size is increased, the performance is not improved.

c. Comparison with Baseline

From the above charts (c.f. Figure 9), we found that the context-based method works better with small text window size (i.e. size=4, 6). We evaluated the same reported pairs of synonym and concept-words with our text mining methods and the above WordNet-based algorithms. Figure 10 shows that our context-based similarity computation methods consistently outperform the best WordNet-based algorithm. Even the less promising *Cent2Cent* method produces performance better than the best case of the WordNet-based similarity algorithms (i.e., RESNIK's algorithm).

The experimental results support our belief that we might not need to rely on the WordNet database to determine similar words. The WordNet-based algorithms have not provided high precision results since many words are compound and/or do not exist in the WordNet database.

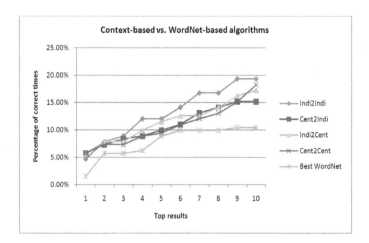

Figure 10. Comparison of our context-based methods vs. WordNet-based algorithms

5.3. Discussion

Our context-based approach was evaluated using synonyms from the amphibian ontology itself as our truth dataset. The experimental results show that our text mining approaches outperform the common similarity calculation algorithms based on WordNet in terms of correctly adding new words to the ontology concepts. Our best algorithm, Indi2Indi, with a window size of 4 and k=30 for kNN, selected the correct concept within the top 10 concepts 19.37% of the time. In comparison, the best WordNet-based algorithm only achieved 8.9% on the same task.

Overall, using WordNet similarity algorithms to assign a new vocabulary to an existing ontology might not be an effective solution since it depends on the WordNet database. One of the main drawbacks of the WordNet database is the unavailability of many words, particularly for narrowly-defined domains. Another problem with WordNet-based algorithms is that, because WordNet is so broad in scope, an extra step is neededfor semantic disambiguation thatcan further decrease accuracy.In contrast, the text mining approach can be applied to any domain and can use information from the Internet to mine new relevant vocabularies.

Compared with the lexical expansion approach, in terms of correctly assigning new words to specific ontology concepts, both context-based and WordNet-based text mining algorithms have lower precision (19.37% and 8.9% vs. 71.9%). This difference is to be expected because, with the lexical expansion approach, we already know the concepts to whichthe new words are to be attached.With that process, we start with a concept and try to find relevant domain-specific words.In contrast, the text mining approach starts with domain-relevant words and then tries to find matching concepts.

	Lexical Expansion	WordNet-based Algorithms	Context-based Algorithms
# Total words	321	191	191
# Correct words added	231	17	37
Precision	71.9%	8.9%	19.3%

Table 6. Comparison of different approaches on number of words added and accuracy.

Table 6 summarizes the results for the various approaches.It is clear that, in spite of the difficulty in finding domain-specific words in WordNet, the lexical expansion approach achieves both the best ontology enrichment, both in terms of the number of words added to the ontology and the quality of those additions.

6. Conclusions

The goal of this research study is to implement and validate an ontology learning framework in order to enrich the vocabulary of the domain ontology from Web documents related to the domain and from the WordNet semantic lexicon. We have presented two approaches, i.e., lexical expansion using WordNet and text mining, to perform these tasks. In the first approach, we built a reference hypernym tree by manually disambiguating top two levels of concepts from the ontology and compared three similarity computation methods to allow us to disambiguate the other concept-words in the ontology using WordNet. For the correct sense, we then enriched the corresponding concept with its synonyms and hypernyms. In our second approach, we implemented a focused crawler that retrieved documents in the domain of amphibian morphology that incorporates an SVM-based filter. The most relevant documents are submitted for information extraction using text mining.

Our approaches were empirically tested based on the seed amphibian ontology with WordNet lexical synsets and with retrieved Web document. While both approaches performed well, the text mining approach had higher precision for extracting relevant vocabulary to enrich the ontology. However, that approach had greater difficulty attaching the new vocabulary to the correct concept. Considering the ultimate utility of these two approaches, the text mining approach depends on the number and quality of the documents collected by the topic specific crawler. In addition, although it extracts good words, these words are not matched with particular concepts within the ontology. A further pairing process, most likely involving WordNet, is needed to complete the ontology enrichment process. In contrast, the lexical expansion approach using WordNet is only dependent on the concept-words in the ontology itself. It also extracts words from WordNet on a concept-by-concept basis, so no extra process is required to match new words with concepts. However, it does suffer from inaccuracies when the incorrect senses of words are used for expansion. It also requires a small amount of manual effort in order to disambiguate a few concept-words in order to construct the reference hypernym tree.

In future, we hope to combine these two approaches to exploit the strengths of each. For example we can use WordNet pair the text mining with concepts and use the documents to identify and disambiguate the multiple senses for the concept-words found in WordNet. In order to mine more vocabularies for the ontology, we will deal with the concept-words that currently do not appear in WordNet due to the very narrowness of the domain. Our other main task is to validate our approach on ontologies from other domains, to confirm that it is domain-independent. Finally, we need to incorporate the results of this work into a complete system to automatically enrich our ontology.

Acknowledgements

This research is partially supported by the NSF grant DBI-0445752: Semi-Automated Construction of an Ontology for Amphibian Morphology.

Author details

Hiep Luong*, Susan Gauch and Qiang Wang

*Address all correspondence to: hluong@uark.edu

Department of Computer Science and Computer Engineering, University of Arkansas, U.S.A.

References

[1] Agirre, E., Ausa, O., Havy, E., & Martinez, D. (2000). Enriching Very Large Ontologies Using the WWW. ECAI 1st Ontology Learning Workshop Berlin, August

[2] Berners-Lee, T., Hendler, J., & Lassila, O. (2001). The Semantic Web. *Scientific American*, 35-43.

[3] Berry, M. W. (2003). Survey of Text Mining. Springer-Verlag New York Inc., Secaucus, NJ,

[4] Buitelaar, P., Cimiano, P., & Magnini, B. (2005). Ontology Learning from Text: Methods, Evaluation and Applications. IOS Press (Frontiers in AI and applications, , 123

[5] Chang, C. C., & Lin, C. J. (2001). LIBSVM : a library for support vector machines. Software available at http://www.csie.ntu.edu.tw/~cjlin/libsvm

[6] Dumais, S. T., Platt, J., Heckerman, D., & Sahami, M. (1998). Inductive learning algorithms and representations for text categorization. Proceedings of CIKM-98, 148-155.

[7] Ester, M., Gross, M., & Kriegel, H. P. (2001). Focused Web Crawling: A Generic Framework for Specifying the User Interest and for Adaptive Crawling Strategies. Paper presented at 27th Int. Conf. on Very Large Databases, Roma, Italy.

[8] Gangemi, A., Navigli, R., & Velardi, P. (2003). The OntoWordNet Project: extension and axiomatization of conceptual relations in WordNet. In Proceedings of OD-BASE03 Conference. Springer

[9] Gauch, S., Madrid, J. M., Induri, S., Ravindran, D., & Chadlavada, S. (2010). KeyConcept: A Conceptual Search Engine. *Center, Technical Report: ITTC-FY2004-TR8646--37*, University of Kansas.

[10] Gómez-Pérez, A., & Manzano-Macho, D. (2003). A survey of ontology learning methods and techniques. *Deliverable 1.5, IST Project IST-20005-29243- OntoWeb*.

[11] Gruber, T. (1994). Towards principles for the design of ontologies used for knowledge sharing. *Int. J. of Human and Computer Studies* [43], 907-928.

[12] Hotho, A., Nürnberger, A., & Paaß, G. (2005). A Brief Survey of Text Mining. *LDV-Forum*, 20(1), 19-62.

[13] Jiang, J., & Conrath, D. (1997). Semantic similarity based on corpus statistics and lexical taxonomy. In Proceedings of International Conference Research on Computational Linguistics Taiwan,

[14] Joachims, T. (1998). Text categorization with support vector machines: learning with many relevant features. Paper presented at Proceedings of the 10th ECML-,1998. 137-142.

[15] Leacock, C., & Chodorow, M. (1998). Combining Local Context and WordNet Similarity for Word Sense Identification. MIT Press, Cambridge, 265-283.

[16] Lin, D. (1998). An information-theoretic definition of similarity. Paper presented at Proceedings of the Fifteenth International Conference on Machine Learning,. 296-304.

[17] Luong, H., Gauch, S., & Wang, Q. (2009, Feb. 1-7). Ontology-based Focused Crawling. Paper presented at International Conference on Information, Process, and Knowledge Management (eKNOW 2009),, Cancun, Mexico,. 123-128.

[18] Luong, H., Gauch, S., & Speretta, M. (2009, August 2-4,). Enriching Concept Descriptions in an Amphibian Ontology with Vocabulary Extracted from WordNet. Paper presented at The 22nd IEEE Symposium on Computer-Based Medical Systems (CBMS 2009), New Mexico, USA. 1-6.

[19] Luong, H., Gauch, S., Wang, Q., & Maglia, A. (2009). An Ontology Learning Framework Using Focused Crawler and Text Mining. *International Journal on Advances in Life Sciences*, 1(23), 99-109.

[20] Maedche, A., & Staab, S. (2001, March). Ontology Learning for the Semantic Web. *IEEE Intelligent Systems, Special Issue on the Semantic Web*, 16(2), 72-79.

[21] Maedche, A., Neumann, G., & Staab, S. (2003). Bootstrapping an Ontology-Based Information Extraction System. *Studies in Fuzziness and Soft Computing, Intelligent exploration of the web*, Springer, 345-359.

[22] Maglia, A. M., Leopold, J. L., Pugener, L. A., & Gauch, S. (2007). An Anatomical Ontology For Amphibians. *Pacific Symposium on Biocomputing* [12], 367-378.

[23] Miller, G. A. (1995). WordNet: a lexical database for English. *Comm. ACM*, 38(11), 39-41.

[24] Omelayenko, B. (2001). Learning of ontologies for the Web: the analysis of existent approaches. Paper presented at Proceedings of the international workshop on Web dynamics, London.

[25] Pedersen, T., Patwardhan, S., & Michelizzi, J. (2004). WordNet::Similarity- Measuring the Relatedness of Concepts. Paper presented at In Proc. of 19th National Conference on Artificial Intelligence, USA. The MIT Press, 1024-1025.

[26] Pirro, G., & Seco, N. (2008). Design, implementation and evaluation of a new semantic similarity metric combining features and intrinsic information content. *OTM Mexico, LCNS 5332*, 1271-1288.

[27] Reiter, N., & Buitelaar, P. (2008). Lexical Enrichment of a Human Anatomy Ontology using WordNet. In: Proc. of GWC08 (Global WordNet Conference), Hungary , 375-387.

[28] Resnik, P. (1995). Using Information Content to evaluate semantic similarity in a taxonomy. In IJCAI-95, Montreal, Canada , 448-453.

[29] Shamsfard, M., & Barforoush, A. (2003). The State of the Art in Ontology Learning. *The Knowledge Engineering Review*, Cambridge Univ. Press, 18(4), 293-316.

[30] Spasic, I., Ananiadou, S., Mc Naught, J., & Kumar, A. (2005). Text mining and ontologies in biomedicine: making sense of raw text. *Brief Bioinform*, 6, 239-251.

[31] Speretta, M., & Gauch, S. (2008). Using Text Mining to Enrich the Vocabulary of Domain Ontologies. Paper presented at ACM International Conference on Web Intelligence, Sydney. 549-552.

[32] Stevenson, M. (2002). Combining disambiguation techniques to enrich anontology. In Proceedings of the 15th ECAI workshop on Machine Learning and Natural Language Processing for Ontology Engineering

[33] Tan, A. H. (1999). Text mining: The state of the art and the challenges. In Proceedings of the Pacific Asia Conf on Knowledge Discovery and Data Mining PAKDD'99 workshop on Knowledge Discovery from Advanced Databases , 65-70.

[34] Vapnik, V. (1995). The Nature of Statistical Learning Theory. Springer-Verlag.

[35] Varelas, G., Voutsakis, E., Raftopoulou, P., Petrakis, E. G., & Milios, E. E. (2005). Semantic similarity methods in WordNet and their application to information retrieval

on the Web. In Proceedings of the 7th Annual ACM International Workshop on Web Information and Data Management (WIDM'05). ACM Press , 10-16.

[36] Velardi, P., Fabriani, P., & Missikoff, M. (2001). Using text processing techniques to automatically enrich a domain ontology. In Proceedings of the international conference on Formal Ontology in Information Systems- Volume 2001 (FOIS'01), ACM New   York,   NY,   USA   DOI=10.1145/505168.505194   http://doi.acm.org/ 10.1145/505168.505194 , 2001, 270-284.

[37] Warin, M., Oxhammer, H., & Volk, M. (2005). Enriching an ontology with wordnet based on similarity measures. In MEANING-2005 Workshop

[38] Wu, Z., & Palmer, M. (1994). Verb semantics and lexical selection. In 32nd Annual Meeting of the Association for Computational Linguistics , 133-138.

[39] Yang, D., & Powers, W. (2005). Measuring semantic similarity in the taxonomy of WordNet. Paper presented at Proc of the 28th Australasian Computer Science Conference. 315-332.

[40] Yang, Y., Zhang, J., & Kisiel, B. (2003, July-August). A scalability analysis of classifiers in text categorization. Paper presented at Proceedings of 26th ACM SIGIR Conference. 96-103.

[41] Yang, Y. (1994). Expert Network: Effective and Efficient Learning from Human Decisions in Text Categorization and Retrieval. *Proceedings of 17th ACM SIGIR*, 13-22.

[42] Yang, Y., & Pederson, J. O. (1997). A comparative study on feature selection in text categorization. *ICML*.

## Chapter 7

Biomedical Named Entity Recognition: A Survey of Machine-Learning Tools

David Campos, Sérgio Matos and José Luís Oliveira

Additional information is available at the end of the chapter

1. Introduction

It is well known that the rapid growth and dissemination of the Internet has resulted in huge amounts of information generated and shared, available in the form of textual data, images, videos or sounds. This overwhelming surge of data is also true for specific areas such as biomedicine, where the number of published documents, such as articles, books and technical reports, is increasing exponentially. For instance, the MEDLINE literature database contains over 20 million references to journal papers, covering a wide range of biomedical fields. In order to organize and manage these data, several manual curation efforts have been set up to identify, in texts, information regarding entities (e.g. genes and proteins) and their relations (e.g. protein-protein interactions). The extracted information is stored in structured knowledge resources, such as Swiss-Prot [1] and GenBank [2]. However, the effort required to continually update these databases makes this a very demanding and expensive task, naturally leading to increasing interest in the application of Text Mining (TM) systems to help perform those tasks.

One major focus of TM research has been on Named Entity Recognition (NER), a crucial initial step in information extraction, aimed at identifying chunks of text that refer to specific entities of interest, such as gene, protein, drug and disease names. Such systems can be integrated in larger biomedical Information Extraction (IE) pipelines, which may use the automatically extracted names to perform other tasks, such as relation extraction, classification or/and topic modeling. However, biomedical names have various characteristics that may difficult their recognition in texts [3]:

- Many entity names are descriptive (e.g. "normal thymic epithelial cells");

- Two or more entity names sharing one head noun (e.g. "91 and 84 kDa proteins" refers to "91 kDa protein" and "84 kDa protein");

- One entity name with several spelling forms (e.g. "N-acetylcysteine", "N-acetyl-cysteine", and "NAcetylCysteine");

- Ambiguous abbreviations are frequently used (e.g. "TCF" may refer to "T cell factor" or to "Tissue Culture Fluid").

Consequently, several NER systems have been developed for the biomedical domain, using different approaches and techniques that can generally be categorized as being based on rules, dictionary matching or Machine Learning (ML). Each approach fulfills different requirements, depending on the linguistic characteristics of the entities being identified. Such heterogeneity is a consequence of the predefined naming standards and how faithfully the biomedical community followed them. Thus, it is recommended to take advantage of the approaches that better fulfill the requirements of each entity type:

- Rule-based: names with a strongly defined orthographic and morphological structure;

- Dictionary-based: closely defined vocabulary of names (e.g. diseases and species);

- ML-based: strong variability and highly dynamic vocabulary of names (e.g. genes and proteins).

Applying the best approaches is not possible in all cases, since each approach presents different technical requirements [4]. However, when the appropriate resources are available, ML-based solutions present several advantages over other methods, and provide the best performance results.

The development of ML-based NER solutions integrates various complex steps that incorporate different processing pipelines. Thus, along the past years, a variety of systems were developed using the most different frameworks, techniques and strategies. This chapter gives an overview of ML-based biomedical NER solutions, providing a brief description of the latest and most significant research techniques, and presenting an in-depth analysis of the available systems and frameworks, considering the technical characteristics, provided features and performance outcomes. In the end, future directions and research opportunities on ML-based NER solutions are discussed.

2. Methods

ML-based solutions use statistical models focused on recognizing specific entity names, using a feature-based representation of the observed data. Such approach solves various problems of rule and dictionary-based solutions, recognizing new entity names and new spelling variations of an entity name. However, ML does not provide identifiers from curated resources, which can be solved by using a dictionary in an extra step. Nonetheless, the main drawback of such solutions is the dependency on annotated documents, which are hard and expensive to obtain. Thus, the absence of such resource for a specific biomedical entity type may limit the applicability of ML solutions.

The development of ML-based solutions requires two essential steps (Figure 1): train and annotate. At first, the ML model must be trained using the annotations present on the annotated documents. This step can take some time depending on the complexity of the model and on the available computational resources. After storing the model in a physical resource, raw documents can be annotated, providing entity names based on the past experience inferred from the annotated documents.

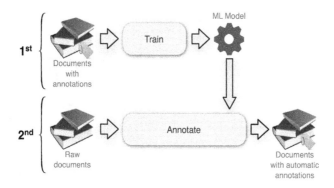

Figure 1. Illustration of the development process of ML-based solutions.

Both training and annotation tasksdepend on various processing steps and resources. Figure 2 presents the pipeline of the required modules to implement ML-based NER solutions:

• Corpora: collection of texts related with the target domain;

• Pre-processing: process the input data in order to simplify the recognition process;

• Feature processing: extract, select and/or induce features from the pre-processed input data;

• ML model: use the generated features to automatically define a set of rules that describe and distinguish the characteristics and patterns ofentity names;

• Post-processing: refinement of the generated annotations, solving problems of the recognition process or extending recognized names;

• Output: input corpora with automatically generated annotations or the extracted information ina structured format.

Each module must perform one or various essential tasks. Moreover, each task can be performed using different algorithms or/and resources, depending on the target goal and predefined requirements. The following sub-sections present the main goals of each module and briefly describe alternative approaches to fulfill the requirements of each task.

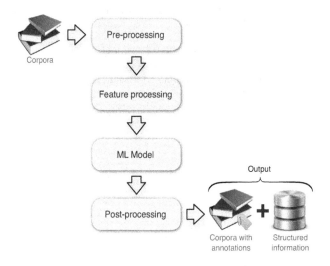

Figure 2. Overall pipeline of the required steps to develop ML-based NER solutions.

2.1. Corpora

In this context, a corpus is a set of text documents that usually contain annotations of one or various entity types. Such annotations are used to train ML models, inferring characteristics and patterns of the annotated entity names. Thus, the trained model is highly dependent on the quality of the annotations present on those corpora. This dependency must be carefully analyzed, since a corpus may contain annotations of a specific entity type but not reflecting the whole spectrum of names. A corpus is also used to obtain performance results, in order to understand the behavior of the system on real-life problems. Such evaluation enables the comparison of distinct solutions to the same problem.

There are two types of annotated corpora, varying with the source of the annotations:

• Gold Standard Corpora (GSC): annotations are performed manually by expert annotators, following specific and detailed guidelines;

• Silver Standard Corpora (SSC): annotations are automatically generated by computerized systems.

Table 1 presents a list of relevant GSC available for the various biomedical entity types. As we can see, most of the research efforts have been on the recognition of gene and protein names, with various corpora containing several thousands of annotated sentences. Such effort is a consequence of two different factors: the importance of genes and proteins on the biomedical domain, and the high variability and no standardization of names. Various challenges were organized for the recognition of gene and protein names, such as BioCreative [5] and JNLPBA [6], and most advances on ML-based NER were achieved in those challenges.

When the amount of annotated documents is not sufficient to reflect the whole spectrum of names, corpora are mostly used for evaluation procedures, as is generally the case for the identification of disorders and species names. The SCAI IUPAC corpus is also a good example of a specific sub-entity type corpus, containing only annotations of chemicals that follow the IUPAC nomenclature. Finally, both AnEM and CellFinder are very recent corpora (released on 2012), showing that the development of manually annotated corpora for the various entity types is still an ongoing work.

Entity	Corpus	Type	Size (sentences)
Gene and Protein	GENETAG [7]	Sentences	20000
	JNLPBA [6] (from GENIA [8])	Abstracts	22402
	FSUPRGE [9]	Abstracts	≈29447*
	PennBioIE [10]	Abstracts	≈22877*
Species	OrganismTagger Corpus [11]	Full texts	9863
	Linnaeus Corpus [12]	Full texts	19491
Disorders	SCAI Disease [13]	Abstracts	≈3640*
	EBI Disease [14]	Sentences	600
	Arizona Disease (AZDC) [15]	Sentences	2500
	BioText [16]	Abstracts	3655
Chemical	SCAI IUPAC [17]	Sentences	20300
	SCAI General [18]	Sentences	914
Anatomy	AnEM[1]	Sentences	4700
Miscellaneous	CellFinder[2]	Full texts	2100

Table 1. List of relevant Gold Standard Corpora (GSC) available for each biomedical entity, presenting the type of documents and its size.
*Each MEDLINE abstract contains on average 7.2±1.9 sentences [19]. We considered the best-case scenario with ≈9 sentences.

As we can see on Table 1, only small sets of documents have been annotated, due to the complexity of generating GSC. The CALBC [20] (Collaborative Annotation of a Large Biomedical Corpus) project aimed to minimize this problem, providing a large-scale biomedical SSC automatically annotated through the harmonization of several NER systems. This large corpus contains one million abstracts with annotations of several biological semantic groups, such as diseases, species, chemicals and genes/proteins.

1 http://www.nactem.ac.uk/anatomy

2 http://www.informatik.hu-berlin.de/forschung/gebiete/wbi/resources/cellfinder

2.2. Pre-processing

Natural Language Processing (NLP) solutions can be accomplished by computerized systems in an effective manner. However, it is necessary firstly to properly delimit the documents into meaningful units. Most NLP solutions expect their input to be segmented into sentences, and each sentence into tokens. Since real-world documents lack such well-defined structure, it is necessary to implement a few methods to perform such tasks.

2.2.1. Sentence splitting

Sentence splitting is the process of breaking a text document into its respective sentences. In the end, each sentence should provide a specific local, logical and meaningful context for future tasks. Various solutions were developed to perform sentence splitting on biomedical documents, such as JSBD [21], OpenNLP[3] and SPECIALIST NLP[4].The best performing solutions can achieve an accuracy of 99.7%.

2.2.2. Tokenization

Tokenisation is the process of breaking a sentence into its constituent meaningful units, called tokens. It is one of the most important tasks of the IE workflow, since all the following tasks will be based on the tokens resulting from this process. Consequently, various tools were developed specifically for the biomedical domain, such as GENIA Tagger [22], JTBD [21] and SPECIALIST NLP. In [23], the authors present a detailed comparison of various biomedical tokenizers. The best solutions achieve accuracies around 96%.

2.2.3. Annotationencoding

In order to internally represent the annotated entity names, it is necessary to use an encoding scheme to give a tag to each token of the text. The simplest is the IO encoding, which tags each token as either being in (tag "I") a particular named entity or outside (tag "O"). This encoding is defective, since it cannot represent two entities next to each other. The BIO encoding is the *de facto* standard, and it extends the IO encoding solving the boundary problem. In this scheme, the "in" tag is subdivided into tag "B", representing the first token or beginning of the entity name, and tag "I" for the remaining tokens. The BMEWO encoding extends the BIO encoding by distinguishing the end of an entity (tag "E") tokens from the middle entity tokens (tag "M"), and adding a new tag ("W") for entities with only one token.

2.3. Feature processing

Feature processing is a crucial NER task, since the predictions will be performed based on the information that they encode, reflecting special phenomena and linguistic characteristics of the naming conventions. Thus, the definition of a rich and carefully selected set of features is required in order to properly represent the target entity names.

3http://opennlp.apache.org

4http://lexsrv3.nlm.nih.gov/Specialist

2.3.1. Linguistic

The most basic internal feature is the token itself. However, in most cases, morphological variants of words have similar semantic interpretations, and can be considered as equivalent. For this reason, stemming or lemmatization can be used to group together all inflected forms of a word, so that they can be analyzed as a single item. The basic idea of stemming is to find the prefix that is common to all variations of the term. On the other hand, lemmatization is a more robust method, because it finds the root term of the variant word (e.g. the lemma of "was" is "be"). Along with normalization techniques, it is also possible to associate each token with a particular grammatical category based on its context, a procedure called Part-of-Speech (POS) tagging. Additionally, chunking can be also used, dividing the text into syntactically correlated parts of words (e.g., noun or verb phrases). These linguistic features only provide a local analysis of the token in the sentence. To complement this, features can be derived from dependency parsing tools to collect the relations between the various tokens in the sentence.

2.3.2. Orthographic

The purpose of orthographic features is to capture knowledge about word formation. For example, a word that starts with a capital letter could indicate the occurrence of an entity name (e.g. in the protein name "MyoD"). Various features can be used, reflecting the presence of uppercase or lowercase characters, the presence of symbols, or counting the number of digits and uppercase characters in a token.

2.3.3. Morphological

Morphological features, on the other hand, reflect common structures and/or sub-sequences of characters among several entity names, thus identifying similarities between distinct tokens. To accomplish this goal, three distinct types of morphological features are commonly considered:

- Suffixes and prefixes:can be used to distinguish entity names. For instance, suffixes like "ase", "ome" and "gen" frequently occur in gene and protein names;

- Char n-grams: are sub-sequences of n characters from a given token. It extends suffixes and prefixes by considering sub-sequences of characters in the middle of tokens;

- Word shape patterns: generate a sequence of characters to reflect how letters, digits and symbols are organized in the token. For instance, "Abc: 1234" could be represented by the following patterns: "Abc: *", "Aaa#1111" and/or "a#1".

2.3.4. Context

Higher-level relations between tokens and extracted features can be established through windows or conjunctions of features, reflecting the local context of each token. The application of windows consists of adding features of preceding and succeeding tokens as features of each token. On the other hand, conjunction of features consists of creating new features by grouping together features of the surrounding tokens. To apply those context methods, it is important to limit the features to use as context information, since using the complete set of features from the surrounding tokens wouldgenerate millions of new features. However, pre-selecting the features used forbuilding the conjunctions may mean that informative conjunctions are not considered. Feature induction solves this problem, by iteratively considering sets of atomic and conjunction features created from the initial feature set. On each iteration, only candidates that provide useful information are included in the updated set of features. Intuitively, features with high gain provide strong evidence for many decisions.

2.3.5. Lexicons

Adding biomedical knowledge to the set of features can further optimize NER systems. To provide this knowledge, dictionaries of specific domain terms and entity names are matched in the text and the resulting tags are used as features. Two different types of dictionaries are commonly used: target entity names (match tokens with dictionaries with a complete set of names of the target entity name), and trigger names (match names that may indicate the presence of biomedical names in the surrounding tokens).

2.4. Machine learning model

As the input to the ML model, each feature should assume the value "1" if it is present on the current token or "0" if it is not (Table 2).

	Feature 1	Feature 2	...	Feature m
Token 1	1	1	...	0
Token 2	0	1	...	0
...	...	...	...	...
Token n	0	0	...	1

Table 2. Illustration of the matrix of features as the input tothe ML model. Each vector defines the features present for the corresponding token.

Each modeling technique uses the feature matrix to create a probabilistic description of the entity names boundaries. The various ML models can be classified as being supervised or semi-supervised, depending on unannotated data being used or not. Supervised learning, which only uses annotated data, has received most research interest in recent years. Consequently, different supervised models have been used on NER systems, namely Conditional Random Fields (CRFs) [24], Support Vector Machines (SVMs) [25], Hidden Markov Models (HMMs) [26] and Maximum Entropy Markov Models (MEMMs) [27]. CRFs have been actively used during the last years, since they present several advantages over other methods. Firstly, CRFs avoid the label bias problem [24], a weakness of MEMMs. In addition, CRFs also have advantages over HMMs, a consequence of their conditional nature that results in relaxation of the independence assumptions [28]. Finally, although SVMs can provide comparable results, more time is required to train complex models.Semi-supervised solutions use both annotated and unannotated data, in order to solve the data sparseness problem. Thus, the main goal is to collect features of the unannotated data that are not present in the annotated data, which may contribute to a better identification of the entity names boundaries. There are various approaches to implement semi-supervised solutions, such as Semi-CRFs [29, 30], Semi-SVMs [31], ASO [32] and FCG [33].

2.5. Model Combination

The most recent results on biomedical NER clearly indicate that better performance results can be achieved by combining several systems with different characteristics. As an example, the top five systems of the BioCreative II gene mention challenge [5] used ensembles of NER systems. In order to generate ML models that reflect different characteristics of the annotated data, it is common to use different parsing directions (forward and backward) or different feature sets. Moreover, different approaches can be used to combine the generated annotations, using union, intersection, machine learning [34] or lexicons [35].

2.6. Post-processing

Post-processing techniques are commonly used to solve some recognition mistakes, which may be easily corrected through simple rules or methods:

- Remove or correct recognition mistakes: annotations with an odd number of brackets may be removed or corrected.

- Extend or make annotations more precise: abbreviation resolution methods can be used to extend detected annotations. Moreover, curated dictionaries can be also used to correct generated annotations.

- Remove uninformative terms: some annotations may be known for being non-informative or unwanted terms, and consequently must be removed.

2.7. Evaluation

In order to understand the behavior of the system, it is important to measure the accuracy of the generated annotations. This can be performed by annotating a corpus and then compare the automatic annotations with the ones provided by expert curators. Thus, each automatic annotation must be classified as being a:

- True Positive (TP): the system provides an annotation that exists in the curated corpus;

- True Negative (TN): the non existence of an annotation is correct according to the curated corpus;

- False Positive (FP): the system provides an annotation that does not exist in the curated corpus;

- False Negative (FN): the system does not provide an annotation that is present in the curated corpus.

Exact and fuzzy matching can be used to obtain performance results and to better understand the behavior of the system. With approximate matching we can find the performance when minor and non-informative mistakes are discarded. Such evaluation is important since various post-NER tasks, such as relation extraction and topic modeling, can be performed with imprecise annotations.

Performance results are obtained using three important measures: precision, recall and F-measure. Those measures assume values between 0 (worst) and 1 (best). Precision measures the ability of a system to present only relevant names, and it is formulated as:

$$Precision = \frac{relevant\ names\ recognized}{total\ names\ recognized} = \frac{TP}{TP + FP} \tag{1}$$

On the other hand, recall measures the ability of a system to present all relevant names, and is formulated as:

$$Recall = \frac{relevant\ names\ recognized}{relevant\ names\ on\ corpus} = \frac{TP}{TP + FN} \tag{2}$$

Finally, F-measure is the harmonic mean of precision and recall. The balanced F-measure is most commonly used, and is formulated as:

$$F - measure = 2\ \frac{Precision \times Recall}{Precision + Recall} \tag{3}$$

3. Tools

In order to understand and expose the current trends of ML-based NER solutions, it is important to study existing tools and respective characteristics, analyzing their applicability on real life problems. Since dozens of tools are available for the recognition of a specific entity type (e.g. gene and protein), we decided to study the systems that better reflect the overall progress of the domain. On the other hand, some entity types do not have any relevant ML-based systems. For instance, species recognition is already efficiently performed by dictionary-based solutions: LINNAEUS [12] and OrganismTagger [11] already achieve ≈95% and ≈97% of F-measure, respectively. Curiously, OrganismTagger uses a simple ML module that gives a small contribution in the recognition of species strains. Also there are no ML solutions for the recognition of anatomy names, since the AnEM corpus was just released (May, 2012). However, due to the characteristics of the corpus and the importance of anatomy enti-ty type in the biomedical domain, we believe that various solutions will be developed soon.

Table 3 presents an overview of the ML-based systems characteristics that we considered for the various entity types, presenting the used programming languages, features, mod-els and post-processing techniques. The tools presented in the miscellaneous section can be applied to more than one entity type, namely on gene/protein and disorders. However, dif-ferent entity types have different characteristics, requiring the applicability of distinct tech-niques and/or feature sets. As we can see, features such as chunking, dependency parsing and conjunctions are only used in gene and protein names recognition, which require a much more complex feature set. Moreover, the BioEnEx authors show that the use of some morphological and orthographic features has a negative impact on the recognition of disor-der names [36].

The application of complex techniques is a reflex of the research effort spent on each entity type. As expected, gene and protein names have been the main research target, with eight systems. Four of those systems, including AIIAGMT and IBM Watson, were developed spe-cifically for these entity types. The other four systems were also adapted for the recognition of disorders, such as ABNER and BANNER. It is also interesting to see that the systems de-veloped for the recognition of chemicals are not used in any other entity type or vice-versa. We believe that this is a consequence of various factors: available corpora do not cover the whole spectrum of chemical names or is sparse; and chemical names present different chal-lenges when compared with gene and protein names, namely high variability but different levels of names standardization.

We also studied the various tools in terms of source code availability, since using and adapt-ing already implemented methods may streamline the development of new and improved IE solutions. For instance, one can use Gimli or BANNER to implement new tools for the recognition of different entity types (e.g., BANNER was used in the development of BioEn-Ex). It is also interesting to see that closed source solutions commonly present more ad-vanced and/or complex techniques. For instance, only IBM Watson applies a semi-supervised algorithm and, with the exception of Gimli, only closed source solutions use model combination strategies.

Regarding used features, we can observe that some features are common to every recogni-tion task, namely some orthographic, morphological and context features. Thus, we may ar-gue that those features are essential in the development of ML-based NER tools. One can also observe that linguistic features are only used in the recognition of entity names that present high variability and low standardization. Moreover, from the results of various tools we can conclude that the use of dictionary matching as features always presents a positive contribution, since adding domain knowledge provides an increased precision.

		Gene and Protein			Chemical			Miscellaneous (gene/protein and disorders)		
Name	Gimli[b]	NERsuite[a]	IBM Watson	AIIAGMT	SCAI	ChemSpot	BioEnEx	BANNER	ABNER	Lingpipe
Year	2011	2010	2007	2008	2008	2012	2010	2008	2005	2007
Reference	-	-	[37]	[35]	[17]	[38]	[36, 39]	[40]	[41]	[42]
Programming Language	Java	C++	-	Java, C++	Java	Java	Java	Java	Java	Java
Open source	x	x				x		x	x	x
Features – Linguistic: Normalization	x	x	x	x			x	x	x	x
Linguistic: POS	x	x	x	x			x	x		
Linguistic: Chunking	x	x								
Linguistic: Dependency	x	x					x			
Orthographic: Capitalization	x	x	x	x	x	x	x	x	x	
Orthographic: Counting	x	x	x	x	x	x	x	x	x	
Orthographic: Symbols	x	x			x	x	x	x	x	
Morphological: Suffix and Prefix	x	x	x	x	x	x	x	x	x	
Morphological: Char n-grams	x									
Morphological: Word Shape	x	x	x	x			x	x	x	
Context: Windows	x	x	x	x	x	x	x	x	x	
Context: Conjunctions	x									
Lexicons: Target names	x	x	x	x			x	x	x	
Lexicons: Trigger names				x						
Model – Supervised	CRF	CRF		CRF	CRF	CRF	CRF	CRF	CRF	HMM
Semi-supervised			ASO							
Model Combination	x		x	x			x			
Post-processing – Parentheses	x		x	x			x	x		
Abbreviation	x		x	x			x	x		
Lexicons	x			x						

Table 3. Overview of the ML-based systems characteristics considering the various target entity types and presenting the used programming languages, features, models and post-processing techniques.

---

5 http://bioinformatics.ua.pt/gimli

6 http://nersuite.nlplab.org

As stated above, nine of the ten tools use supervised models. From those, all the systems developed in the last four years (from 2008 to 2012) take advantage of CRFs, which shows the success of this modeling technique. However, there is a growing research interest in the application of semi-supervised models, since they may provide more general and non-corpus specific solutions.

Finally, post-processing methods are commonly applied by closed source solutions, with the exception of Gimli and BANNER that already take advantage of several high-end techniques. Thus, we can argue that parentheses processing and abbreviation resolution are essential tasks, since its applicability is independent of the entity type.

Besides the study of the characteristics of each tool, we have also conducted a set of evaluation experiments to help elucidating about the solutions that perform the best. Figure 3 presents a performance comparison of the analyzed tools per entity type.

3.1. Gene and Protein names

Most of the developed solutions are focused on two main corpora, GENETAG and JNLPBA. GENETAG is not restricted to a specific domain, containing annotations of proteins, DNA and RNA (grouped in only one semantic type), which were performed by experts in biochemistry, genetics and molecular biology. This corpus was used in the BioCreative II challenge [5], and it contains 15000 sentences for training and 5000 sentences for testing. For evaluation, the matching is performed allowing alternative names provided by the expert annotators. On the other hand, the JNLPBA corpus is a sub-set of the GENIA corpus, containing 2404 abstracts extracted from MEDLINE using the MeSH terms "human", "blood-cell" and "transcription factor". The manual annotation of these abstracts was based on five classes of the GENIA ontology, namely protein, DNA, RNA, cell line, and cell type. This corpus was used in the BioEntity Recognition Task in BioNLP/NLPBA 2004 [6], providing 2000 abstracts for training and the remaining 404 abstracts for testing. On this challenge, the evaluation was performed using exact matching. Since GENETAG is not focused on any specific biomedical domain, its annotations are more heterogeneous than those of JNLPBA. A brief analysis, considering protein, DNA and RNA classes, shows that GENETAG contains almost 65% of distinct names, as opposed to the 36% found on JNLPBA.

As expected, a model trained on GENETAG provides annotations not focused on any specific biomedical domain, which may be recommended for general real life applications. However, the same semantic group contains annotations of DNA, RNA and gene/protein. On the other hand, a model trained on the JNLPBA corpus may provide annotations optimized for research on human blood cell transcription factors. On this corpus, the various entity types are split on different semantic groups.

Overall, the systems present high performance results on both corpora, where the best performing systems achieve an F-measure of 88.30% on GENETAG and 73.05% on JNLPBA. Both systems, AIIAGMT and Gimli, present complex solutions that include the application of linguistic and lexicon features and the combination of various CRF models with different characteristics. When comparing open with closed source solutions, there is no significant difference, since both apply high-end techniques and high performance results. Moreover, Gimli is the open-source solution that provides more implemented features,with the best performance results. Nevertheless, BANNER, BioEnEx and NER Suite also present positive outcomes using simpler models and no combination techniques.

The high performance results achieved on this task, on both general and specific corpora, indicate that the recognition of gene and protein names is ready to be used on real life problems, presenting an acceptable error margin.

3.2. Disorder names

Following the UMLS description of disorder, it includes various semantic sub-groups with different interpretations. Thus, a corpus must contain names of diseases, symptoms, abnormalities and dysfunctions in order to reflect the whole spectrum of disorder names in the best way as possible.Some of those sub-groups are important since new diseases are often referred as a set of signs and symptoms until the disease receives an official name.

Only two corpora were used for the development of ML solutions: Arizona Disease Corpus (AZDC) and BioText. AZDC presents a set of annotations that reflect the whole spectrum of disorder names. The annotation process was performed manually by one expert and revised by another. On the other hand, the BioText corpus was annotated for the identification of disease and treatment mentions, not covering the whole spectrum of names. Moreover, the primary goal of this corpus was to explore different types of relationships between diseases and treatments. Thus, a high degree of annotation consistency was not required at the token level. Regarding both corpora, we consider that the amount of annotated sentences (2500 and 3655) may not be sufficient to train an accurate ML model for real life applications. For instance, the AZDC corpus provides 3228 disease mentions. In comparison, GENETAG contains ≈24000 primary gene and protein annotations and more than 17000 alternative mentions for approximate matching.

Due to the restrictions of the available corpora, most solutions for the recognition of disorders are typically implemented through the application of dictionary-based approaches. Nevertheless, various solutions were developed using only ML and the existing corpora. Overall, those solutions present a simpler feature set when comparing with gene and protein models.

As expected, a model trained on the AZDC corpus may provide general annotations considering the whole spectrum of disorder names in one semantic group. On the other hand, a model trained on the BioText corpus only provides annotations of diseases and treatments. However, on both cases, a large amount of disorder names are missed since their statistical description is not present on the training corpus.

Considering exact matching, the best system achieves an F-measure of 81.08% on the AZDC corpus, which is a good performance result. The improved performance of BioEnEx in comparison to BANNER may be justified by the use of dependency parsing and the absence of some orthographic features. On the other hand, the BioText inconsistencies cause the performance of systems to be overly pessimistic. As we can see, the best performing system only achieves an F-measure of 54.84%.

In summary, we believe that the AZDC corpus provides a good benchmark for the recognition of disorder names. However, the implementation of systems based only on that specific corpus is doubtful, due to the small amount of annotated documents. Moreover, we also believe that the BioText corpus is not the best solution for systems comparison, due to the reported inconsistences and achieved results.

3.3. Chemical names

Chemical names can be divided into two classes [38]: a closed (finite) class for trivial names, and an open (infinite) class for names following strictly defined nomenclatures (e.g. IUPAC names). The SCAI General corpus contains manual annotations of both classes. However, we believe that 914 sentences with only 1206 mentions is not sufficient for development and evaluation procedures, due to the amount and complexity of chemical names. On the other hand, the SCAI IUPAC corpus only contains annotations of chemical names that follow the IUPAC nomenclature. In this case, we believe that 20300 sentences are sufficient for ML models to infer the patterns of the rule-based convention with success.

As expected, the systems developed using the IUPAC corpus deliver good results. The best performing solution achieves 85.60% of F-measure using exact matching. As we can see, ChemSpot and SCAI have similar characteristics in terms of model and features. However, the achieved results are quite different. Such difference may be related with specific characteristics of the CRF training. The authors of ChemSpot argue that SCAI uses a third-order CRF (instead of second-order) with optimized meta-parameters, which may over fit the model and consequently provide worse performance on unseen instances.

The same model of ChemSpot that was trained on the IUPAC corpus was tested on the SCAI corpus. As expected, it provides low recall results, since only IUPAC annotations are generated. Overall, it presents an F-measure of 42.60%, which is a good result considering that IUPAC annotations represent around 32% of all names present on the SCAI corpus.

Since the systems for IUPAC entity names provide positive outcomes, we believe that an optimal solution for the recognition of chemical names must be hybrid, combining ML and dictionary-based solutions. Thus, ML may be used for IUPAC names and the dictionary matching for trivial names and drugs. Actually, ChemSpot does exactly that, and achieved an F-measure of 68.10% on the SCAI corpus, presenting an improvement of ≈11% against previous solutions.

Genes and Proteins

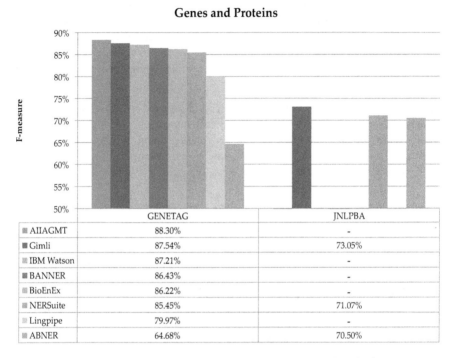

	GENETAG	JNLPBA
▨ AIIAGMT	88.30%	–
▪ Gimli	87.54%	73.05%
▨ IBM Watson	87.21%	–
▪ BANNER	86.43%	–
▨ BioEnEx	86.22%	–
▪ NERSuite	85.45%	71.07%
▨ Lingpipe	79.97%	–
▪ ABNER	64.68%	70.50%

Disorders   ## Chemicals

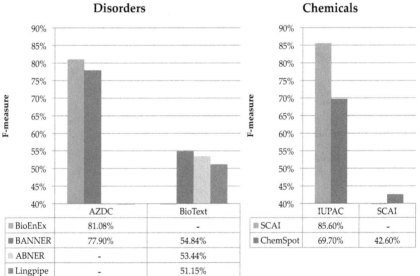

	AZDC	BioText
▪ BioEnEx	81.08%	–
▪ BANNER	77.90%	54.84%
▨ ABNER	–	53.44%
▪ Lingpipe	–	51.15%

	IUPAC	SCAI
▨ SCAI	85.60%	–
▪ ChemSpot	69.70%	42.60%

Figure 3. Performance comparison of the various ML-based NER solutions per entity type and corpus.

4. Conclusion

This chapter presented a detailed survey of machine learning tools for biomedical named entity recognition. We started by introducing the various fundamental steps for the development of such tools. Afterwards, we described each step in detail, presenting the required methods and alternative techniques used by the various solutions. Using that knowledge, we presented various tools for each biomedical entity, describing the used methodologies and provided features. Thus, solutions for recognition of gene/protein, disorder and chemical names were studied in detail, exposing the main differences between the various systems characteristics. Such analysis allowed us to expose the current trends of ML-based solutions for biomedical NER, and compare the performance outcomes considering the different systems' characteristics. Thus, we can summarize the current trends by task:

- Corpora: annotated abstracts are the most used corpus type;

- Pre-processing: sentence splitting, tokenization and annotation encoding are fundamental for input data processing;

- Features: most of orthographic, morphological, lexicon and context features are essential in the recognition of any biomedical entity type. Linguistic features and conjunctions present an important contribution in the recognition of non-standardized entity names;

- Model: supervised CRF models are widely used and present positive outcomes on all biomedical entity types;

- Post-processing: parentheses processing and abbreviation resolution are essential tasks and provided positive contributions on all entity types.

Overall, we can argue that the amount and quality of ML-based tools already provide a significant number of advanced features with good performances results. Such results show that most tools are ready to be used on real life applications, providing acceptable error margins.

Regarding future steps, we believe that using full text documents will be fundamental, since they provide more information and completely different challenges, due to the increased ambiguity. Moreover, the application of semi-supervised algorithms will take advantage of the millions of unannotated documents. Such strategy presents various advantages, contributing to the development of ML-based solutions for entity types that have a reduced amount of annotated corpora, and allowing the development of general models, independent of the training corpora and ready to annotate any text with high accuracy. Finally, we also believe that feature induction will be essential, enabling automatic generation of informative features to extract new and unknown characteristics of entity names.

5. Nomenclature

CRFs - Conditional Random Fields
HMMs - Hidden Markov Models
IE - Information Extraction
MEMMs - Maximum Entropy Markov Models
ML - Machine Learning
NLP - Natural Language Processing
POS - Part-of-Speech
SVMs - Support Vector Machines

Acknowledgements

This work received funding from FEDER through the COMPETE programme and from Fundação para a Ciência e a Tecnologia (FCT) under grant agreement FCOMP-01-0124-FEDER-010029. S. Matos is funded by FCT under the Ciência2007 programme.

Author details

David Campos*, Sérgio Matos and José Luís Oliveira

*Address all correspondence to: david.campos@ua.pt

IEETA/DETI, University of Aveiro, Portugal

References

[1] Bairoch, A., & Boeckmann, B. (1992). The SWISS-PROT protein sequence data bank. *Nucleic acids research*, 20, 2019-2022.

[2] Benson, D. A., Karsch-Mizrachi, I., Clark, K., Lipman, D. J., Ostell, J., & Sayers, E. W. (2012). GenBank. *Nucleic acids research*, 40, D48-53.

[3] Zhou, G., Zhang, J., Su, J., Shen, D., & Tan, C. (2004). Recognizing names in biomedical texts: a machine learning approach. *Bioinformatics*, 20, 1178-1190.

[4] Campos, D., Matos, S., & Oliveira, J. L. (2012). Current methodologies for biomedical Named Entity Recognition. *In Biological Knowledge Discovery Handbook: Preprocessing, Mining and Postprocessing of Biological Data (to appear)*, Edited by Elloumi M, Zomaya AY: John Wiley & Sons, Inc.

[5] Smith, L., Tanabe, L. K., Ando, R. J., Kuo, C. J., Chung, I. F., Hsu, C. N., Lin, Y. S., Klinger, R., Friedrich, C. M., Ganchev, K., et al. (2008). Overview of BioCreative II gene mention recognition. *Genome biology*, 9(2), S2.

[6] Kim, J. D., Ohta, T., Tsuruoka, Y., Tateisi, Y., & Collier, N. (2004). Introduction to the bio-entity recognition task at JNLPBA. *In International Joint Workshop on Natural Language Processing in Biomedicine and its Application*, Geneva, Switzerland. Association for Computational Linguistics: 70-75.

[7] Tanabe, L., Xie, N., Thom, L. H., Matten, W., & Wilbur, W. J. (2005). GENETAG: a tagged corpus for gene/protein named entity recognition. *BMC bioinformatics*, 6(1), S3.

[8] Kim, J. D., Ohta, T., Tateisi, Y., & Tsujii, J. (2003). GENIA corpus-semantically annotated corpus for bio-textmining. *Bioinformatics*, 19(1), i180-182.

[9] Hahn, U., Beisswanger, E., Buyko, E., Poprat, M., Tomanek, K., & Wermter, J. (2008). Semantic Annotations for Biology-A Corpus Development Initiative at the Jena University Language & Information Engineering (JULIE) Lab. *In Proceedings of the 6th International Conference on Language Resources and Evaluation*, 28-30.

[10] Kulick, S., Bies, A., Liberman, M., Mandel, M., Mc Donald, R., Palmer, M., Schein, A., Ungar, L., Winters, S., & White, P. (2004). Integrated annotation for biomedical information extraction. *In Workshop on Linking Biological Literature, Ontologies and Databases (Human Language Technology conference)*, Association for Computational Linguistics, 61-68.

[11] Naderi, N., Kappler, T., Baker, C. J., & Witte, R. (2011). OrganismTagger: detection, normalization and grounding of organism entities in biomedical documents. *Bioinformatics*, 27, 2721-2729.

[12] Gerner, M., Nenadic, G., & Bergman, C. M. (2010). LINNAEUS: a species name identification system for biomedical literature. *BMC bioinformatics*, 11, 85.

[13] Gurulingappa, H., Klinger, R., Hofmann-Apitius, M., & Fluck, J. (2010). An Empirical Evaluation of Resources for the Identification of Diseases and Adverse Effects in Biomedical Literature. *In 2nd Workshop on Building and evaluating resources for biomedical text mining*, (7th edition of the Language Resources and Evaluation Conference); Valetta, Malta, 15.

[14] Jimeno, A., Jimenez-Ruiz, E., Lee, V., Gaudan, S., Berlanga, R., & Rebholz-Schuhmann, D. (2008). Assessment of disease named entity recognition on a corpus of annotated sentences. *BMC bioinformatics*, 9(3), S3.

[15] Leaman, R., Miller, C., & Gonzalez, G. (2009). Enabling recognition of diseases in biomedical text with machine learning: Corpus and benchmark. *In 3rd International Symposium on Languages in Biology and Medicine*, Jeju Island, South Korea, 82-89.

[16] Rosario, B., & Hearst, M. A. (2004). Classifying semantic relations in bioscience texts. *In 42nd annual meeting of the Association for Computational Linguistics*, Barcelona, Spain. Association for Computational Linguistics, 430.

[17] Klinger, R., Kolarik, C., Fluck, J., Hofmann-Apitius, M., & Friedrich, C. M. (2008). Detection of IUPAC and IUPAC-like chemical names. *Bioinformatics*, 24, i268-276.

[18] Kolárik, C., Klinger, R., Friedrich, C. M., Hofmann-Apitius, M., & Fluck, J. (2008). Chemical names: terminological resources and corpora annotation. *In Workshop on Building and evaluating resources for biomedical text mining (Language Resources and Evaluation Conference)*, 51-58.

[19] Yu, H. (2006). Towards answering biological questions with experimental evidence: automatically identifying text that summarize image content in full-text articles. *In Proceedings of the AMIA Annual Symposium*, American Medical Informatics Association, 834-838.

[20] Rebholz-Schuhmann, D., Yepes, A. J., Van Mulligen, E. M., Kang, N., Kors, J., Milward, D., Corbett, P., Buyko, E., Beisswanger, E., & Hahn, U. (2010). CALBC silver standard corpus. *Journal of bioinformatics and computational biology*, 8, 163-179.

[21] Tomanek, K., Wermter, J., & Hahn, U. (2007). A reappraisal of sentence and token splitting for life sciences documents. *Studies in health technology and informatics*, 129, 524-528.

[22] Tsuruoka, Y., Tateishi, Y., Kim, J. D., Ohta, T., McNaught, J., Ananiadou, S., & Tsujii, J. (2005). Developing a robust part-of-speech tagger for biomedical text. *Advances in informatics*, 382-392.

[23] He, Y., & Kayaalp, M. (2006). A Comparison of 13 Tokenizers on MEDLINE. Bethesda, MD: The Lister Hill National Center for Biomedical Communications.

[24] Lafferty, J., McCallum, A., & Pereira, F. C. N. (2001). Conditional random fields: Probabilistic models for segmenting and labeling sequence data. *In International Conference on Machine Learning*, Williamstown, Massachusetts, USA. Morgan Kaufmann.

[25] Cherkassky, V. (1997). The nature of statistical learning theory. IEEE transactions on neural networks / a publication of the IEEE Neural Networks Council , 8, 1564.

[26] Baum, L. E., & Petrie, T. (1966). Statistical inference for probabilistic functions of finite state Markov chains. *The Annals of Mathematical Statistics*, 37, 1554-1563.

[27] McCallum, A., Freitag, D., & Pereira, F. (2000). Maximum entropy Markov models for information extraction and segmentation. *In International Conference on Machine Learning*, Stanford, California, USA. Morgan Kaufmann, 591-598.

[28] Wallach, H. M. (2004). Conditional random fields: An introduction. *University of Pennsylvania CIS Technical Report MS-CIS-04-21*.

[29] Mann, G. S., & Mc Callum, A. (2007). Efficient computation of entropy gradient for semi-supervised conditional random fields. *In Proceedings of the North American Association for Computational Linguistics*, Rochester, New York, USA. Association for Computational Linguistics, 109-112.

[30] Mann, G., & Mc Callum, A. (2008). Generalized expectation criteria for semi-supervised learning of conditional random fields. *In Proceedings of Association of Computational Linguistics*, Association of Computational Linguistics, 870-878.

[31] Bennett, K., & Demiriz, A. (1999). Semi-supervised support vector machines. *Advances in Neural Information processing systems*, 368-374.

[32] Ando, R. K., & Zhang, T. (2005). A framework for learning predictive structures from multiple tasks and unlabeled data. *The Journal of Machine Learning Research*, 6, 1817-1853.

[33] Li, Y., Hu, X., Lin, H., & Yang, Z. (2011). A Framework for Semisupervised Feature Generation and Its Applications in Biomedical Literature Mining. *IEEE/ACM Transactions on Computational Biology and Bioinformatics (TCBB)*, 8, 294-307.

[34] Campos, D., Matos, S., Lewin, I., Oliveira, J. L., & Rebholz-Schuhmann, D. (2012). Harmonisation of gene/protein annotations: towards a gold standard MEDLINE. *Bioinformatics*, 28, 1253-1261.

[35] Hsu, C. N., Chang, Y. M., Kuo, C. J., Lin, Y. S., Huang, H. S., & Chung, I. F. (2008). Integrating high dimensional bi-directional parsing models for gene mention tagging. *Bioinformatics*, 24, i286-294.

[36] Chowdhury, M., & Faisal, M. (2010). Disease mention recognition with specific features. *In Proceedings of Association for Computational Linguistics*, Association for Computational Linguistics, 83-90.

[37] Ando, R. K. (2007). BioCreative II gene mention tagging system at IBM Watson. *In Proceedings of the Second BioCreative Challenge Evaluation Workshop*, Madrid, Spain, 101-103.

[38] Rocktaschel, T., Weidlich, M., & Leser, U. (2012). ChemSpot: A Hybrid System for Chemical Named Entity Recognition. *Bioinformatics*.

[39] Chowdhury, F. M., & Lavelli, A. (2011). Assessing the practical usability of an automatically annotated corpus. *In Proceedings of the Fifth Linguistic Annotation Workshop*, Portland, Oregon, USA. Association for Computational Linguistics, 101-109.

[40] Leaman, R., & Gonzalez, G. (2008). BANNER: an executable survey of advances in biomedical named entity recognition. *Pacific Symposium on Biocomputing Pacific Symposium on Biocomputing*, 652-663.

[41] Settles, B. (2005). ABNER: an open source tool for automatically tagging genes, proteins and other entity names in text. *Bioinformatics*, 21, 3191-3192.

[42] Carpenter, B. (2007). LingPipe for 99.99% recall of gene mentions. *In Proceedings of the Second BioCreative Workshop*, Madrid, Spain, 307-309.

## Chapter 8

Analyses on Text Data Related to the Safety of Drug Use Based on Text Mining Techniques

Masaomi Kimura

Additional information is available at the end of the chapter

1. Introduction

One of main raison d'etre of medical care should cure patients and save their lives. Drug safety has attracted attention for a long time, with an emphasis on toxicity and side effects of drugs. Additional to this, the safety of drug use is attracting increasing attention from the perspective of medical accident prevention. In order to prevent medical accidents, such as errors involving medicines, double dosage and insufficient dosage, it is necessary to ensure the proper treatment of the right medicines, namely, safety of drug use. The confirmation of usage should be one of the keys to identifying errors and prevention from misuse. Consider the case when a doctor inputs prescription data into a computerized order entry system for medicines. If the system shows him information concerning therapeutic indications, he can subsequently avoid the errors. To enable this, the order entry system requires the databases containing information on dosage regimens so that the proper usage can be verified.

The most reliable data, which can be a source of the databases, is a package insert published by pharmaceutical companies as an official document attached to its medicine. Original package inserts are, however, distributed as paper documents and unsuitable for processing by a computer system. In Japan, Pharmaceutical and Medical Devices Agency (PMDA), which is an extra-departmental body of the Japanese Ministry of Health, Labor and Welfare, has released SGML formatted package insert data. SGML is an old-established markup language, which adds metadata and structures to data by tagging, which is defined by DTD. In fact, it is difficult to leverage the data structure defined in the DTD for analysis of the data. This is because the definition of data structure is ambiguous and because the information is not well structured, namely, described by the sentences in tagged elements. This hinders the utilization of the SGML formatted package insert data, especially as a database used in computer systems that ensure the safety of medicinal usage. We should also note that the SGML version package inserts usually describe their contents as sentences, as is described in the original paper version package inserts. In order to obtain information from package insert data, we need to analyze the sentences in package insert data.

Other important sources of knowledge besides official packge inserts are practices of medical experts. One of the useful and important ways to understand what people think is to conduct a survey in the form of a questionnaire. In particular, the freely described data included in the questionnaire responses represent an important source to let us know the real thoughts of the people. However, it is not easy to analyze such freely described data by hand, since a large number of responses are anticipated and subsequent analysis using manual counting may be influenced by the individual prejudice of the analysts involved. It is, therefore, suitable to apply a text mining approach to objectively analyze such freely described data. As readers know, text mining is an analytical technique based on data mining / statistical analysis algorithms and NLP algorithms. It has wide applicability — including clustering research papers or newspaper articles, finding trends in call center logs or blogged articles, and so on. The clustering of textual data is popular as a commonly-available method to classify data and understand their structure. Unlike such applications, however, the freely described data contained in the responses of a questionnaire have characteristics such as a small number of short sentences in each piece of data and wide-ranging content that precludes the application of clustering algorithms to classify it. In this chapter, we review the cases of application of our method to questionnaire data.

As we mentioned above, it is necessary to avoid medical accidents. In order to take a countermeasure, past cases must be investigated to identify their causes and suitable countermeasures. Medical incidents, caused by treatment with the wrong medicines, are strongly related to medical accidents occurring due to a lack of safety in drug usage. Medical incidents are the ones that may potentially become medical accidents without certain suppression factors, and tend to occur more frequently than medical accidents. Incorporating Heinrich's law, which shows the tendency of frequency and seriousness of industrial accidents, we can estimate that for every serious medical accident, there are 300 incidents and thirty minor accidents. This can be interpreted as medical accidents having many causes, most of which are eliminated by certain suppression factors, which lead to incidents, while the remaining causes lead to medical accidents. From this perspective, we can expect both medical accidents and incidents to originate from identical causes, which suggests that the analysis of data concerning incidents is valid in order to investigate the cause of medical accidents, since their occurrence frequency tends to be much larger than that of medical accidents. Though simple aggregation calculations and descriptive statistics have already been applied to drug-related medical incident data, the analyses are too simple to extract sufficient information, such as the reasons behind incidents depending on the circumstances. To ensure such analyses could be properly performed, we should apply text mining technique to the texts describing incidents.

In this chapter, we introduce the techniques that we have developed, Word-link method and Dependency-link method, and review their application to the following data:

- Package inserts
  - Application to an analysis on descriptions of dosage regimens described in package inserts of medicines
- Questionnaire data
  - Application to data obtained by nation-wide investigations based on questionnaires about the 'therapeutic classification mark' printed on transdermal cardiac patches
- Medical incident data
  - Application to incident data disclosed by Government of Japan

2. Method

2.1. Word-link method and dependency-link method [3]

2.1.1. Introduction

In order to determine the features of freely described data, the easiest and simplest way is to apply morphological analysis and count the number of the root (main part) of morphemes, which shows us particular words recurring frequently and suggests the nature of the themes discussed by respondents. This method, however, derives a difficult result to interpret in the case where there are several different topics contained in the entire free descriptions contained in the questionnaire responses. This is because that method can show the appearance of words but does not preserve their inter-relations. This method cannot, therefore, provide us with more in-depth information, such as how matters related to the topic are evaluated by the respondents.

Regarding the syntax tree of a sentence based on modification relationships as semi-structured data, Matsuzawa et al. [1] and Kudo et al. [2] have applied pattern mining algorithms to extract frequently appearing subtrees, namely, sub-sentences recurring frequently in plural sentences more than a specified number of times (support). These represent rigorous means to determine the pattern of sub-sentences, which preserves the co-occurrence relationships of words and their structure in sentences.

As for the freely described data written by respondents, there is no guarantee of them expressing the same opinion in sentence of the same structure. If the respondents write similar sentences but with slightly different structures, it is difficult to identify the sentences by only matching their substructures alone. In addition, we have to maintain the entire data in memory at the same time when we use the pattern mining algorithm, which prunes the substructure appearing less than the support during the process. It is preferable that the algorithm be applicable to the huge size of data to a sufficient extent to cover surveillance in the form of a large-scale questionnaire.

In this section, we, therefore, suggest a method featuring summarized description data, by initially aggregating modification relations and then limiting them to instances appearing more than the support. By connecting the resultant modification relations and finding word sequences which can be reconstituted into understandable sentences, we can expect to extract sentences which contain the main opinions of the respondents.

2.1.2. Theory

Let s_i ($i = 1 \cdots n$) denote the sentences in freely described text data. Applying morphological analysis to s_i, we obtain a series of words $W(s_i) = \{w^i_1, w^i_2, \cdots \}$, where w^i_j denotes a word in the sentence s_i. We also define a set of dependency relations $D(s_i) = \{d^i_1, d^i_2, \cdots \}$, where d^i_j denotes a dependency relation in the sentence s_i, and their union set $D = \cup_i D(s_i)$.

For instance, if we target the two sentences, s_1="医薬品の安全性は重要だ"(the safety of drug is important) and s_2="医薬品の安全性は改善が必要だ"(the safety of drug needs improved),

- $W(s_1) = \{$ 医薬品(drug), 安全性(safety), 重要だ(important) $\}$,
- $W(s_2) = \{$ 医薬品(drug), 安全性(safety), 改善(improved), 必要だ(needs)$\}$,

- $D(s_1) = \{$ 医薬品(drug)→ 安全性(safety), 安全性(safety)→重要だ(important)$\}$,
- $D(s_2) = \{$ 医薬品(drug)→ 安全性(safety), 安全性(safety) →必要だ(needs), 改善(improved)→必要だ(needs) $\}$
- $D = \{$ 医薬品(drug)→ 安全性(safety), 安全性(safety)→重要だ(important), 安全性(safety) →必要だ(needs), 改善(improved)→必要だ(needs)$\}$.

Note that, following the linkage of $d^i_j \in D(s_i)$, we can reproduce the original sentence s_i except for the order of appearance of modifications which modify the same word. If the word w^i_j modifies another word w^i_k and the dependency relation $d^i \in D(s_i)$ is related to these words, we can define 'counterpart' functions such as

$$d^i = L(w^i_j, w^i_k) \tag{1}$$

$$w^i_j = S(d^i) \tag{2}$$

$$w^i_k = E(d^i). \tag{3}$$

The function L denotes dependency linkage between w^i_j, w^i_k and S and E returns a modifying word and a modified word respectively. For instance, as for the dependency医薬品(drug)→ 安全性(safety), $d = L($医薬品(drug), 安全性(safety)$)$, 医薬品(drug)$= S(d)$ and 安全性(safety)$=E(d)$.

Note that some relations between these functions hold as follows:

$$d^i = L(S(d^i), E(d^i)) \tag{4}$$

$$w^i_j = S(L(w^i_j, w^i_k)) \tag{5}$$

$$w^i_k = E(L(w^i_j, w^i_k)). \tag{6}$$

Let us assume the verb of the main clause is modified by other words but does not modify another word in the target language. For all dependency relations $d^i \in D(s_i)$ whose $E(d^i)$ is not the verb of the main clause of s_i, there exists another $d'^i \in D(s_i)$ which satisfies

$$E(d^i) = S(d'^i),$$

because each word but the verb of the main clause necessarily modifies other word in the sentence.

Thus, there exists $d' \in D$ satisfying $E(d) = S(d')$ for each $d \in D$, if d is not the verb of the main clause of the original sentences $\{s_i\}$. Since $D(s_i) \subset D$ because of the definition of D, we can find a series of modification relations which satisfy the Eq.2.1.2 in D and reproduce all the original sentences $\{s_i\}$ by following their linkage.

However, rather than all sentences, we are only interested in the sentences described by plural respondents. If the same sentences appear η times, the dependency relations in the sentences will also recur (more than) η times. Let us define a 'support' function:

$$supp_D(d) = card\{s_i \mid d \in D(s_i)\},$$

where 'card' denotes the cardinality of a set. The above statement can be described via $supp_D(d)$ as follows: if there are η sentences, which have the same dependency structure as s_i, the number of sentences is equivalent to η, which contains $d_k^i \in D(s_i)$. Thus the following inequality holds for each $d_k^i \in D(s_i)$

$$supp_D(d_k^i) \geq \eta.$$

Therefore, If we limit D to the set with the constraint of Eq.2.1.2:

$$D^\eta = \{d \mid d \in D, supp_D(d) \geq \eta\},$$

each modification relation in sentences with the same dependency structure, namely more than η times, is a member of D^η. These dependency relations satisfy the same relation as Eq.2.1.2, though, in general, we cannot necessarily expect the existence of the dependency relation $d \in D^\eta$ such that $E(d) = S(d')$ for each $d' \in D^\eta$. We can therefore expect to find sentences described by plural respondents and with an equivalent dependency structure by following the linkage of dependency relations in D^η, which satisfies the relation Eq.2.1.2. (We call this method using a series of dependency relations the 'word-link method'.)

In fact, we should be aware that the extraction of a series of dependency relations in D^η satisfying Eq.2.1.2 is a necessary condition to find such sentences and the co-occurrence of dependency relations is not preserved in this operation. In other words, the elements of D^η, d and d', which satisfy the relation $E(d) = S(d')$, do not necessarily appear in the same sentence. In order to ensure the co-occurrence of dependency relations, it is necessary to confirm that the dependency relations d and d' satisfying $E(d) = S(d')$ are included in the same sentence. If more sentences exist than the support, which contains a series of dependency relations satisfying $E(d) = S(d')$, we can conclude that the sentences are written by more respondents than the number preliminarily determined. Taking the calculation cost and the degree of freedom of expression into account, we relax the above restriction as follows:

1. Firstly, find the pairs of dependency relations $d, d' \in D$ satisfying $E(d) = S(d')$, both of which are contained in the same sentence. Let $d \to d'$ denotes such a pair of dependency relations (First step).

2. Next, find the two pairs $d \to d'$ and $d' \to d''$, where the dependency relationship d' in both pairs is identical. If such pairs exist, we presume there is a link connecting these pairs (Second step).

3. Finally, follow the linkages of such pairs which appear more than η' times and reproduce sentences (Third step). η' is the threshold to limit the lower boundary of the number of appearances.

In this method, each of two pairs of dependency relations $d \to d'$ and $d' \to d''$ contains a common pair of words $E(d) = S(d')$ and $E(d') = S(d'')$, which appears in the same sentence. Since the variations of the structures of descriptions related to common opinions in a set of questionnaire data tend to be small, such overlap of words is (at least empirically) sufficient to approximately reproduce sentences summarizing original sentences. (We call this method using the series of the pairs of modification relations the 'dependency-link method'.)

In addition, our method helps us find the sentences which have similar dependency structures. We usually visualize the result as a graph structure, whose nodes denote modifying or modified words and edges denote dependency relationships between the words. We can expect that such sentences are placed in the same graph structure since they share the same words and the similar dependency relations.

3. Application

3.1. Analysis on descriptions of dosage regimens in package inserts of medicines [4]

To prevent medical accidents, such as mix-ups involving medicines, double dosage and insufficient dosage, it is necessary to ensure the proper treatment of the right medicines, namely, 'safety of usage' of medicines.

There occurred, in some Japanese hospitals, fatal accidents due to mix-ups involving a steroid, Saxizon, with a similarly-titled medicine, Succine, which is a muscle relaxant. There are two conceivable ways to avoid such accidents, one of which is to prevent the naming and use of medicines resembling other medicines in their name, both in terms of appearance and sound. Another method is to confirm the medicine by checking the actual usage based on their dosage regimens. Though the former method can be realized by utilizing a name checking system provided by the Japan Pharmaceutical Information Center or making a rule to adopt medicines which have confusing names, the accident is known to have occurred despite the existence of a rule to reject Succine due to its confusing name.

This suggests to us that the latter, namely the confirmation of usage, should be the key to identifying error. Consider the case when a doctor inputs prescription data into a computerized order entry system for medicines. If the system shows him information concerning therapeutic indications, he can subsequently avoid mix-ups of medicines such as the case in question. To enable this, the order entry system requires a database containing information on dosage regimens so that the proper usage can be verified.

As is described in Introduction in this chapter, the structure of the portion of dosage regimens in package insert data does not achieve sufficiently fine granularity to enable its effective utilization in a computer system, such as the order entry system mentioned above. In this section, we show the method to find the description patterns of the sentences in the dosage regimen portion of the SGML formatted package inserts data. Based on this result, we also propose the data structure of dosage regimen information, which will be the basis of a drug information database to ensure safe usage.

The target data in this section is the SGML formatted package insert data of medicines for medical care, which can be downloaded from the PMDA web site. Since we need the list of medicines to retrieve the data, we utilize the standard medicine master data (the version released on September 30, 2007), which is provided with The Medical Information System Development Center (MEDIS-DC). Using the master data, we obtained 11,685 SGML files, which are our target data.

The part of dosage regimens contain 'detail' elements. They describe information concerning dosage regimens as sentences and are suitable to apply a text mining technique in order to find potential meta data of dosage regimens.

We applied the word-link method to descriptions in 'detail' elements concerning the dosage regimens in each SGML package insert. Since, as a minimum, dosage, administration and adaptation diseases will differ for each medicine, with a considerable scope of expression, our original method, whereby attempts are made to find patterns, including the use of nouns, might result in a failure to find the common sentences. We thus extend it to determine the tendency for the co-occurrence of nouns and particles (parts of speech which play roles similar to prepositions in English) and extract structural patterns except for noun variations. The analytical steps are as follows:

1. We retrieve sentences in the 'detail' elements and apply dependency analysis to them.

2. If the segment in the dependency contains a noun, we differentiate the latter from the segment. The resultant characters are expected to be particles, hence we name a 'particle candidate' in this paper.

3. We aggregate nouns that appear in segments including each particle candidate and find the characteristics of the particle candidates in use. We call the part of the segment obtained by removing a particle segment the 'main part of segment'.

4. We replace the found nouns with a symbol such as '○○○' in order to mask them, and apply the word-link method. If there are certain rules governing the way in which particles should be used, this method extracts the common structures of sentences and suggests us the idea of data items, for which descriptions must be converted into a structured data form.

value	ratio	%	freq.
		53.67	155411
を	(to)	8.67	25094
に	(to)	6.74	19516
として	(as)	4.67	13512
の	(of)	3.97	11506
により	(depending on)	3.31	9578
には	(for)	3.0	8698
は	(is)	2.12	6143
$null$		2.08	6011
.		1.84	5331
が	(is)	1.54	4448
と	(with/and)	1.15	3333
で	(with/by)	0.76	2195
まで	(to/untill)	0.4	1163
な	(like)	0.36	1053
も	(too/also)	0.28	817
後	(after)	0.28	813
では	(as for)	0.24	688
から	(from)	0.22	634
までと	(until)	0.2	593

Figure 1. The particle candidates of segments included in the 'detail' elements.

Fig. 1 shows the distribution chart of particle candidates with their frequencies. First, we investigate the nature of the nouns involved in the segments containing the particle candidates appearing frequently in the sentences of dosage regimens. Fig. 1 indicates that the particle candidate of more than 50% of the segments is a null character, namely the segments contain only their main part. Since the targets in Fig. 1 are all segments contained in sentences of dosage regimens, they involve not only nouns but also other part of speech such as verbs. The particle candidate of segments whose main word is not a noun is expected to be a null character. In the following analysis, we thus exclude segments whose main word is not a noun.

Fig. 2 shows nouns in the segments whose particle candidate is a null character. This indicates that such segments contain information about units of administration, '日' (days), '回' (times), 'mg', the manner of administration, '適宜' (arbitrarily), '通常' (usually), and the condition of age such as '年齢' (age) and '成人' (adult) and so on.

value	ratio	%	freq.
日	(day)	17.84	15125
適宜	(proper extent)	12.52	10620
回	(times)	11.37	9640
通常	(ordinary)	10.03	8503
年齢	(age)	7.31	6200
m g		4.89	4148
通常成人	(ordinary adult)	3.34	2834
成人	(adult)	2.29	1942
体重	(weight)	1.65	1403
こと	(thing)	1.36	1154
g		1.17	994
日量	(daily amount)	1.07	904
m l		0.85	724
本剤	(this medicine)	0.78	659
錠	(tablet)	0.76	648
症状	(symptom)	0.56	479
場合	(case)	0.56	473
時間	(time)	0.54	458
日間	(during ... days)	0.42	356
力価	(titer)	0.41	348

Figure 2. The nouns whose segment has a null character as the particle candidate.

値 (value)	割合 (ratio)	%	度数 (freq)
m g		26.	6530
g		7.12	1787
m l		4.82	1209
錠	(tablet)	3.73	935
力価	(titer)	3.49	877
投与	(dosage)	2.85	715
m g／k g		2.28	573
適量	(proper amount)	1.77	445
これ	(this)	1.49	373
体表面積	(body surface area)	1.47	369
力価／k g	(titer/kg)	1.19	299
本剤	(this medicine)	1.15	288
μg／k g		0.99	248
単位	(unit)	0.97	243
日量	(daily dose)	0.91	229
本剤錠	(this tablet)	0.7	175
用量	(dosage)	0.65	164
回m g	(times mg)	0.64	160
投与量	(dosage amount)	0.63	158
回	(times)	0.57	143
カプセル	(capsule)	0.49	122

Figure 3. The nouns whose segment has a particle candidate 'を'. (top 20)

We outline the nouns in the segments, including each particle segment, as follows:

- Fig. 3 shows nouns in the segments, including 'を' as a particle segment. We can see that they express amounts of medication such as 'mg', '錠' (tablets) and '力価' (titers).
- The nouns in the segments whose particle segment is 'に' (at/to) are shown in Fig. 4, which shows that the particle segments tend to be used with frequency-related words such as '回' (times) and '数回' (sometimes), and concerning the timing of administration, such as '食間' (inter cibos) and '就寝前' (before bedtime), administration site such as '静脈内' (in a vein).

値 (value)	割合 (ratio)	%	度数 (freq.)
回 (times)		23.2	4527
症状 (symptom)		5.46	1066
食間 (inter cibos)		4.7	918
就寝前 (before bedtime)		3.28	641
静脈内 (in the veins)		3.21	626
必要 (necessity)		2.53	494
患部 (affected area)		2.18	425
緩徐 (moderation)		2.08	406
m l		1.92	375
食後 (after meal)		1.9	370
回食後 (times after meal)		1.43	280
成人 (adult)		1.13	221
就回 (some times)		1.01	197
回患部 (times affected area)		0.92	180
時間ごと (each ... hour)		0.87	169
経口投与 (oral administration)		0.81	158
筋肉内 (intramuscular)		0.81	158
週間ごと (each ... weeks)		0.75	147
年齢症状 (age and symptom)		0.67	131
食前 (before meal)		0.61	119

Figure 4. The nouns whose segment has a particle candidate 'に' (at/to).(top 20)

値 (value)	割合 (ratio)	%	度数 (freq.)
原則 (principle)		2.9	392
クラリスロマイシン (clarithromycin)		1.18	159
日量 (daily dose)		1.17	158
ファモチジン (famotidine)		1.04	141
回アシクロビル (times acyclovir)		1.03	139
回アルファカルシドール (times alfacalcidol)		0.97	131
フルオロウラシル (fluorouracil)		0.94	127
維持量 (maintainance dosage)		0.94	127
シメチジン (cimetidine)		0.85	115
ドンペリドン (domperidone)		0.78	106
ドライシロップ (dry syrup)		0.74	100
ケトチフェン (ketotifen)		0.72	97
アモキシシリン (amoxicillin)		0.68	92
レボホリナート (Levofolinate)		0.65	88
ランソプラゾール (lansoprazole)		0.64	86
オメプラゾール (Omeprazole)		0.62	84
ジクロフェナクナトリウム (diclofenac sodium)		0.62	84
メシル酸ナファモスタット (nafamostat mesilate)		0.61	83
プランルカスト水和物 (pranlukast hydrate)		0.61	82
ラニチジン (ranitidine)		0.61	82

Figure 5. The nouns whose segment has a particle candidate 'として' (as). (top 20)

値 (value)	割合 (ratio)	%	度数 (freq.)
(adult) 成人		49.28	3976
(case) 場合		13.94	1125
(ordinary adult) 通常成人		8.96	723
(child) 小児		7.11	574
(severe infection) 重症感染症		1.72	139
(elder people) 高齢者		0.71	57
(improvement) 改善		0.66	53
(dissolution and dilution) 溶解希釈		0.57	46
(patient) 患者		0.56	45
(case) 症例		0.48	39
(ordinary child) 通常小児		0.43	35
(hepatic disease) 肝疾患		0.37	30
(less than ... years old) 歳未満		0.36	29
(after) 後		0.33	27
(objective) 目的		0.33	27
(severe hypertension) 重症高血圧症		0.33	27
(astriction) 便秘		0.32	26
(insomnia) 不眠症		0.29	23
(severe refractory infection) 重症難治性感染症		0.29	23
(baby and child) 幼小児		0.27	22

Figure 6. The nouns whose segment has a particle candidate 'には' (for). (top 20)

値 (value)	割合 (ratio)	%	度数 (freq.)
症状 (symptom)		80.27	7688
年齢症状 (age and symptom)		7.49	717
体重 (weight)		2.14	205
目的 (objective)		1.41	135
年齢体重症状 (age, weight and symptom)		0.67	64
体質 (diathesis)		0.56	54
病型 (pattern of disease)		0.55	53
経口投与年齢症状 (oral administration, age and symptom)		0.41	39
年令症状 (age and symptom)		0.41	39
疾患 (disease)		0.39	37
こと (thing)		0.32	31
程度 (extent)		0.31	30
年齢症状等 (age and symptom etc.)		0.28	27
尿量 (urinary volume)		0.28	27
患者 (patient)		0.25	24
抗悪性腫瘍剤 (anticancer drug)		0.24	23
状態 (state)		0.22	21
次式 (next equation)		0.2	19
生理食塩液 (normal saline)		0.19	18
大きさ (size)		0.18	17

Figure 7. The nouns whose segment has a particle candidate 'により' (depending on). (top 20)

- The particle segment 'として' (as) is included in the segments whose main words are nouns, as shown in Fig. 5. Besides the nouns for the formulaic phrases, '原則として' (as a rule), '(1) 日量として' (as a daily dosage) and '維持量として' (as a maintenance dosage), the other nouns shown in the figure represent active ingredients of medicines.

- Fig. 6 shows nouns in the segments including the particle segment 'には' (for). This mainly contains nouns showing an object person such as '成人' (adult), '小児' (child) and '高齢者' (elder person). It also shows the name of symptoms such as '重症感染症' (severe infection) and '肝疾患' (hepatic disease).

- In Fig. 7, segments whose particle candidate is 'により' (depending on) tend to contain the word '症状' (symptom). In this figure, we can also read words such as '体重' (body weight), '年齢' (age), '目的' (objective) and so on. This results and the meaning of the particle candidate suggest that these segments show the condition to adjust a dose.

値 (value)	割合 (ratio)	%	度数 (freq.)
増減する (increase and decrease)		17.23	10115
経口投与する (administer orally)		9.72	5708
する (do)		5.81	3409
分ける (split)		3.64	2135
応じる (respond)		3.61	2122
投与する (administer)		2.85	1676
用いる (use)		2.57	1512
分割する (divide)		2.39	1402
分割経口投与する (take orally in fractional amounts)		2.26	1330
溶解する (dissolve)		1.75	1026
増量する (increase)		1.73	1018
できる (be possible)		1.67	983
点滴静注する (infuse intravenously)		1.65	970
使用する (make use of)		1.44	843
注射する (inject)		1.41	827
かける (source)		1.4	822
3回経口投与する (administer orally thrice)		1.29	757
開始する (begin)		1.1	645
塗布する (apply)		1.04	608
行う (perform)		1.01	596

Figure 8. The verbs included in 'detail' elements describing dosage regimens.(top 20)

Based on the results shown above, we can find the tendency of contents in the segments including each particle segment. We replaced each segment containing nouns with the symbol '○○○', and applied the word-link method to the replaced sentences. Fig. 8

shows the verbs used in the sentences of dosage regimens. To absorb the difference in verb expressions, we replace verbs of similar meanings with a representative verb. For instance, the verbs, '経口投与する' (dose orally) and '点滴静注する' (drip-feed intravenously) have analogous meanings in terms of medication and are hence consolidated into a single verb. In this paper, to enhance comprehension, we consolidated them into '投与・使用する' (administrate/use). Moreover, we consolidated the verbs that mean increase or decrease into '増減する' (escalate) and replaced the verb '分割する' (divide) with '分ける' (split).

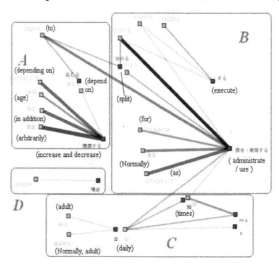

Figure 9. The result of the word-link method applied to 'detail' elements (the links show co-occurrence more than 1149 times). Blue nodes denote modifying words and red nodes denote modified words.

Following this consolidation, we applied the word-link method and obtained sentence structures based on dependency relationships. Fig. 9 shows the links of dependency relationships appearing more than 1149 times. Based on this figure, we can read the following contents:

- Increase or decrease according to conditions such as indication (disease) and age (Part A in Fig. 9).
- Dosage based on the information concerning the administration site, frequency, object person, symptoms, amount of medication and (the amount of) active gradients (Part B).
- Daily dosage (Part C) and description of conditions (Part D)

Based on these and the fact that verbs indicate the method of administration, we can see that the data structure to describe dosage regimens needs the following items:

- Indication (disease)
- Objective person
- Administration site
- Amount of medication

No.	Questions (Originally Japanese)	Respondents	Num of responses
Q1	Why did you select the transdermal patch?	Doctors, Pharmacists, Nurses	737
Q2	What are the preventive measures to avoid medical accidents related to the transdermal patch?	Doctors, Pharmacists, Nurses	2115
Q3	What is your opinion of the cardiac transdermal patch?	Patients	529
Q4	Have you ever been asked by patients about the transdermal patch with the therapeutic classification mark on it?	Pharmacists, Nurses	533

Table 1. The free description part of the questionnaire concrening the therapeutic classification mark printed on a cardiac transdermal patch.

- Amount of active gradient
- The way of administration
- Frequency
- Conditions of increase or decrease

3.2. A questionnaire concerning the therapeutic classification mark printed on a cardiac transdermal patch [5]

In certain hospitals in Japan, medical accidents have occurred, whereby patients suffering from lung ailments and those suffering from heart disease were mixed up and operations were performed without any modification. It is known that the incident happened because a cardiac transdermal patch was placed on the body of the heart disease sufferer, which indicated when the patients were delivered. If surgeons had known what the patch signified, they would have avoided making a mistake with the surgery. To prevent recurrences, the pharmaceutical company marketing the patches voluntarily printed a 'therapeutic classification mark' on them. The 'therapeutic classification mark' is a security feature linked to the use of the drug and shows that the patch is a cardiac medicine. We applied our method to the free description part of a questionnaire, which is conducted as a nationwide investigation into the 'therapeutic classification mark' printed on isosorbide dinitrate transdermal patches. The respondents were doctors, pharmacists, nurses and patients and the number of respondents and the questions asked are listed in Table 1.

Table 2 lists the resulting sentences for the dependency-linking method($\eta' = 3$), where we filled postpositions and implemented classification by respondent and topic. We only presented representative sentences in the content columns where there are many sentences with similar meanings.

Respondents	[A typical sentence (translated)]
	Examples of sentences originally obtained by the method.
Doctors, Pharmacists, Nurses	[It is usable for the patients who have a difficulty in taking the medicine orally.] 飲めない患者に使用可 経口が難しい患者に使用可
Doctors, Nurses	[Easy to use.] 簡単
Pharmacists	[There are few burdens for patients.] 患者の負担軽減
Nurses	[I do not know well.] よくわからない
Doctors	[The number of oral drugs decreases.] 経口薬の数が減る 経口薬の種類が減る 経口の量が減る [The medicine works slowly.] 効果が穏やか / 効果が弱い [For the hope/ease of patients] 患者の希望 / 患者の安心 [Mental effects] 心理的効果

Table 2. The resultant sentences obtained by the dependency-link method for Q1. In this table we show the typical sentences translated in English with some examples of original sentences in Japanese.

The table shows that all medical experts prioritized reducing the load of patients as the reason for selecting the transdermal patch, since it could be used by patients who were unable to take medicines orally. In addition, this shows that doctors and nurses focused on the ease of use and that doctors also prioritized the effect of the medicine.

The following is a summary of the results for Q2 -Q4 obtained by the dependency-link method:

For Q 2, the result shows that medical experts appreciated the name of the medicine and the therapeutic classification mark printed on the patch in order to prevent medical accidents and considered it necessary to have a space for the date. The doctors also required a patch that was much smaller and that changed color depending on the amount of time having elapsed. The nurses focused on the behavior of patients, while the pharmacists emphasized the widespread need for awareness regarding correct use of the medicine.

The result of Q 3 shows numerous patients' opinions concerning the medicine, skin symptoms, mentality, and the site of the patch. We can also see that patients in their 40s and 50s mainly commented on skin symptoms, although those in their 60s to 80s covered all these opinions. This suggests that the younger generation focused on the functions of the medicine, while older patients focused on other factors, like ease of mind.

For Q 4, we obtained a result showing that patients asked nurses and pharmacists questions about where to place the patch and how to use it. Nurses also asked questions concerning the effect of the medicine, while pharmacists asked about displays on the patch or packaging and when to use it. This suggests that patients expect nurses to tell them about the efficacy of the medicine and pharmacists to tell them about usage.

The result clarifies that opinions differed depending on the viewpoints of the respondents, although they all wanted to use the same medicine safely. This meant that it is necessary to collect and analyze people's opinions from various backgrounds to ensure drugs are being used safely.

3.3. Incident data related to the safety of drug use [6]

The target data were reports of medical near-miss cases related to medicines and collected by the surveys of the Japan Council for Quality Health Care, which is an extra-departmental body of the Japanese Ministry of Health, Labor and Welfare. We analyzed 858 records from the 12th - 14th surveys, whose data attributes are shown in Table 3. This is because they contain free-description data such as 'Background / cause of the incident' and 'Candidates of counter measures'. Applying text mining to such data required the deletion of characters such as symbols and unnecessary line feed characters. We must also standardize synonyms, since it is difficult to control by making respondents use standard terms to reduce the number of diverse expressions. For this reason, we standardized the words using the dictionary prepared for this analysis.

Day of the week
Weekday or holiday
Time
Place
Department
Content of incident
Psychosomatic state of the patient
Job title
Experience (year/month)
Affiliation (year/month)
Medical benefit class
Nonproprietary name
Name of wrong drug
Dosage form of wrong drug
Effect of wrong drug
Name of right drug
Dosage form of right drug
Medical benefit of right drug
Discussed cause
Concrete descriptions of the incident
Background/cause of the incidents
Candidates of counter measures
Comment

Table 3. Data attributes of records corrected by 12th - 14th surveys.

3.3.1. background/cause of incidents

We applied the Word-link method to data in the field 'background/cause of incidents' in order to determine the concrete information concerning the cause of incidents. The method was applied by occupation to determine the difference in backgrounds and the causes of incidents depending on the job title. We fixed the value of each η so as to make a resultant graph understandable for us. Figure 10 and Fig. 11 show the result of nurses' and pharmacists' comments, respectively. Both figures contain the common opinions, namely, 'the problem of the checking system of the protocol and the rule' (A) and 'confirmation is insufficient' (B), nurses point out 'the systematic problem of communication'(C) and pharmacists 'the problem of adoption of medicines' (C'). We can see that, though B arises due to individual faults, A, C and C' are systematic problems.

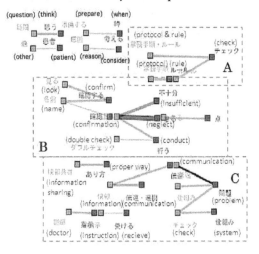

Figure 10. The backgrounds and causes of incidents caused by nurses ($\eta = 4$).

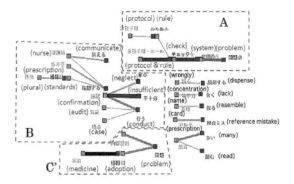

Figure 11. The backgrounds and causes of incidents caused by pharmacists ($\eta = 3$).

3.3.2. Countermeasures

We applied Word-link method to the field 'Candidates of countermeasures' to summarize the nurses' and the pharmacists' opinions concerning the countermeasures to prevent the incidents. Fig. 12 is the summary of the counter measures described by nurses, and suggests that there are many opinions stating '(it is necessary to) instruct to confirm and check', 'make a speech' and 'ensure confirmation'. Fig. 13 shows the summary of the countermeasures proposed by pharmacists. This explains that, besides the confirmation and audit, it is also necessary to attract (pharmacists') attention and to devise ways of displaying medicines such as labels.

Compared with the both results, except for the pharmacists' opinion concerning the innovation of labels, only few opinions exist on the countermeasures related to the system of the medical scenarios. This suggests that the medical experts such as nurses and pharmacists tend to try to find solutions to problems within themselves. To solve the structural problems of medical situations, it is important not only to promote the efforts of each medical expert, but also to strive to improve the organization to which they belong. It is also desirable for them to be aware of the importance of organizational innovation, and to combat the systematic error.

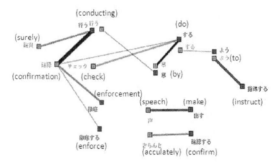

Figure 12. The countermeasures of incidents caused by nurses. ($\eta = 5$)

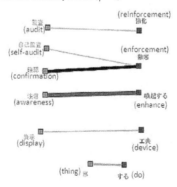

Figure 13. The countermeasures of incidents caused by pharmacists. ($\eta = 4$)

4. Discussion

4.1. Methods

The three analyses suggest that our method can be a powerful tool to extract the parts of sentences that commonly appear in original sentences. The target data have been Japanese sentences. Let us discuss whether our method is applicable to the data in the other language, English. As we introduced in Section 2.1, Word-link method and Dependency-link method utilize dependency relationships in target sentences. One of the representative dependency parsers for English sentences is Stanford parser [7–9], which provides us with the dependency relationships in Stanford Dependencies format. In principle, it enables us to perform our method.

The difference between Japanese and English data comes from the followings:

- Directions of dependency relationships. The dependency relationships in a Japanese sentence always have forward direction, whereas the relationships in an English sentence can have both forward and backward direction. Let us show an example that illustrates this. The Japanese sentence 'ジョンが太郎に話した' corresponds to the English sentence 'John talked to Taro'. In the both sentences, there exist dependency relationships, "ジョン(John) → 話す(talk)" and "太郎(Taro) → 話す(talk)". We should note that both 'ジョン'(John) and '太郎'(Taro) also appear prior to the verb '話す'(talk) in the Japanese sentence. This coincidence of order helps us to suggest the sentences that frequently appear in original data. [1] However, in the English sentence, the noun 'Taro' follows the verb 'talked'. Though this helps to distinguish a subject and an object, it does not preserve the order of words that appear in original sentences. Because of this, as for the dependency relationship between an object and a verb, we should swap their order (e.g. 話す(talk) → 太郎(Taro)) to reproduce summarizing sentences.

- Treatment of a relative pronoun. In English sentences, we frequently use a relative pronoun. It essentially requires reference resolution to identify an antecedent that is modified by the relative pronoun. Reference resolution often requires semantics of words and the knowledge related to them. Because of this, it is currently a difficult problem to find a right antecedent. In contrast, Japanese language does not have a relative pronoun. The relationship between a relative clause and its antecedent is built in normal modification relationships. Therefore, Japanese sentences do not cause the difficulty that originates from a relative pronoun.

- Zero pronoun. In Japanese language, we often omits a subject in a sentence. Such omission is usually called as 'zero pronoun'. In contrast, a subject in an English sentence is seldom omitted. This fact tells us that we can expect the patterns that include subjects in English sentences. If there are only the patterns without subjects, this indicates no definite subjects that appear in the target sentences. However, as for Japanese sentences, we cannot necessarily obtain information about subjects and may have to guess them based on the semantics of words included in the obtained patterns.

---

[1] Of course, if you need to distinguish which is a subject or an object, you should focus on particles as we did in Section 3.1.

4.2. Application

In this subsection, let us briefly review related works and discuss text mining applied to the description data related to medical safety.

4.2.1. Package inserts

U.S. Food and Drug Administration [14] also defines a specification of a package insert document markup standard, Structured Product Labeling (SPL), and . This is similar to SGML formatted package inserts disclosed by PMDA. Thus, in this chapter, we identify SPL with package inserts.

Recently, there emerge several studies which analyze descriptions in drug package inserts. Let us review some of them.

Duke et al. [10, 11] developed a tool, SPLICER, which utilized natural language processing to extract information from SPLs. It parses SPL by identification of target parts, removal of XML tags and extraction of terms. It also identify sysnonymns of the extracted terms by mapping them to medical dictionary, MedDRA. In their study, they applied their tool to quantitatively show the "overwarning" of adverse events in the package inserts of newer and more commonly prescribed drugs. They also showed that recent FDA guide lines do not succeed in reducing overwarning.

Bisgin et al. [12] applied a text mining method, topic modeling, to package insert data. A topic modeling method, latent Dirichlet allocation (LDA), explores the probabilistic patterns of 'topics', implicitly expressed by words in documents. They identified topics corresponding to adverse events or therapeutic application. This enabled them to identify potential adverse events that might arise from specific drugs.

Richard et al. [13] applied machine learning techniques to package insert data. It is a trial to automatically identify pharmacokinetic drug-drug interaction based on unstructured data. They created a corpus of package inserts, which is manually annotated by a pharmacist and a drug information expert. Using the corpus data as a training set, they evaluated the accuracy of identification and obtained F-measure of 0.8-0.9.

The number of the studies that deal with adverse events seems to be much more than the ones that deal with safety of drug usage. For the purpose of finding adverse events, package inserts are just one of text sources. Other sources are academic papers or Medline abstracts. We expect that there emerge more studies from the various viewpoint of safety to utilize package insert data.

4.2.2. Questionnaire data

There are many studies where text mining approach is applied to questionnaire data. However, as for application in the area of medication, there are only a few studies. This might be because analysts tend to take a traditional approach, manual reading, because it captures the written information more precisely than text mining. However, it is obviously time and cost consuming.

Suzuki et al. [15] applied a text mining technique to questionnaire data about clinical practice pre-education conducted to pharmacists, providers of clinical practices. Their method was correspondence analysis between keywords appearing in sentences and attributes of respondents, such as a type of their affiliation and their profession. As a result, they obtained the tendency that mentors in hospitals feel anxious about mismatch between learning contents and real situation.

4.2.3. Medical incident data

Malpractice reduction is one of important themes of medical safety. A lot of governments or institutions construct incident reporting system and analyze the collected report data to find knowledge therein.

Kawanaka et al. [16, 17] utilized Self Organizing Map (SOM) to make a map expressing the relationships of sentences in incident report data. They calculated the co-occurrence possibility of keywords in sentences and defined a characteristic vector for each keyword. They also defined a vector to characterize a report by summing up the vectors whose corresponding keywords appear in it. They input a vector for each report to SOM algorithm. As a result, they found two clusters of reports, the former of which is summarized as "Forget of inscription to medication note" and the latter is as "Forget of administration of medicine taken before sleep". Based on this technique, they also proposed an incident report analysis system.

Baba et al. [18] proposed a method to analyze the co-occurrence relation of the words that appear in the medical incident reports using concept lattice.

Classification is a start point to analyze incident reports. Empirically, the incident types seem to obey Zipf's law. This makes it difficult to classify reports by naive application of clustering algorithms, because they generate too many small-size clusters or a large-size cluster of . If we target major incidents, the better strategy to understand reports is to focus on relative large-size clusters and to summarize the reports in them. However, one should also note that there exist important but less frequently occurring cases. Thus, it is expected to introduce a parameter to measure importance and use it to narrow down clusters to focus on.

All of the above studies suggest that text mining studies tend to focus on words not syntactic structures. Remember that stochastical approach and data mining assume table-type structured data.This might be the reason why it is more difficult to analyze syntactic structures than words. However, as Richard et al. pointed out the importance of the use of syntactic information [13], syntactic structures include information much richer than just a collection of words. They also provide us with easier interpretation of results. This is a basis of the strategy of our method.

5. Conclusion

In this chapter, we introduced the text mining method to analyze text data such as documents and questionnaire response data, and reviewed the studies where we used the method.

Our method utilizes syntactical information of target sentences. We extract a dependency relations from each sentence and restrict them to the ones that appear more than frequency threshold. Connecting common words in the resultant dependencies produces the patterns that contain the frequently appearing portions of sentences. We reviewed the study where we applied the method to drug package inserts, questionnaire data and medical incident reports. We discussed the consideration points to apply our method to English sentences. We also introduced the related works and discussed their tendency.

Though an analysis on medical safety data is important, most of the data are untouched to be analyzed. It is expected that not only text mining techniques are developed but also they are applied to medical safety data.

Author details

Masaomi Kimura

Shibaura Institute of Technology, Japan

References

[1] Matsuzawa, H. (2001) Mining Structured Association Patterns from Large Databases, *Transactions of Information Processing Society of Japan*, Vol.42, No.SIG 8(TOD 10), pp.21-35.

[2] Kudo, T., Yamamoto, K., Tsuboi, Y., Matsumoto, Y. (2002) Mining Syntactic Structures from Text Database, *IPSJ SIG Notes. ICS*, Vol.2002, No.45(20020523), pp.139-144.

[3] Kimura, M. (2009) The Method to Analyze Freely Described Data from Questionnaires *Journal of Advanced Computational Intelligence and Intelligent Informatics* , Vol.13 No.3 pp.268-274.

[4] Kimura, M.; Okada, K.; Nabeta, K.; Ohkura,M.; Tsuchiya, F. (2009) Analysis on Descriptions of Dosage Regimens in Package Inserts of Medicines, In: *Human Interface and the Management of Information. Information and Interaction*, Vol.5618 pp.539-548.

[5] Kimura, M.; Furukawa, H.; Tsukamoto, H.; Tasaki, H.; Kuga, M.; Ohkura,M.; Tsuchiya, F. (2005) Analysis of Questionnaires Regarding Safety of Drug Use, Application of Text Mining to Free Description Questionnaires, *The Japanese Journal of Ergonomics*, Vol.41 No.5 pp.297-305.

[6] Kimura,M.; Tatsuno,K.; Hayasaka,T.; Takahashi,Y.; Aoto,T.; Ohkura,M.; Tsuchiya,F.(2007) The Analysis of Near-Miss Cases Using Data-Mining Approach. *Human-Computer Interaction. HCI Applications and Services* pp.474-483, Beijing.

[7] Klein, D. & Manning, C. (2003a) Accurate Unlexicalized Parsing. *Proceedings of the 41st Meeting of the Association for Computational Linguistics*, pp. 423-430.

[8] Klein, D. & Manning, C. (2003b). Fast Exact Inference with a Factored Model for Natural Language Parsing. In: *Advances in Neural Information Processing Systems 15*, Cambridge, MA: MIT Press, pp. 3-10.

[9] Marneffe, M.C.; Bill MacCartney, B.; Manning, C.(2006) Generating Typed Dependency Parses from Phrase Structure Parses. In *LREC*.

[10] Duke, J. & Friedlin, J. (2010) ADESSA: A Real-Time Decision Support Service for Delivery of Semantically Coded Adverse Drug Event Data. *AMIA Annu Symp Proc. 2010*, pp.177-181.

[11] Duke, J.; Friedlin, J.; Ryan, P. (2011) A Quantitative Analysis of Adverse Events and "Overwarning" in Drug Labeling, *Arch Intern Med* Vol.171, No.10, 2011, 944–946.

[12] Bisgin, H.; Liu, Z.; Fang, H.; Xu, X.;Tong, W.(2011) Mining FDA drug labels using an unsupervised learning technique - topic modeling, *BMC Bioinformatics*12(Suppl 10), S11.

[13] Richard, B.; Gregory, G.; Henk, H.(2012) Using Natural Language Processing to Extract Drug-Drug Interaction Information from Package Inserts, *Proceedings of the 2012 Workshop on Biomedical Natural Language Processing*, pp.206-213, Montréal, Canada, 2012, Association for Computational Linguistics.

[14] FDA   (2008)   Structured   Product   Labeling   Resources http://www.fda.gov/ForIndustry/DataStandards/.

[15] Suzuki, S.; Koinuma, M.; Hidaka, Y.; Koike, K.; Nakamura, H.(2009) The Consciousness Research and Analysis on the Directive Pharmacists Who Provide Pre-education Prior to Clinical Practice?An Effort in the College of Pharmacy Nihon University?*YAKUGAKU ZASSHI* Vol. 129, No.9, 1103-1112, 2009

[16] Otani, Y.; Kawanaka, H.; Yoshikawa T.; Yamamoto, K.; Shinogi, T.; Tsuruoka S.(2005) Keyword Extraction from Incident Reports and Keyword Map Generation Method Using Self Organizing Map *Proceedings of IEEE International Conference on Systems, Man and Cybernetics 2005*, pp.1030–1035 .

[17] Kawanaka, H.; Otani, Y.; Yamamoto, K.; Shinogi, T.; Tsuruoka S.(2007) Tendency Discovery from Incident Report Map Generated by Self Organizing Map and its Development *Proceedings of IEEE International Conference on Systems, Man and Cybernetics 2007*, pp.2016–2021.

[18] Baba, T.; Liu, L.; Hirokawa S.(2010) Formal Concept Analysis of Medical Incident Reports *KES 2010*, Part III, LNAI 6278, pp. 207–214.

## Chapter 9

Towards Computational Processing of Less Resourced Languages: Primarily Experiments for Moroccan Amazigh Language

Fadoua Ataa Allah and Siham Boulaknadel

Additional information is available at the end of the chapter

1. Introduction

The world is undergoing a huge transformation from industrial economies into an information economy, in which the indices of value are shifting from material to non-material resources. This transformation has been rightly described as a revolution that is accompanied by considerable dangers for the future and the survival of many languages and their associated cultures. The last years have seen a growing tendency in investigating applying language processing methods to other languages than English. However, most of tools and methods' development on language processing has so far concentrated on a fairly small and limited number of languages, mainly European and East-Asian languages.

Nevertheless, there is a mandatory requirement for all people over the world to be able to employ their own language when accessing information on the Internet or using computers. To this end, a variety of applications is needed, and lots funds are involved. But the fact that the most of the research sponsored around the world has focused only on the economically and politically important languages makes the language technology gap between the languages of the developed countries and those of the less developed ones leading up to a larger and a largest gap.

According to some linguists' estimations in 1995, half of the 6000 world's languages is being disappearing, 2000 among the 3000 remaining will be threatened in the next century [1]. This means that if there are no efforts put in place to reduce the technology gap and to preserve these languages so many of them will disappear completely by the end of this century. Unfortunately, there are numerous obstacles to advance in language processing for this kind of languages. In the first hand, the language features themselves might impose specific strategies to be undertaken. In the second hand, the lack of previously existing language resources produces a vicious circle: having resources makes creating electronic ones and processing tools easier, but not having resources makes the development and testing of new ones more difficult and time-consuming. Furthermore, there is usually a disturbing lack of interest that people needs to be able to employ their own language in computer applications.

In the aim to help in revitalizing endangered languages, that are generally under or less resourced languages, many efforts need to be made. One way is to encourage younger generations to use their mother tongue by building e-learning platforms, and creating instructive games. Oral documenting can be used to preserve the culture of endangered languages; especially that many of these languages are only spoken. They have rich oral cultures with stories, sayings, songs, chants and histories, but no written forms. So, the extinction of such language will quickly lead to the annihilation of its culture. Machine translation system can also be employed to produce translations from other languages, in order to extend the use of these languages from familiar and home use to more formal social contexts such as media, administration, and commercial relations. Another way to contribute in preserving endangered languages is the use of Internet. This later might be handy to raise awareness about the issues of language extinction and language preservation.

In this context, this paper presents the key strategies for improving endangered languages on human language technologies. It describes the experiments currently underway on Amazigh at Computer Science Studies, Information Systems and Communications Center (CEISIC) in the Royal Institute of the Amazigh Culture (IRCAM), in order to let this language becoming more intercommunicated and widely used in the community.

2. Strategies for enhancing under and less resourced languages

Recently, several private companies, technology centers, and public institutes have begun to get interested and to invest in developing technology for under and less resourced languages. To successfully deal with this task some studies have focused on studying the main strategies that could be taken in order to promote and develop this set of languages.

2.1. Linguistic contribution

Generally, the computational processing of a language involves linguistic contributions that consist on matching or modeling language competence by discovering and presenting formally the rules governing this language. These linguistic contributions can be efficiently shared by a collaborative work on the web [2], substituting a local development team with potentially bigger distributed team. This idea avoids reduplication and wastage of efforts and resources. It has been investigated in an early Montaigne project (1996), and has been implemented at GETA for the Lao language. It has also been applied by Oki to the Japanese language and by NII/NECTEC to a Japanese-Thai dictionary [3].

2.2. Resource recycling

Building electronic resources is indispensable parts of any computational language process. However, this task requires time and valuable human competence. An alternative solution for developing such resources is to get firstly electronic files by using Optical Character Recognition (OCR) [4], then to generate from these files a standardized suitable format of resources that will be exploitable for automated task.

The resource standardization is an important step in the process of resource building. It allows the reuse of resources in different researches, tools and applications. Furthermore, it facilitates the maintenance of a coherent document life cycle through various processing stages, and enables the enrichment of existing data with new information.

2.3. Adapting CLP techniques

Adapting Computational Language Processing (CLP) techniques is an interesting way to build new tools for a specific language while taking the advantages of the similarity between languages' features. Such experiment has been particularly applied in machine translation projects. One of these project is the 'MAJO system', where the investment of syntactical and morphological similarities between Japanese and Uighur has helped sufficiently to obtain good results [5].

2.4. Extensibility focused

The philosophy of this direction suggests that the conception of any project should be made in such a way that others can easily come and extend the work to another level. This means that the project's development should not focus only on getting results, but looking for others to be able to continue the work [6]. In this context, there are several examples: The 'Acabit system' has been developed firstly for the extraction of French multiword. Then, it has been extended to Japanese and Arabic languages [7]. Similarly, the 'NOOJ framework' has been built for European languages. Whereas, the work is still continuing on this framework for other languages such as Arabic [8], and Amazigh [9].

2.5. Open source focused

In general, the under and less resourced languages are economically poor. Whereas, doing computational language processing involves lots funds. To get around this obstacle and to cut down on the financial issues, it is suggested to adopt the open source strategy. Furthermore, this strategy will allow the adoption of the two previous directions (adapting CLP techniques and extensibility focused).

2.6. Professional documentation

Documentation will also greatly help in the continuation and the extension of projects. This documentation could be in terms of manuals or Websites, assisting people who may be interested in the use of a project, or allowing them to access to any phase of the work and continue its development.

2.7. Evaluation system

The evaluation system can be defined as a process allowing measuring the gap between fixed objectives and attained results. The choice of the time of the evaluation depends on the aim of the evaluation. Generally, the evaluation of a project could be done before its realization, to make a diagnostic that determines the objectives of this project and its prerequisites; during the development, to make a progressive evaluation that pilots and directs the progress of the development; and after the implementation, to make a final evaluation which yields the results of the level of satisfaction, relevance, durability of the project, and finally of the continuity and the extensibility of the project.

2.8. Road map

Conscious that search engine, machine translation, human-machine dialogue, and e-learning play a key role in the survival of under and less resourced languages, in manner that they will strongly help these languages to find their way into our daily lives by extending their use from familiar use to social one, we have organized and prepared a clear vision to realize these specific projects in a progressive approach.

While studying these projects, we have noted that:

- Search engine is designed to look for the information needed of the user by understanding his/her query, retrieving the relevant information related to the given query independently of the used language, and presenting a list of ranked search results. To this end, most of the search engines are based on automatic web crawlers, ranking algorithm, and relevance techniques of automatic indexing. These later either rely on keyword-based indexing, linguistic analysis indexing, concept-based indexing, or multilingual indexing.

- Machine translation objective is to allow translating text with roughly the skill of a human, by ensuring a high quality of hierarchical phrase-based translation. In this aim, most of the machine translation systems combine the strengths of rule-based and statistical approaches to reduce the amount of the required linguistic information and training data, and also reduce the size of the statistical models while maintaining high performance. The rule-based machine translation (RBMT) approach is described as interlingual or transfer-based machine translation. It is based on lexicons with morphological, syntactic, and semantic information, and sets of rules. While the statistical machine translation (SMT) approach is based on parallel corpora to properly train the translation system. The two approaches can be merged in different ways: either translation is performed using a rules based engine, then statistics are used in an attempt to adjust/correct the output from the rules engine; rules are used to pre-process data in an attempt to better guide the statistical engine; or rules are used to post-process the statistical output.

- Human-machine dialogue aims to support interactions between users and machines by designing receptive products to the user's needs. The Human-machine dialogue systems can be represented as a four process: Speech recognition process to transcribe sentences spoken into written text, natural language understanding process to extract the meaning from the text, execution process to perform actions on the conversation meaning, and response generation process to give feedback to the user.

- E-learning increases access to learning opportunities, by offering knowledge and skills' online transfer that can be ensured anytime and anywhere through a variety of electronic learning and teaching solutions such as Web-based courseware, online discussion groups, live virtual classes, video and audio streaming. Nowadays, modern technology, especially computational language processing, is strongly used in e-learning to assist reading, writing, and speaking a language. While a person writes a sentence or reads a text aloud, the system can correct and monitor which words are not right or even analyze and tutor particular problems.

From this study we have noticed that these projects are mutually related to each other, and one can act as a part of the other. Furthermore, they are based on various processing which requires a large amount of specialized knowledge. Therefore, we have identified a list of the necessary processes needed to ensure the functionality of these projects, and we have suggested arranging them in a road map chronologically for short, medium, and long term *according to the availability of resources and the level of functionality expected within each term* [10].

As discussed, the achievement of our goal requires a large amount of specialized knowledge that is mainly encoded in complex systems of linguistic rules and descriptions, such as grammars and lexicons, which will in turn involve a considerable amount of specialized manpower. Thus depending on the availability of linguistic expertise and resources, we have estimated that short term phase will necessitate at least 5-year to 10-year plan to establish the low level processing and resources, and pave the way for medium and long terms applications. While, based on the undertaken studies for well resourced language, we have gauged that the two other phases will demand only 5-year plan. Figure 1 represents the road map structured on these three phases.

2.8.1. Short term phase

This phase is considered as an initial step. It consists mainly on the identification of the language encoding, and the foundation of the primarily resources namely keyboard, fonts, basic lexical database (list of lemmas and affixes), and the elementary corpora that serve in the elaboration of most computational language processing applications (text raw corpus, corpus for evaluating search engine and information retrieval systems, manually part of speech tagged corpus, and speech corpus). Furthermore, basic tools and applications such encoding converter, sentence and token splitter, basic concordancer and web search engine, morphological generator, and optical character recognition system also need to be developed in this phase.

2.8.2. Medium term phase

After paving the way by the elaboration of the fundamental and the basic resources in the first phase, this one needs to be focused on advanced tools and applications. Based on the size and the representativity of the elaborated resources, the processing tools of this phase could be even rule-based or statistical. The most important processing to undertake, in this step, are stemming or lemmatization (depending on the morphological features of the stud-

ied language), part of speech tagging, morphological analyzer, chunker, syntactical analyzer, and speech recognition. These processing tools will enable to build a spell checker, a
terminology extractor, a text generator, and human-machine dialogue. Furthermore, they
will allow the enhancement of the first phase tools and applications.

The medium term phase represents also the time to prepare the necessary resources for the
next step, including multilingual dictionaries, multilingual aligned corpora, and semantic
annotated corpora.

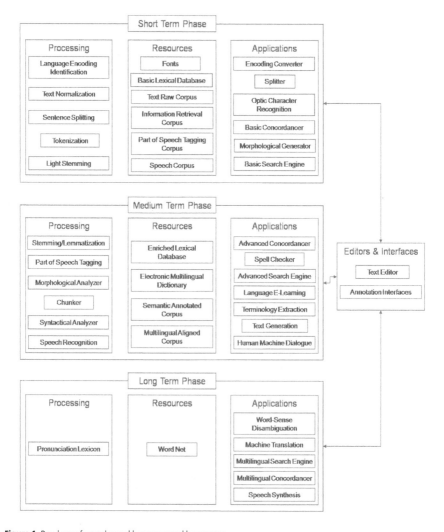

Figure 1. Road map for under and less resourced languages.

2.8.3. Long term phase

The third step of the road map could be considered as the synthesis phase of the realized work. Beside the elaboration of a pronunciation lexicon, Word Net, word-sense disambiguation and speech synthesis, this phase is also focused on the multilingualism applications, mainly machine translation system.

3. Amazigh language features

The Amazigh language, known as Berber or Tamazight, is a branch of the Afro-Asiatic (Hamito-Semitic) languages [11, 12]. Nowadays, it covers the Northern part of Africa which extends from the Red Sea to the Canary Isles and from the Niger in the Sahara to the Mediterranean Sea.

3.1. Sociolinguistic context

In Morocco, this language is divided, due to historical, geographical and sociolinguistic factors, into three main regional varieties, depending on the area and the communities: Tarifite in North, Tamazight in Central Morocco and South-East, and Tachelhite in the South-West and the High Atlas.

The Amazigh is spoken approximately by the half of Moroccan population, either as a first language or bilingually with the spoken Arabic dialect. However, it was until 1994 reserved only to family domain [13]. But in 2001, thanks to the King Mohammed VI Speech, which has established by a Dahir the creation of the Royal Institute of the Amazigh Culture, the Amazigh language has become an institutional language nationally recognized; and in July 2011, it has become an official language beside the classical Arabic.

3.2. Tifinaghe-IRCAM graphical system

Since the ancient time, the Amazigh language has its own script called Tifinaghe. It is found engraved in stones and tombs in some historical sites attested from 25 centuries. Its writing form has continued to change from the traditional Tuareg writing to the Neo-Tifinaghe in the end of the sixties, and to the Tifinaghe-IRCAM in 2003.

The Tifinaghe-IRCAM graphical system has been adapted, and computerized, in order to provide the Amazigh language an adequate and usable standard writing system. While, it has been chosen to represent to the best all the Moroccan Amazigh varieties, it tends to be phonological [14].

However, before adopting Tifinaghe-IRCAM as an official graphic system in Morocco, the Arabic script was widely used for religion and rural poetry writing, and the Latin script supported by the International Phonetic Alphabet (IPA) was used particularly in missionaries' works.

The Tifinaghe-IRCAM graphical system contains:

- 27 consonants including: the labials (ⵝ, ⵀ, ⵞ), the dentals (ⵜ, ⵠ, ⴻ, ⴻ, ⵉ, ⵔ, ⵇ, ⵀ), the alveo-lars (ⵔ, ⵥ, ⵕ, ⵥ), the palatals (ⵛ, ⵉ), the velar (ⵕ, ⵅ), the labiovelars (ⵕ, ⵅ), the uvulars (ⵥ, ⵅ, ⵖ), the pharyngeals (ⴽ, ⵕ) and the laryngeal (ⵔ);

- 2 semi-consonants: ⵢ and ⵓ;

- 4 vowels: three full vowels ⵔ, ⵥ, ⵖ and neutral vowel (or schwa) ⵖ which has a rather special status in Amazigh phonology.

3.3. Punctuation and numeral

No particular punctuation is known for Tifinaghe. IRCAM has recommended the use of the international symbols (" " (space), ".", ",", ";", ":", "?", "!", "…") for punctuation markers; and the standard numeral used in Morocco (0, 1, 2, 3, 4, 5, 6, 7, 8, 9) for the Tifinaghe system writing.

3.4. Directionality

Historically, in ancient inscriptions, the Amazigh language was written horizontally from left to right, and from right to left; vertically upwards and downwards; or in boustrophe-don. However, the orientation most often adopted in Amazigh language script is horizontal and from left to right, which is also adopted in Tifinaghe-IRCAM writing system.

3.5. Amazigh morphological properties

The main syntactic categories of the Amazigh language are the noun, the verb, and the parti-cles [14, 15, 16].

3.5.1. Noun

In the Amazigh language, noun is a lexical unit, formed from a root and a pattern. It could occur in a simple form (ⵔⵔⵅⵔⵝ 'argaz' *the man*), compound form (ⵀⵖⵔⵢⵢⵖⵝ 'buhyyuf' *the fam-ine*), or derived one (ⵔⵞⵢⵔⵓⵔⴻ 'amyawaḍ' *the communication*). This unit varies in gender (mas-culine, feminine), number (singular, plural) and case (free case, construct case).

3.5.2. Verb

The verb, in Amazigh, has two forms: basic and derived forms. The basic form is composed of a root and a radical, while the derived one is based on the combination of a basic form and one of the following prefixes morphemes: ⵔ 's' / ⵔⵔ 'ss' indicating the factitive form, ⵜⵜ 'tt' marking the passive form, and ⵞ 'm' / ⵞⵞ 'mm' designating the reciprocal form. Whether basic or derived, the verb is conjugated in four aspects: aorist, imperfective, perfect, and negative perfect.

3.5.3. Particles

In the Amazigh language, particle is a function word that is not assignable to noun neither to verb. It contains pronouns, conjunctions, prepositions, aspectual, orientation and negative particles, adverbs, and subordinates. Generally, particles are uninflected words. However in Amazigh, some of these particles are flectional, such as the possessive and demonstrative pronouns (+o 'ta' *this* (fem.)) ⁕ +ɛlo 'tina' *these* (fem.)).

4. The complexity of Amazigh in CLP

Amazigh is an official language in Morocco. However, it has been less studied from the computational point of view for many years. Moreover, it is among the languages having rich morphology and different writing forms. Below we describe the difficulties that the Amazigh language confronts in developing computational language applications.

4.1. Amazigh script

Amazigh is one of the languages with complex and challenging pre-processing tasks. Its writing system poses three main difficulties:

• Writing forms' variation that requires a transliterator to convert all writing prescriptions into the standard form 'Tifinaghe – Unicode'. This process is confronted with spelling variation related to regional varieties ([tfucht] [tafukt] (sun)), and transcription systems ([tafuct] [tafukt]), especially when Latin or Arabic alphabet is used.

• The standard form adopted 'Tifinaghe – Unicode' requires special consideration even in simple applications. Most of the existed CLP applications were developed for Latin script. Therefore, those that will be used for Tifinaghe – Unicode require localization and adjustment.

• Different prescriptions differ in the style of writing words using or elimination of spaces within or between words ([tadartino] [tadart ino] (my house)).

4.2. Phonetic and phonology

The Amazigh phonetic and phonological problems depend particularly on the regional varieties. These problems consist on allophones and two kinds of correlations: the contrast between constrictive and occlusive consonants, and that between lax and tense ones.

• The allophone problems concern single phonemes that realized in different ways, such as /ll/ and /k/ that are pronounced respectively as [dž] and [š] in the North.

• The contrast between constrictive and occlusive consonants concern particularly the Riffian and the Central varieties. Those have a strong tendency to plosive spirantization, where b, t, d, ḍ, k, g become respectively b̲, t̲, d̲, k̲, g̲.

- In the phonological Amazigh system, all phonemes can alternate from lax to tense, which is characterized by greater articulator energy and often a longer duration. Some phonetic and phonological evidence consider the opposition lax versus tense as a tense correlation and not a gemination [17], while others consider this opposition as gemination [14]. Moreover, the realization of this opposition varies from region to region and from consonant to consonant.

4.3. Amazigh morphology

An additional reason for the difficulties of computational processing of the Amazigh language is its rich and complex morphology. Inflectional processes in Amazigh are based primarily on both prefix and suffix concatenations. Furthermore, the base form itself can be modified in different paradigms such as the derivational one. Where in case of the presence of geminated letter in the base form, this later will be altered in the derivational form (ⵇⵇⵉⵎ 'qqim' • ⵙⵓⵢⵙⵎ 'svim' (make sit)).

5. Primarily experiments for the Amazigh language

For many decades the Amazigh language was solely oral, exclusively reserved for familial and informal domains, although 50% of the Moroccan population are Amazigh speakers [14]. Since the colonial period, many studies have been undertaken, but most of them have contributed to the collection of the Amazigh oral tradition or have focused on linguistic features. Whereas, the computational studies have been neglect until the creation of the IRCAM in 2001. This creation has enabled the Amazigh language to get an official spelling [18], proper encoding in the Unicode Standard [19], appropriate standards for keyboard realization, and linguistic structures [15, 18].

Nevertheless, this is not sufficient for a less-resourced language as Amazigh to join the well-resourced languages in information technology. In this context, many researches, based on the approaches used for well-resourced languages, are undertaken at national level to improve the current situation [20, 21, 22]. In the remainder of this paper we present existing systems and resources built for Amazigh languages.

5.1. Amazigh encoding

5.1.1. Tifinaghe encoding

Over several years, the Amazigh language has been writing in Latin alphabet supported by the IPA, or in Arabic script. While after adopting Tifinaghe as an official script in Morocco, the Unicode encoding of this script has become a necessity. To this end considerable efforts have been invested. However, this process took ample time to be done, which required the use of ANSI encoding as a first step to integrate the Amazigh language into the educational system at time.

Considering Tifinaghe variants used in all parts of the Amazigh world, the Unicode encoding is composed of four character subsets: the basic set of IRCAM, the extended IRCAM set, other Neo-Tifinaghe letters in use, and modern Touareg letters. The two first subsets constitute the sets of characters chosen by IRCAM. While, the first is used to arrange the orthography of different Moroccan Amazigh varieties, the second subset is used for historical and scientific use. The letters are classified in accordance with the order specified by IRCAM. Other Neo-Tifinaghe and Touareg letters are interspersed according to their pronunciation. Thus, the Unicode Consortium accepts the 55 Tifinaghe characters for encoding in the range U+2D30..U+2D65, U+2D6F, with Tifinaghe block at U+2D30..U+2D7F [19].

5.1.2. Keyboard and fonts

Amazigh integration in international standard prescription keyboards ISO/IEC 9995 has fixed two keyboards: a basic one containing the Tifinaghe characters recommended by IRCAM, and an enhanced keyboard including all characters adopted by ISO. To facilitate keyboarding, Tifinaghe characters' position was chosen in a manner that matches their Latin correspondent position of Azerty keyboard (see Table 2).

In order to integrate the Amazigh language in the Moroccan education system in 2003, eight Tifinaghe fonts, associated with the ANSI encoding, were developed. Then a new Unicode font generation was succeeded [23].

5.2. Optical character recognition

In the aim to achieve perfection on Amazigh optical character recognition systems many studies have been undertaken using different approaches. Most of these approaches have achieved a recognition rate around 92%. In the following, we present briefly some Amazigh optical character recognition systems. Es Saady et al. focused on isolated printed characters recognition based on a syntactic approach using finite automata [24]. Amrouch et al. proposed a global approach based on Hidden Markov Models for recognizing handwritten characters [20]. El Ayachi et al. presented a method using invariant moments for recognizing printed script [25]. Ait Ouguengay et al. proposed an artificial neural network approach to recognize printed characters [26].

5.3. Fundamental processing tools

5.3.1. Transliterator

The Amazigh language has known through its existence different forms of writing: Latin supported by the International Phonetic Alphabet, Arabic script, and Tifinaghe character based on ANSI and Unicode encoding. In the aim to allow an automatically passage from one form to another, a transliterator tool has been developed [27]. This later allows users to read or write in a suitable form, and converts all writing prescriptions into a standard unique form for text pre-processing tasks.

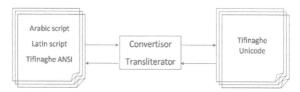

Figure 2. Transliterator tool conception.

The Amazigh transliterator consists of two processes: Convertisor and transliterator.

• Convertisor: This process allows the passage from ANSI representation of Tifinaghe into Unicode representation and vice versa.

• Transliterator: The transliterator process aims to transcribe words from one script to another, while conserving the phonetic pronunciation of the words. This process is based on direct mapping between the pairs of scripts (Latin, Tifinaghe Unicode) and (Arabic, Tifinaghe Unicode). In the Latin - Tifinaghe Unicode mapping the correspondences illustrated in Table 2 are used. While in the Arabic - Tifinaghe Unicode mapping, there are more constrained rules to use the correspondences represented in Table 2. These constraints depend mainly on the writing cursivity of the Arabic language, the phonetic pronunciation, and the use of Amazigh and Arabic vowels. Thus, some Arabic - Tifinaghe correspondences have been adapted (c.f. Table 1), and orthographic rules have been specified mainly on the transliteration from Arabic script into Tifinaghe one.

These rules are as follow:

• If the word contains any emphatic letter (E, Q, Ø, E, ✹), the letter 'ⴵ' will be represented by 'Q'.

• If the letter 'ⵉ' is preceded by a vowel, it will be represented by the semi-consonants 'ⵢ'. Otherwise, it will be represented by the vowel 'ⴻ'.

• If the letter 'ⵓ' is preceded by the vowel 'ⵍ', it will be represented by the semi-consonants 'ⵍ'. If it is preceded by the vowel 'ⵉ' or preceded and succeeded by a consonant, it will be represented by the vowel 'ⴻ'.

English appellation	Tifinaghe	Latin correspondence	New Arabic correspondence
yag	ⵅ	g	ﮔ
yagw	ⵅ	gʷ	ﮔ'
yakw	ⴿ	kʷ	ﮎ
yi	ⵉ	i	ﮄ (in the beginning of a word)
you	ⵓ	u	ﻭ (in the beginning of a word)
yarr	ⵇ	r	ﺭ
yaw	ⵍ	w	ﻭ
yay	ⵢ	y	ﻱ

Table 1. Tifinaghe – Arabic adapted correspondences.

5.3.2. Stemmer

To enhance the performance of information retrieval systems for the Amazigh language a computational stemming process was realized. This process consists in splitting Amazigh words into constituent parts (stem, prefix, suffix) without doing complete morphological analysis, in order to conflate word variants into a common stem [28].

The algorithm is merely based on an explicit list of prefixes and suffixes that need to be stripped in a certain order. This list is derived from the common inflectional morphemes of gender, number and case for nouns; personal markers, aspect and mood for verbs; and affix pronouns for kinship nouns and prepositions. While, the derivational morphemes are not included in order to keep the semantic meaning of words. See Figure 3 for more details.

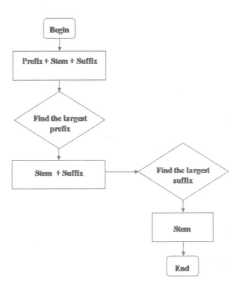

Figure 3. Amazigh light stemming process.

The set of prefixes and suffixes, that has been identified, are classified to five groups ranged from one character to five characters.

Prefix Set

- One-character: ⴰ 'a', ⵉ 'i', ⵏ 'n', ⵓ 'u', ⵜ 't'.

- Two-character: ⵏⴰ 'na', ⵏⵉ 'ni', ⵏⵓ 'nu', ⵜⴰ 'ta', ⵜⵉ 'ti', ⵜⵓ 'tu', ⵜⵜ 'tt', ⵡⴰ 'wa', ⵡⵓ 'wu', ⵢⴰ 'ya', ⵢⵉ 'yi', ⵢⵓ 'yu'.

- Three-character: ⵉⵜⵜ 'itt', ⵏⵜⵜ 'ntt', ⵜⵜⴰ 'tta', ⵜⵜⵉ 'tti'.

- Four-character: ⵉⵜⵜⴰ 'itta', ⵉⵜⵜⵉ 'itti', ⵏⵜⵜⴰ 'ntta', ⵏⵜⵜⵉ 'ntti', ⵜⴻⵜⵜ 'tett'.

- Five-character: ⵜⴻⵜⵜⴰ 'tetta', ⵜⴻⵜⵜⵉ 'tetti'.

Suffix Set

- One-character: ₀ 'a', Λ 'd', Ɛ 'i', Ʀ 'k', Ϲ 'm', Ι 'n', Ψ 'γ', Ο 's', ϯ 't'.

- Two-character: ₀Ι 'an', ₀ϯ 'at', ƐΛ 'id', ƐϹ 'im', ƐΙ 'in', ƐΨ 'iγ', Ϲϯ 'mt', ΙΨ 'nγ', Ιϯ 'nt', ℓΙ 'un', ΟΙ 'sn', ϯΙ 'tn', ЦϹ 'wm', ЦΙ 'wn', ЯΙ 'yn'.

- Three-character: ₀Ϲϯ 'amt', ₀Ιϯ 'ant', ₀ЦΙ 'awn', ƐϹϯ 'imt', ƐΙϯ 'int', ƐЦΙ 'iwn', ΙƐΙ 'nin', ℓΙϯ 'unt', ϯƐΙ 'tin', ϯΙΨ 'tnγ', ϯℓΙ 'tun', ϯΟΙ 'tsn', ΟΙϯ 'snt', ЦϹϯ 'wmt'.

- Four-character: ϯℓΙϯ 'tunt', ϯΟΙϯ 'tsnt'.

5.3.3. Search engine

As the number of Amazigh documents grew, searching algorithms have become one of the most essential tools for managing information. Thus, Ataa Allah and Boulaknadel have been proposed a first tentative in order to develop a search engine that could support the Amazigh language characteristics [21]. They have tried to develop an Amazigh search engine that is mainly structured on three parts: data crawling, indexing, and searching.

- Data crawling: Data crawling is a process behind the search engine, based on spiders or web robots, to fetch web pages. In this context, they have developed a spider that collects automatically and daily all the pages containing Tifinaghe script from the IRCAM Website. All the fetched pages are stored in a web pages' repository, and associated to an ID number. To this ID, called also docID, a web page is assigned whenever a new URL is parsed.

- Data indexing: Based on vector space model [29], the data indexing system creates an index for a set of documents and assigns the Okapi BM-25 weight to each term-document association. The Okapi formulas, especially the BM-25 scheme, attack the problem of higher term frequencies in long documents, and the chances of retrieving long documents over shorter ones [30]. Considering the common use of infixes for both Arabic and Amazigh languages, and based on the study undertaken in Arabic information retrieval [31], the data indexing system of this search engine performs four steps on each document: word identification, stop-word removal, light stemming, and indexing. First, it identifies individual words in the document. Second, all the "stop words" in a document are removed based on a pre-defined list. Then, it reduces the words to their light stem. Finally, it records the information about the relationships between these words and the documents to support searching.

- Data searching: The data searching system includes query engine and a web user interface. The query engine accepts search queries from users, applies the light stemming, represents the query as a vector in term-document space, and assigns a weight to each term-query. Then, it calculates scores between the user query and the set of documents. After retrieving search results, the query engine ranks the search results according to content analysis scores, generates a summary for each search result, based on the web pages' repository, and renders its link. Whereas, the web user interface allows submitting queries and view the search results. When a user performs a search through the web interface, the query is passed to the query engine, which retrieves the search results and passes them back to the user, who can specify the number of retrieved web pages per each result page.

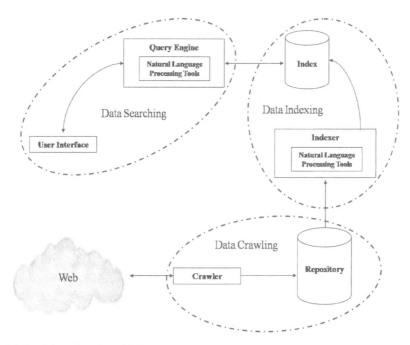

Figure 4. Amazigh search engine architecture.

5.3.4. Concordancer

Amazigh linguistics corpora are currently enjoying a surge activity. As the growth in the number of available Amazigh corpora continues, there is an increased need for robust tools that can process this data, whether it is for research or teaching. One such tool that is useful for both groups is the concordancer, which is displaying a specified target word in its context. However, obtaining one that can reliably cope with the Amazigh language characteristics has proved an extreme difficulty. Therefore, an online concordancer that supports all Moroccan Amazigh language scripts was developed [32].

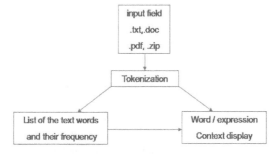

Figure 5. Amazigh concordancer conception.

This concordancer is relatively simple to get up and running. Its interface ensures:

- Corpus selection: The Amazigh concordancer accepts compressed file format and most common text file formats including proprietary and non-proprietary formats such as Microsoft Word, RTF, and PDF files.

- Query keyboarding: The goal of the Amazigh concordance system is to allow a user to look for instances of specific words or expressions. For this purpose, the system opens up two ways for the user to enter his/her query in any one of the scripts involved. The first way is by specifying one of the following kinds of query: exact single word query, or exact string query. Whereas, the second way allows choosing a word from a list in the frequency panel.

- Word frequency panel: The Amazigh concordancer displays a list of the corpus words and their frequency.

- Display of results: Concordances generated by the Amazigh concordancer can be sent either to screen, to printer as hard copy, or to file for future manipulation.

- Context size choice.

5.3.5. Tagging assistance tool

The use of corpora in CLP, especially those annotated morphosyntactically, has become an indispensable step in the language tools' production and in the process of language computerization. In this context, an initiative has been taken to build a morphosyntactic corpus, which has elicited the development of a tool providing support and linguists' assistance [33].

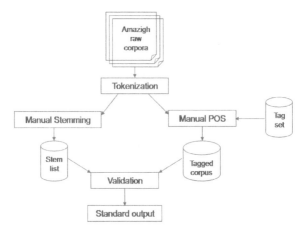

Figure 6. Tagging assistance tool conception.

This tool is structured in three-step process: management, annotation, and validation processes.

- Management: Management is a process for managing user's account and electronic documents. It allows creating or deleting user account, and modifying user information or privileges. Also, it provides to store different range of data, namely original documents, transliterated or corrected ones. Furthermore, it provides a standardized format of the annotated corpus.

- Annotation: This process assists linguists to grammatically annotate a text, by providing them sentences segmented into single words, and allowing them the ability to select for each word its morphological tag from a list of tags that has been elaborated in collaboration with some linguists. Moreover, it requires them to specify the appropriate lemma of each word. Then, the process stores the triples (word, tag, lemma) in the database for further processing.

- Validation: Validation process consists on comparing tags and lemmas specified by all linguists working on the same document, and extracting a list of anomalies. Then, the process returns the context of each word in the list and the information related to, namely the name of linguists that have annotated the word along with the selected tags and the specified lemmas. After, the process allows the correction by updating inconsistent annotations.

5.4. Language resources

Human language technologies are showing more interest in the Amazigh language in recent years. Suitable resources for Amazigh are becoming a vital necessity for the progress of this research. In this context some efforts are currently underway.

5.4.1. Corpora

Corpora are a very valuable resource for CLP tasks, but Amazigh lacks such resources. Therefore, researchers at IRCAM have tried to build Amazigh corpora in progressive way until reaching a large-scale corpus that follows TREC's standards. Thus, three parallel works are undertaking [[34], [35], [36]]. The first consists in building a general corpus based on texts dealing with different literary genres: novels, poems, stories, newspaper articles, and covering various topics; while the second is based on POS tagged data that was collected from IRCAM's newspapers, websites and pedagogical supports; whereas the third work is dealing with the construction of a corpus for evaluating information retrieval system, where the queries' creation and the relevance assessment are manually performed by narrative speakers.

5.4.2. Dictionary

Although many paper dictionaries are available for the Amazigh language, none of them is computational. To deal with this lack, an application that is helping in collecting and accessing Amazigh words has been elaborated [22]. This application has provided all necessary information such as definition, Arabic French and English equivalent words, synonyms, classification by domains, and derivational families. Moreover, it provides the possibility to generate a word copy of the dictionary.

5.4.3. Terminology database

While the Amazigh language is given new status, it becomes necessary, even inevitable to own a terminology covering the largest number of lexical fields. Thus, a tool managing terminology database has been developed to facilitate the work of researchers allowing an efficient exploitation of users. This tool allows the processing of new terminology data, the compilation, and the management of existing terminology [37].

6. Conclusion and future directions

In this paper, we have outlined the key strategies to uphold under and less resourced languages on human language technologies. We have specified a road map based on the elementary and necessary processing, resources and applications needed to ensure the survival of under and less resourced languages in "information society". Moreover, we have discussed the main challenges in processing the Amazigh language, and we have attempted to survey the research work on Amazigh CLP in Morocco.

In the aim to convert Amazigh language from a less resourced language into a resourced and well studied language from computational point of view we need to expedite the basic research on Amazigh CLP tools development by addressing the following issues:

• Building a large and representative Amazigh corpus which will be helpful for spelling and grammar checking, speech generation, and many other related topics.

• Re-use the existing language technologies developed over the years for resourced languages and particularly for Arabic that shares with Amazigh a number of linguistic properties, which will allow saving time and funds.

• Elaborating an E-learning application to ensure the language and culture transmission to young generation.

• Developing a machine translation system which will immensely contribute to promote and disseminate the Amazigh language.

• Creating a pool of competent human resources to carry out research work on Amazigh CLP by offering scholarship for higher degrees and attracting young researchers with attractive salary.

However, there are other research tracks, especially those related to recent technologies, that need to be taken into account to attract young generations, namely:

• Investing on media social contents will strongly contribute in the salvation of many less resourced languages.

• Developing mobile phone and tablet applications will also keep language alive for future generations and help foreign visitors to discover the region for better understanding of the local culture.

• Elaborating special applications in Amazigh language for people with disabilities, in order to offer them opportunities to access information and services in their native language.

Appendix

English appellation	Tifinaghe	Latin correspondence	Arabic correspondence
ya	ⵄ	a	ا
yab	ⴱ	b	ب
yag	ⴳ	g	گ
yagw	ⴳ	gʷ	گ'
yad	ⴷ	d	د
yadd	ⴹ	ḍ	ض
yey	ⴻ	e	
yaf	ⴼ	f	ف
yak	ⴽ	k	ک
yakw	ⴽ	kʷ	ک'
yah	ⵀ	h	ﮬ
yahh	ⵃ	ḥ	ح
yaa	ⵄ	ɛ	ع
yakh	ⵅ	x	خ
yaq	ⵇ	q	ق
yi	ⵉ	i	ي
yazh	ⵊ	j	ج
yal	ⵍ	l	ل
yam	ⵎ	m	م
yan	ⵏ	n	ن
you	ⵓ	u	و
yar	ⵔ	r	ر
yarr	ⵕ	ṛ	ر
yagh	ⵖ	ɣ	غ
yas	ⵙ	s	س
yass	ⵚ	ṣ	ص
yash	ⵛ	c	ش
yat	ⵜ	t	ت
yatt	ⵟ	ṭ	ط
yaw	ⵡ	w	ۉ
yay	ⵢ	y	ˆي
yaz	ⵣ	z	ز
yazz	ⵥ	ẓ	ژ

Table 2. Tifinaghe-Ircam Alphabet.

Author details

Fadoua Ataa Allah and Siham Boulaknadel

Computer Science Studies, Information Systems and Communications Center, The Royal Institute of the Amazigh Culture, Rabat, Morocco

References

[1] Brickley, D. A. (1995). The Conservation of Endangered Languages. In: Seminar at the centre for theories of language and learning. *University of Bristol department of philosophy, Bristol, UK.*

[2] Boitet, C. (1999). A research perspective on how to democratize machine translation and translation aids aiming at high quality final output. *In: proceeding of VII Summit of Machine Translation in the Great Translation Era*, MT VII, 13-17 September, Singapore.

[3] Shimohata, S., Kitamura, M., Sukehiro, T., & Murata, T. (2001). Collaborative translation environment on the Web., *In: proceeding of VIII Summit of Machine Translation in the Information Age*, MT, 18-22 September, Santiago de Compostela, Spain.

[4] Nguyen, H. D. (1998). Techniques génériques d'accumulation d'ensembles lexicaux structurés à partir de ressources dictionnairiques informatisées multilingues hétérogènes. PhD thesis. *University of Joseph Fourier.*

[5] Mahsut, M., Ogawa, Y., Sugino, K., & Inagaki, Y. (2001). Utilizing agglutinative features in Japanese-Uighur machine translation. *In: proceeding of VIII Summit of Machine Translation in the Information Age*, MT, 18-22 September, Santiago de Compostela, Spain.

[6] Muhirwe, J. (2007). Towards Human Language Technologies for Under-resourced languages. *In Joseph Kizza et al. (ed.) Series in Computing and ICT Research*, 2Fountain Publishers, 123-128.

[7] Boulaknadel, S. (2008). TAL et recherche d'information dans un domaine de spécialité : apport des connaissances morphologiques et syntaxique pour l'arabe. *Ph.D. Thesis. University Mohamed V.*

[8] Mesfar, S. (2008). Etude linguistique de la langue arabe. *Ph.D. Thesis. University of Franche Comté.*

[9] Nejm, F. Z., & Boulaknadel, S. (2012). Formalisation de l'amazighe standard avec NooJ. *In: proceeding of atelier de traitement automatique des langues africaines*, TALAF, 04-08 June, Grenoble, France.

[10] Ataa Allah, F., & Boulaknadel, S. (2009). Note méthodologique pour la réalisation des outils et ressources linguistiques de la langue amazighe. *Intern Report. IRCAM, Rabat, Morocco.*

[11] Greenberg, J. (1966). The Languages of Africa. *The Hague.*

[12] Ouakrim, O. (1995). Fonética y fonología del Bereber. *Survey, University of Autònoma de Barcelona.*

[13] Boukous, A. (1995). Société, langues et cultures au Maroc : Enjeux symboliques. *Najah El Jadida.*

[14] Ameur, M., Bouhjar, A., Boukhris, F., Boukouss, A., Boumalk, A., Elmedlaoui, M., Iazzi, E. M., & Souifi, H. (2004). Initiation à la langue amazighe. *IRCAM.*

[15] Boukhris, F., Boumalk, A., Elmoujahid, E., & Souifi, H. (2008). La nouvelle grammaire de l'amazighe. *IRCAM, Rabat, Morocco.*

[16] Ataa Allah, F., & Boulaknadel, S. (2010). Light Morphology Processing for Amazighe Language. *In: proceeding of the Workshop on Language Resources and Human Language Technology for Semitic Languages,* 17 May, Valletta, Malta.

[17] Galand, L. (1953). La phonétique en dialectologie berbère. *In : Bulletin Internationale de Documentation Linguistique. Orbis,* 225-233.

[18] Ameur, M., Bouhjar, A., Boukhris, F., Boumalk, A., Elmedlaoui, M., & Iazzi, E. (2006). Graphie et orthographe de l'amazighe. *IRCAM, Rabat, Morocco.*

[19] Andries, P. (2008). Unicode 5.0 en pratique : Codage des caractères et internationalisation des logiciels et des documents. *Dunod, Collection InfoPro, France.*

[20] Amrouch, M., Rachidi, A., El Yassa, M., & Mammass, D. (2010). Handwritten Amazigh Character Recognition Based On Hidden Markov Models. *International Journal on Graphics, Vision and Image Processing,* 10(5), 11-18.

[21] Ataa Allah, F., & Boulaknadel, S. (2010). Amazigh Search Engine: Tifinaghe Character Based Approach. *In: proceeding of International Conference on Information and Knowledge Engineering, IKE,* 14-16 July, Las Vegas, Nevada, USA.

[22] Iazzi, E., & Outahajala, M. (2008). Amazigh Data Base. *In: proceeding of HLT & NLP Workshop within the Arabic world: Arabic language and local languages processing status updates and prospects,* 31 May, Marrakech, Morocco.

[23] Ait Ouguengay, Y. (2007). Quelques aspects de la numérisation des polices de caractères : Cas de Tifinaghe. *In : Zenkouar L. (ed.) La typographie entre les domaines de l'art et de l'informatique. IRCAM,* 159-181.

[24] Es Saady, Y., Rachidi, A., El Yassa, M., & Mammas, D. (2010). Printed Amazigh Character Recognition by a Syntactic Approach using Finite Automata. *International Journal on Graphics Vision and Image Processing,* 10(2), 1-8.

[25] El Yachi, R., Moro, K., Fakir, M., & Bouikhalene, B. (2010). On the Recognition of Tifinaghe Scripts. *Journal of Theoretical and Applied Information Technology,* 20(2), 61-66.

[26] Ait Ouguengay, Y., & Taalabi, M. (2009). Elaboration d'un réseau de neurones artificiels pour la reconnaissance optique de la graphie amazighe : Phase d'apprentissage. *In : Bellafkih M., Ramdani M., Zreik K. (ed.) Systèmes intelligents-Théories et applications. Europia productions.*

[27] Ataa Allah, F., & Boulaknadel, S. (2011). Convertisseur pour la langue amazighe : script arabe- latin- tifinaghe. *In: proceeding of the 2ème Symposium International sur le Traitement Automatique de la Culture Amazighe, SITACAM,* 6-7 May, Agadir, Morocco.

[28] Ataa Allah, F., & Boulaknadel, S. (2010). Pseudo-racinisation de la langue amazighe. *In: proceeding of Traitement Automatique des Langues Naturelles, TALN,* 19-23 July, Montreal, Canada.

[29] Gerard, Salton. (1968). Automatic Information Organization and Retrieval. *McGraw-Hill.*

[30] Stephen, E. R., Steve, W., Susan, J., Micheline, H. B., & Mike, G. (1994). Okapi at TREC-3. *In: proceeding of the 3rd Text Retrieval Conference, TREC,* November, Gaithersburg, Maryland, USA.

[31] Ataa Allah, F., Boulaknadel, S., El Qadi, A., & Aboutajdine, D. (2008). Evaluation de l'Analyse Sémantique Latente et du Modèle Vectoriel Standard Appliqués à la Langue Arabe. *Revue de Technique et Science Informatiques,* 27(7), 851-877.

[32] Ataa Allah, F., & Boulaknadel, S. (2010). Online Amazigh Concordancer. *In: proceeding of the international Symposium on Image Video Communications and Mobile Networks, ISIVC,* 30 September-2 October, Rabat, Morocco.

[33] Ataa Allah, F., & Jaa, H. (2009). Etiquetage morphosyntaxique : outil d'assistance dédié à la langue amazighe. *In: proceeding of the 1er Symposium International sur le Traitement Automatique de la Culture Amazighe, SITACAM,* 12-13 December, Agadir, Morocco.

[34] Boulaknadel, S., & Ataa Allah, F. (2011). Building a standard Amazigh corpus. *In: proceeding of the International Conference on Intelligent Human Computer Interaction, IHCI,* 29-31 August, Prague, Tchec.

[35] Outahajala, M., Zekouar, L., Rosso, P., & Martí, M. A. (2010). Tagging Amazigh with AnCoraPipe. *In: proceeding of the Workshop on Language Resources and Human Language Technology for Semitic Languages,* 17 May, Valletta, Malta.

[36] Ataa Allah, F., & Boulaknadel, S. (2011). Les ressources langagières pour la recherche d'information textuelle: Cas de la langue amazighe. *In: proceeding of colloque sur l'Amazighe et les Nouvelles Technologies de l'Information et de Communication, NTIC,* 24-25 February, Rabat, Morocco.

[37] EL Azrak, N., & EL Hamdaoui, A. (2011). Référentiel de la Terminologie Amazighe : Outil d'aide à l'aménagement linguistique. *In: proceeding of colloque sur l'Amazighe et les Nouvelles Technologies de l'Information et de Communication, NTIC,* 24-25 February, Rabat, Morocco.

Permissions

The contributors of this book come from diverse backgrounds, making this book a truly international effort. This book will bring forth new frontiers with its revolutionizing research information and detailed analysis of the nascent developments around the world.

We would like to thank Shigeaki Sakurai, for lending his expertise to make the book truly unique. He has played a crucial role in the development of this book. Without his invaluable contribution this book wouldn't have been possible. He has made vital efforts to compile up to date information on the varied aspects of this subject to make this book a valuable addition to the collection of many professionals and students.

This book was conceptualized with the vision of imparting up-to-date information and advanced data in this field. To ensure the same, a matchless editorial board was set up. Every individual on the board went through rigorous rounds of assessment to prove their worth. After which they invested a large part of their time researching and compiling the most relevant data for our readers. Conferences and sessions were held from time to time between the editorial board and the contributing authors to present the data in the most comprehensible form. The editorial team has worked tirelessly to provide valuable and valid information to help people across the globe.

Every chapter published in this book has been scrutinized by our experts. Their significance has been extensively debated. The topics covered herein carry significant findings which will fuel the growth of the discipline. They may even be implemented as practical applications or may be referred to as a beginning point for another development. Chapters in this book were first published by InTech; hereby published with permission under the Creative Commons Attribution License or equivalent.

The editorial board has been involved in producing this book since its inception. They have spent rigorous hours researching and exploring the diverse topics which have resulted in the successful publishing of this book. They have passed on their knowledge of decades through this book. To expedite this challenging task, the publisher supported the team at every step. A small team of assistant editors was also appointed to further simplify the editing procedure and attain best results for the readers.

Our editorial team has been hand-picked from every corner of the world. Their multi-ethnicity adds dynamic inputs to the discussions which result in innovative outcomes. These outcomes are then further discussed with the researchers and contributors who give their valuable feedback and opinion regarding the same. The feedback is then collaborated with the researches and they are edited in a comprehensive manner to aid the understanding of the subject.

Apart from the editorial board, the designing team has also invested a significant amount of their time in understanding the subject and creating the most relevant covers. They scrutinized every image to scout for the most suitable representation of the subject and create an appropriate cover for the book.

The publishing team has been involved in this book since its early stages. They were actively engaged in every process, be it collecting the data, connecting with the contributors or procuring relevant information. The team has been an ardent support to the editorial, designing and production team. Their endless efforts to recruit the best for this project, has resulted in the accomplishment of this book. They are a veteran in the field of academics and their pool of knowledge is as vast as their experience in printing. Their expertise and guidance has proved useful at every step. Their uncompromising quality standards have made this book an exceptional effort. Their encouragement from time to time has been an inspiration for everyone.

The publisher and the editorial board hope that this book will prove to be a valuable piece of knowledge for researchers, students, practitioners and scholars across the globe.

List of Contributors

Hanmin Jung, Sung-Pil Choi, Seungwoo Lee and Sa-Kwang Song
Korea Institute of Science and Technology Information, Korea

Alan L. Porter
Search Technology, Inc., Norcross, Georgia, USA
Technology Policy & Assessment Center, Georgia Tech, Atlanta, Georgia, USA

Yi Zhang
School of Management and Economics, Beijing Institute of Technology, Beijing, China

Hidenao Abe
Department of Information Systems, Faculty of Information and Communications, Bunkyo University, Japan

Hidetsugu Nanba, Aya Ishino and Toshiyuki Takezawa
Graduate School of Information Sciences, Hiroshima City University, Japan

Alessio Leoncini, Fabio Sangiacomo, Paolo Gastaldo and Rodolfo Zunino
Department of naval, electric, electronic and telecommunications engineering (DITEN), University of Genoa, Genoa, Italy

Hiep Luong, Susan Gauch and Qiang Wang
Department of Computer Science and Computer Engineering, University of Arkansas, U.S.A

David Campos, Sérgio Matos and José Luís Oliveira
IEETA/DETI, University of Aveiro, Portugal

Masaomi Kimura
Shibaura Institute of Technology, Japan

Fadoua Ataa Allah and Siham Boulaknadel
Computer Science Studies, Information Systems and Communications Center, The Royal Institute of the Amazigh Culture, Rabat, Morocco

Printed in the USA
CPSIA information can be obtained
at www.ICGtesting.com
JSHW011412221024
72173JS00003B/519